BAKE UON AMERICA

THE GENEROUS ART OF BROWNIES, CUPCAKES, WHOOPIES, MUFFINS AND MORE

DAVID LESNIAK & DAVID MUNIZ

EBURY
PRESS

RECIPE NOTES:

We Americans have an odd way of doing things. When it comes to measuring ingredients we use cups. To make these recipes attainable for all, we provide equivalents to suit preference or technique as well as the basis for converting other recipes. Ingredient quantities throughout are listed as such:

Imperial / Metric / American measured in *Ounces / Grams / Cups*

American recipes measure butter like so:

1 cup of butter = 8 ounces = 16 tablespoons = 2 sticks

We've tested and edited a number of times so it is entirely possible something slipped through the cracks. For that we apologize in advance. If need be, please feel free to contact us with any questions/problems and we'll be happy to help: info@outsidertart.com

CONTENTS

FOREWORD

Rachel Allen

In the summer of 2008, while filming for my *Bake* series, I travelled around Ireland and the UK visiting lots of different chefs and bakers who were all doing something quite unique, and often extraordinary, with their baking. On one of the days, the crew and I invaded the home of David and David to see what all the fuss was about over these two guys with the same name – they had been causing quite a stir at local farmers' markets with their authentic American treats. Within five minutes of entering their gorgeous home I had a warming cup of coffee in one hand and a sweet fudgy chocolate brownie in the other.

We cooked, filmed and ate all day and, fortunately for me, we had to reshoot my sampling of their scones and cupcakes a few times over. I left that day certain they were going to go on to do more great things. I couldn't wait for their café to open and knew a beautiful book would inevitably follow.

The Davids do nothing by half. Their style is not just generous but full on. If something is to be gooey then it must seriously ooze goo. If chocolate's involved then only a huge hit of chocolate intensity will do. I love that style of baking, with no flavours diluted or half-fat options. This is uncompromising cooking and the results are fantastic. Each recipe has a twist but is grounded in serious American baking.

The Davids have established their café, Outsider Tart, as one of the best places in the UK for authentically indulgent baking. They've drawn people from far and wide to their beautiful shop to taste their famous whoopie pies, cupcakes, cookies and more. Now they've given us their secrets in this book full of fabulous recipes that are innovative, impressive and uncompromisingly decadent. Many of the recipes in this book should come with a warning – I urge you to try the Snickers brownies and the Blackout cake. No, I urge you to try them all.

INTRODUCTION

Two American Davids decide to move to London and open a cake shop. Blimey. What on earth for? We often ask ourselves the very same question. David No. 1 is older and wiser. Having grown up in New Jersey just outside of New York City, his primary education was a bit more evolved than that of David No. 2 (henceforth referred to as OD, for Other David) whose education in Hattiesburg, Mississippi, caused him to believe *'Grease'* is a country. It is a widely known fact that Mississippi's educational system ranks among the lowest in the 50 states. For that reason, David No. 1 will be your author. But don't be fooled; OD is really the brains behind the organization, having been a successful serial entrepreneur his entire adult life. David No. 1, (aka the tall, good-looking one) comes from an architectural background. No. 1 makes things look pretty. No. 2 pays for it. Dearly.

Several years after we met in 2002, OD had an opportunity to run a radio station in London. Not knowing a thing about radio, he figured it would be a once-in-a-lifetime chance and we agreed it would be a personal adventure for us both. So in October 2005 we set sail for London. Literally. Fact is we have two large dogs, Mabel and Otis, who are littermates and have never been separated from each other, let alone us. Otis was born with a heart condition that has required a few surgeries and medications along the way. As a result, he is unable to be sedated, pretty much ruling out any flights across the ocean. So on to the ship we went. After 6 long days of staring at nothing but water (M&O had a lovely top-deck perch at the back of the boat), we settled in the Richmond area of London.

While still in New York, we had toyed with the idea of one day opening a bakeshop. No clear plans but we dabbled with a name and even some logos. We were both self-employed at the time and, it seemed, professionally fulfilled. Daydreaming had its benefits but we never felt the need to pursue it further. Upon arriving in London, OD was attempting to ensconce himself in his new job. To date, I had known nothing but residential design, architecture and construction and wasn't sure if that was the path on which to continue. In the States we were both weekend warriors in the kitchen. We never cooked or baked during the week: too many restaurants, too much take-out, too much delivery. But we enjoyed the hunt for equipment, ingredients and the perfect whatever it was we were making and weekends proved ideal for that. Upon our arrival on UK soil, we continued our culinary quests.

Fortunately for us, Richmond has a lovely farmers' market overlooking the Thames, a picture-perfect London setting if ever there was one. Most weekends we would head to the market, buy up all sorts of produce then walk home to enjoy it. Eventually we came to learn of all the farmers' markets throughout London and we expanded our circle to include them. We journeyed. We shopped. We cooked and baked. We ate.

Conscious of our ever-expanding waistlines, we then started to send the fruits of our labors into OD's office each week. After a month or so of this, we took note of our overly positive feedback and things started to gel. Because the office staff was large and diverse we

thought we had a fairly reliable focus group at our fingertips. We started thinking … why not have a go at selling our goodies at the farmers' market? How difficult could it be? Given some of the things we sampled at the markets ourselves it seemed we would, at the very least, be moderately successful. To date, no one had spat out what we offered up (or so they said) and we gained enough confidence to think this newly formed thought just might work. And so we set out to establish a market pitch in, where else, Richmond. And before we knew it, OUTSIDER TART was born. Never really trained, certainly not local and sassy when we want to be, we opted to do what we knew best and spread some American frosting as far as it would go, convinced we should offer up nothing but the best baking from American kitchens far and wide. Did we have grand plans for turning a hobby into a vocation?
Not really, no.

After weeks of planning and anticipation, we pitched our first stall in East Sheen in March 2007. In preparation for that event, we researched all sorts of recipes, determining what might appeal to a larger audience than to our loyal focus group. When people asked if we did traditional English treats, we would enquire what they were and then head to the bookshelves to suss out an American equivalent. We tried to bridge the culinary and cultural divide between the two sides of the pond whenever and wherever possible. For obvious reasons it wasn't uncommon to find direct links. Certain things, however, were best left where they belong. Suet, for example, used in traditional mince pies, made the trans-Atlantic journey to arrive in the US ultimately in the form of bird food, so why mess with that success? Christmas cake? Personally we saw no reason for any baked good to have a shelf life beyond a week, let alone 52. Or more. Some things worked. Many

things didn't. But we were learning all along. The best inspiration always came from family recipes, if not always ours, then from our adoptive families across America. So onward we read, page after page, learning about local recipes, regional histories, family traditions and all things butter and sugar. Otherwise the lesson we learned is easy as pie: you needn't have the best technique, nor any as the case may be, in order to achieve the best results. Our hope is that by sharing our experience and methods you will recognize the difference between the foundation of a recipe and its inclusions and embellishments. How the former is a bit more rigid (even foundations can vary), but the latter is totally subjective and up to you. We merely make a few suggestions but it's not our place to dictate. We aim to give you the tools and instill enough culinary confidence for you to gain your footing, build as you see fit and create unique favourites all your own.

Who cares if you don't know the exact technique for folding or reasons why leavening agents work their magic. Do you enjoy doing it? Are your kids having fun while you navigate a recipe together? Do your friends enjoy teasing you when the results are less than stellar? Do you enjoy frosting with a partner while bickering about how best to distribute sprinkles in a pretty pattern for a party you knew nothing about but your partner swears s/he mentioned? Should you substitute raisins because you loathe the currants called for in the recipe? Better yet, why use fruit when chocolate will do just fine? Eat a few nuts if it's fiber you want. Then again, add the nuts.

More to the point … never ever use a recipe as the be-all and end-all. Gospel it is not. Substitutions in the kitchen are a given either by need (logistics) or want (just because). They will happen no matter how hard you try to avoid them. Know that baking is not the exact science it's made out to be. When you are forced or opt to adapt a recipe the only 'trick' is to keep the proportion of the basic batter or dough close to the original. A little more of this or that never hurts. How else to explain the thousands of recipes for the same thing? Doubling the butter? Not good. Doubling the nuts? Go right ahead. One might cause problems while the other simply makes it more to your taste. To us, the best results come from within and will be a result of your mood at any given moment. Market forces also play a role since some ingredients might not be available when you thought they'd be, or the aforementioned partner may have bought oranges when it was clearly, clearly specified lemons were required. Clearly. Nonetheless, research plays a role, in that it will expose you to new ideas and give you the confidence to try something new or change your method and achieve something different or better. Rest assured, the world of architecture calls it practice for a reason. The same should apply in the kitchen. Don't become the best baker, just become the best practice baker you can by simply trying it. Again and again and again.

A FEW WORDS FROM OD

The question we often hear is how did you get started baking? For me, it was a two-staged process. I first got the urge to cook when my loving sister Elena or, to us, Nen, almost killed me with a meal when I was 10. Picture it: a young angelic boy left alone with his much older sister while their parents were away on vacation. Nen, bless her heart, decided to make my favourite meal of Picadillo, a Cuban chili of sorts loaded with raisins, olives and capers. The only problem was my mother's recipe is written in Spanish and my dear sister doesn't speak a word of Spanish, 'gracias' notwithstanding Can you see where this is going? Dinner is served and even at the tender age of 10 it's clear from the get-go what's been

placed before me looks all wrong. Not wanting to hurt my sister's feelings (I told you I was angelic) our dog, Ace, became the recipient of her efforts. He was more than happy to help. At first. Two hours later the poor dog was listless and gassy. After a quick visit to the vet, the little guy was right as rain and my sister's cooking lives on in infamy within our family.

A few short years later (2.5 decades' worth), I met OD. Early on, he invited me to dinner and he whipped up an amazing meal at his house. I enjoyed the night, but I kept thinking, I have to reciprocate. Oh God, I have to reciprocate. The dinner I planned definitely made an impression. I threw everything I knew how to make at him. First there was an Elvis sandwich: peanut butter, honey, banana and bacon sandwich assembled and pan-fried in butter for a little something extra. It didn't stop there. I followed that with a PBBJ sandwich: peanut butter, fried baloney and jelly sandwich. Clearly I pulled out all the stops. OD survived the evening and in spite of my attempts decided to stick around. He felt I needed a hobby, something that spoke to my 'neurotic and compulsive nature'. I know. Isn't he sweet? Since he loved to cook, we settled on baking together. Our time in the kitchen is something I wouldn't trade for the world because that hobby has turned into my passion. You hear about people being fulfilled with what they do for a living, but I didn't really understand what that meant until now. We have spent years learning and experimenting in the kitchen together which actually feels like just a few days. We spend our days feeding and (hopefully) bringing happiness to our customers. Without OD, I never would have found my place, the one thing that without question never feels like effort or work, but makes me shine.

I hope this book fills your stomach and keeps you smiling for years to come.

POTAYTO / POTAHTO

You like potayto and I like potahto,
You like tomayto and I like tomahto;
Potayto, potahto, tomayto, tomahto!
Let's call the whole thing off!

George and Ira Gershwin, 1937

Wow. Not the most auspicious beginning to a cookbook, now is it? While we're a bit loath to cite musical references, it does seem a fitting place to start.

When we first arrived on these shores in November 2005, we anticipated a new adventure in a familiar city. Sure we figured on odd bits here and there with regard to cultures clashing, but never in a million years did we think that language would be an issue. English is English. Same alphabet. Same words. Almost the same grammar. Why even give it a moment's consideration? When we first began to suspect language was, indeed, some sort of barrier, we moved on to the how-hard-could-this-be frame of mind. And when we started to zero in on opening a bakeshop, we begrudgingly accepted the harder-than-you-think frame of mind. But we're both a bit stubborn so we set forth undeterred.

Given our mission is to create a cookbook focused on American baking (cakebook is more like it) we thought it best to remain true to our roots and present the facts as we know them. How best to inform people of the American way other than to use American terminology? They say the best way to learn a new language is by immersing yourself in it, so we offer up this guide to American baking, immersion style. As far as we can tell, no one bothered to translate 'quiche' when it first became popular and now everyone knows the term, let alone just how good it can be.

By no means is there anything as specific as quiche to what we do, but you get the idea. Our goal is to provide recipes for success. Our responsibility in ensuring a positive outcome in your kitchen is to clarify the very few differences in American ingredients and their British cousins; the few differences in terminology and equipment and the slightly more than few differences in methods of measurement. We have chosen to include all manners of measurement be it the 'standard' American, imperial or metric units. In so doing, we hope to also create a reference book so no matter what your preferred method may be, you can easily switch from one to the other and back again. We also hope that your newly developed skills give you the confidence to tackle other recipes written as these are. What follows is an item-by-item explanation of why we say potayto and you say potahto but in the end we're both saying root vegetable. No need to call the whole thing off. To the contrary, turn the oven on and let's get baking.

WHAT THESE AVERAGE AMERICAN BAKERS HAVE TO WORK WITH

Herein we offer an item-by-item list of what we have in our kitchen and kit bag, so to speak. At times it will be a decoder ring translating American baking lingo for British terminology, be it colloquial, formal and technical. These are the things we keep available for use on a day-to-day basis. We've broken it down into three categories: in the pantry we keep dry goods and stable liquids such as flavorings; in the fridge is where most of the wet ingredients are kept (certainly the dairy); and the cabinets and cupboards are where we keep bakeware and assorted kitchenalia to get the job done. For the first two categories we offer substitutes should something prove difficult to find, or, as happens to us constantly, you find yourself short of what's required. The last category includes our preferred 'tools of the trade' but by no means are they a prerequisite for success. Very little of it is professional. In fact much of it can be had at a well-equipped kitchen store. No need to be overwhelmed. Just curious.

Off you go…

IN THE PANTRY

Bicarbonate of Soda is Baking Soda: Also known as sodium bicarbonate. It is an alkali used to neutralize acidic ingredients to promote leavening. Molasses, treacle, honey, chocolate, sour cream, yoghurt and buttermilk are examples of acidic ingredients, the effects of which need to be tempered with baking soda.

Cream of Tartar: Known to geeks as potassium hydrogen tartrate. Believe it or not, cream of tartar is obtained from sediment produced during wine-making, as grapes are the most significant source of tartaric acid. As wine ages, a salt is produced which is found in the sediment and this becomes cream of tartar. Used in combination with baking soda it will produce baking powder. Used on its own, it will help to give more volume to beaten egg whites and, because it helps prevent sugar crystals from forming, it will make certain frostings creamier.

Baking Powder: Most commercially available baking powders contain metallic additives as a type of acid in addition to the alkali baking

soda and cornstarch to keep them separate in the jar. Because it contains both acids and alkali, baking powder is in a state of flux, meaning its efficacy will diminish over time since, ostensibly, the acid and alkali are reacting as it sits on the shelf. Once opened, it will work its magic for 4 months or so. After that, all bets are off. It is used to assist in leavening baked goods when in the oven. Unfortunately, given the presence of aluminium in the additives, baking powder can have a metallic aftertaste. We prefer to make our own to ensure freshness and eliminate unwanted flavor. Simply combine two parts cream of tartar to one part baking/bicarbonate of soda and keep it sealed in an airtight container. Or mix as needed at the time of baking.

Cornstarch is Cornflour: More scientific talk … it is the dried and powdered endosperm of the corn kernel. Extremely fine in texture, it adds tenderness to cakes and is also used for thickening puddings and sauces both sweet and savory. As an additive to baking powder and ground grains like wheat flour, it acts as an anti-caking agent.

Kosher Salt: We use kosher salt exclusively for all our baking and cooking. It has a larger granule than table salt, has no additives and therefore a more pure taste. It derives its name not from religious guidelines for its production nor from having been blessed, rather it comes from its use: koshering meat. According to Hebrew law, no animal blood can be consumed. In order to extract blood, meat is prepared according to tradition by smothering it with kosher salt. The size and shape of the salt granule causes it to sit on the surface longer to draw fluids out of the meat. We have yet to be disappointed by substituting kosher salt for table salt in our baking. Weight for weight it is the same, however, the larger granule is about double the size of regular salt so if one is measuring by volume, roughly half the amount of table salt would be needed when substituting for kosher salt. As always, salt is a matter of preference so regardless of the salt specified, it can be adjusted to suit one's tastes. Eliminating it altogether would be problematic but adding or subtracting ¼ teaspoon here and there won't hurt.

All-purpose is Plain Flour: Nearly every American recipe uses all-purpose flour not self-raising. Sometimes it is fortified or further refined and called cake flour and pastry flour but we have focused on nothing but the versatile all-purpose. The type of flour used will affect the final product. The amount of flour protein varies depending on the growing season, the type of wheat, the region in which the wheat was grown and milling technique. When proteins interact with liquid and heat they produce gluten, which gives structure and texture to the baked good. The simple process of kneading can generate enough heat to produce protein and is the main reason why we often refrigerate dough after mixing: to break down any gluten formed and make a more tender product. On the flour protein continuum, cake flour is the lowest with 6 to 8% protein, pastry flour is next with 8 to 10%, all-purpose or plain is 10 to 12% and last there is bread flour with 12 to 14%. Lower protein content means soft wheat was used for milling and, conversely, higher protein means hard wheat was used. In the UK bread flour is often referred to as strong flour. Depending on where the wheat was grown and its method of milling, the protein content can vary within the same type (or in some cases brand) of flour. All-purpose flour can be bleached or unbleached; they can be used interchangeably. It is also a mix of soft and hard wheat therefore lending itself to a wide variety of recipes. Self-raising flour is rarely specified or used in American baking. We prefer to add our own leavening agents

and salt to better control the outcome. If self-raising flour is stored for too long the strength of the additives will fade and so will your results. If, however, you are in need of a substitution, combine 5oz/150g/1 cup of all-purpose flour with 1 teaspoon of baking powder, ½ teaspoon of kosher salt and ¼ teaspoon of baking soda.

Whole Wheat is Wholemeal Flour: Because whole wheat flour contains all the components of the wheat kernel, it is packed with more minerals, vitamins and fiber than ordinary all-purpose flour. It has higher nutritional value and depth of flavor. Stone-ground whole wheat flour, such as Shipton Mill, produces less heat during production thus preserving more of the nutrients than flour produced with a steel mill. We use it in conjunction with all-purpose but never as a full-on substitute. It lends a more rustic texture and nutty flavor.

A quick note about measuring flour: since we measure flour by volume not weight, we use calibrated dry measuring cups. First we sort of fluff the flour by digging the cup into the container and tossing the flour about to break up any clumps and aerate it a bit. Then we use the 'dip and sweep' method: dip the measuring cup into the flour, pull it toward you to fill it up and then some, raise it out of the flour then sweep the top mound off to level it using your finger or a knife. Try not to compact the flour into the cup.

Cornmeal is Polenta: We use quite a bit of cornmeal in American baking. Nothing beats corn bread stuffing at Thanksgiving, cornbread with chili or a corn muffin toasted with butter and jam. Depending on region and technique, cornmeal is usually ground to a medium texture but can be ground fine as well. The former is best for baking. Rarely is the latter called for. Most commercially available cornmeal has been processed to prolong shelf life almost indefinitely. Stone-ground cornmeal is the most flavorsome since it contains the entire grain. As such it is more perishable – it only keeps for about 6 months but you can prolong its shelf life considerably by storing it in the freezer.

Slow Oats are Jumbo Oats: These are the little rounded, oval oats used in making oatmeal or porridge. Used in baking they tend to keep their shape and thus add a nubbly, almost chewy texture. Since they are more intact, they need more time in the pot or oven to let them absorb liquid and become tender.

Quick Oats are Rolled Oats: These are the little oatmeal crumbs that result from crushing the intact jumbo oat grain. They, too, are used when making oatmeal or porridge and in baking but require less time on the stove. Since they are reduced in size they cook quicker and break down more readily. They lend a little less texture than slow oats but no less flavor. They are interchangeable depending on your preference for texture.

Instant oats are Useless. Period.

Gluten-free Flour: A lot has been said of late regarding the desire or need to be gluten-free. While we have had moderate success, we do it only upon request since we feel it simply isn't a strong suit. That said, we have found Dove Farm gluten-free flour to be the best direct substitute for all-purpose flour and so keep a stock of it on hand for when it's needed.

Granulated Sugar: This one's the same on either side of the pond. It has a larger granule than caster sugar. We use it for most recipes. When we need a finer crumb for a cake or a particular finish as with brownies and certain layer or whoopie recipes, we will let you know and specify something else instead. It can be used interchangeably with caster sugar just

know your results will vary slightly but the taste will remain the same.

Caster Sugar: Here is one we've adopted from the UK. At home this is called superfine sugar but ours is ground finer than caster. It is refined further and the granules are smaller than granulated sugar so they melt faster or cream better. We use this when making certain brownies to achieve a shiny paper-thin top crust. We also use this for Red Velvet recipes since the granule disappears more giving the finished product its smooth velvety namesake. Some bakers use this exclusively for making any cake layer for a more delicate, refined texture.

Powdered Sugar is Confectioner's Sugar is Icing Sugar: This can also, though rarely, be referred to as 10x sugar because of the way the package reads back home. Supposedly it is processed 10 times to produce the silky powder common to any of these names. Others posit it is 10 times finer than granulated sugar. Mostly it is used when making icings, frostings and buttercreams. Of course, you can dust just about anything with it for a simple yet elegant finish. Occasionally we use it for making cake batter and cookies. Depending on the brand, how it was made and stored, it can clump. Typically cornstarch has been added to avoid this but not always. Sifting may be required. When making a glaze or icing, you may want to heat your sugar and liquid mixture to help in breaking up the clumps and create a smoother finish.

Light Brown Sugar is Soft Light Brown Sugar: One of our favorite ingredients, it is less refined than any white sugar. Less molasses has been removed. We often substitute some amount of granulated sugar for brown sugar in just about any recipe to give a richer, less sweet taste. In cakes it will make a layer denser and chewier just as it does in cookies or brownies. Used in frostings, it will impart a caramel flavor. We use this or dark brown sugar, depending on what's in stock or closer at hand.

Dark Brown Sugar is Soft Dark Brown Sugar: Really, same as above only with even less molasses removed so it gives an even deeper, richer taste. American recipes stipulate either of the brown sugars to be measured and 'packed'. Because they are less refined they contain more moisture and tend to be quite sticky. At home we always measure brown sugar by spooning it out of the box and then smushing it into the measuring cup. Never quick nor neat. Once we started determining weight equivalents we learned that 1 cup of packed brown sugar weighs the same as 1 cup of granulated: (8oz or 225g). We never turned back and we've saved oodles of time not having to wash and dry the measuring cups. This was one of those 'what were we thinking' moments. Keep sealed tightly otherwise they dry out and become hard. We've found by resealing the bag and being a bit patient, hardened sugar will soften up again. If not, toss a halved apple in there to add moisture.

Demerara Sugar: In America we don't really have this. We do have brown granulated sugar which has a larger crystal than granulated sugar. Demerara sugar originally came from the South African colony of the same name. Supposedly it can be measured and used in place of granulated or other brown sugars. We use it to sprinkle on the tops of muffins and quick breads for a glittering finish.

Corn Syrup is almost Golden Syrup: Corn syrup comes either light (clear) or dark. Because it is what is known as an inverted sugar (read liquid), it will lend moisture as well as sweetness to any recipe. For the most part we don't use either of these. We prefer a more natural option such as molasses or sorghum

(see opposite). However, if a recipe called for it and we couldn't get hold of either of our preferred choices, we would reach for golden syrup instead since we find it has better flavor than corn syrup. Light or dark, you can use any of these equally.

Honey: For yet another level of flavor, use any runny honey in place of the above. If it should crystallize over time, remove the lid and place the jar in a pot of simmering water. Stir occasionally and the crystals will dissolve to become the liquid it once was.

Maple Syrup is not necessarily Maple Syrup: Okay, so maybe it is. But we grew up with Vermont Maple Syrup not the Canadian. Since we're purists and miss home on occasion, we import the Vermont stuff for a taste of home. But that's just us.

Molasses is almost Treacle: When refining sugar cane or sugar beets to make granulated sugar the byproduct molasses is born. Juice is extracted from sugar cane leaves and then boiled or reduced into a concentrate. After boiling sugar cane juice once, first molasses is made (mild and sweeter), then after boiling it again second molasses is made (darker with a rich, slightly bitter flavor) and after the third boiling blackstrap is made (used as a health supplement). Boiling creates sugar crystals that are then removed and refined into granulated sugars. The most commonly known brand here in the UK and at home is Grandma's Molasses which is unprocessed cane juice without any sugar extraction. It has been reduced, not boiled, and is very distinct in its smell and taste. To some it gives a mineral flavor but it is superlative when making something rich and spicy for a cold winter's night. Grandma's also makes first molasses marketed as 'robust'. Depending on the age of the sugar cane used, molasses can be sulphured or unsulphured: younger cane requires additives for purification while older cane does not. For a more moderate yet similar taste we prefer sorghum. Treacle is akin to molasses but with a less distinct flavor and a thicker consistency. When measuring any inverted sugar, first wipe the spoon or measuring cup with oil or butter and it will slip out as opposed to clinging for dear life.

Sorghum: This is OD's Southern American baby. Up north in New Jersey we've never heard of the stuff. Sorghum syrup is sometimes referred to as molasses or sorghum molasses but, to nitpick, it shouldn't be. It is the pure, condensed juice of sweet sorghum cane, a subtropical grass imported to America in the mid-1800s, resembling a corn stalk without the ears. Sorghum's taste varies depending on weather, soil, variety and method of production. Most sorghum production takes place on smaller farms and thus is subject to vagaries of personal technique versus the consistency of mass-production. To us, that's its precise charm. We keep a stock of this in the shop and online but any inverted sugar will work in its place.

Cane Syrup: Another Southern US specialty, this is the very first step in making molasses. Its closest cousin would be maple syrup in terms of consistency. By keeping this on the heat a while longer, you would eventually end up with thicker molasses.

Vegetable Shortening: In the States we use Crisco or Spry. Here Trex, Flora and Stork are all widely available. Broadly defined, it is any semisolid fat used to achieve a 'short' or crumbly texture. It can be derived from either animal or vegetable but typically the term is used to refer to the latter. It is 100% fat compared to roughly 80% fat for butter. When used in combination with butter it helps make tender, flaky crusts and pastries but with less flavor than when only butter is used. Some crust recipes use only vegetable shortening. No thanks. We think it imparts an aftertaste let alone a sensation on your tongue. However, for those with a vegetarian diet, this would be the way to go. OD prefers to make his crusts with half butter and half lard for the ultimate in flaky, flavorful pies. If a cake recipe calls for shortening, we replace it with a flavorless oil such as sunflower. The results are the same and it's a healthier alternative since shortening contains trans-fats.

Canola Oil is Rapeseed Oil: When oil is called for in place of or in combination with butter for the fat in a recipe, we use any flavorless oil such as canola (in the US) or rapeseed (in the UK), safflower, sunflower or corn. The versatile all-rounder vegetable oil is good as well. We prefer the lightest possible texture and color with the least amount of viscosity. Of late, we have been using mainly sunflower oil, more specifically Flora. Rapeseed oil appears to be following in olive oil's footsteps in that it is being first-pressed, cold-pressed and pressed any which way you can think of. These preparations can be more viscous and have more flavor than other commercially available rapeseed oils. They would be good for savory recipes and salad dressings but not at all good for baking. Just be careful what you choose. In finished baked goods, we look for a moist crumb, not the feel or aftertaste some oils can leave on the tongue.

Sweetened Condensed Milk: Very sweet and thick, this is made by evaporating milk then simmering it with sugar. It appears in a few recipes so it's a great thing to buy when you see it and keep in the pantry to grab when you need it.

Evaporated Milk: Unlike condensed milk, this is not sweetened. It is what it says it is: milk with the water removed. Originally it was devised for long shelf life. Some

recipes use it straight out of the can while others 'reconstitute' it by adding water. Like condensed milk, it's good to have around if you find yourself short of the real deal.

Vanilla Extract: Most if not all vanilla extracts commercially available are alcohol based. Our preferred brand both here and at home is Nielsen-Massey Madagascar Bourbon because of its superior flavor and staying power once exposed to heat. When adding vanilla or any alcohol-based flavoring or liqueur to hot liquids, it's best to do so off the heat so the alcohol doesn't evaporate taking flavor with it. Vanilla beans, or pods, are the fruit of a Central American orchid. Like all orchids they are labor-intensive to grow therefore the price of quality beans and extracts reflects that. Imitation or synthetic vanilla contains no vanilla whatsoever. While it may be less costly, the quality of your baking will suffer immensely for using it. In our experience we've also found organic vanilla extract to be less flavorsome. To make your own, take 4 vanilla beans and 12fl oz/350ml of good-quality brandy, bourbon, vodka, etc. Split the beans in half lengthwise then cut each section into thirds again. Combine the chopped vanilla bean and liquor in a Mason jar and seal tightly. Store the jar in a cool, dark place. Shake it periodically just to keep things stewing evenly. After about a month, you have the most delicious, aromatic vanilla. Simply replace the liquid you use with a fresh pour of liquor. You can keep the vanilla beans stewing for several years so really, there is no need to suffer the misery of imitation vanilla.

Almond Extract: Not one of our favorites but that could be because only imitation was available until recently. Real, pure extracts more widely available. Used sparingly it will enhance the nut flavor of any recipe regardless of what nuts are used. In general, it's best to use almond extract cautiously. It

can permeate a recipe and mouthful in no time so unless you want that just be careful. Very, very rarely will you see a large quantity of this being used.

Citrus Extracts or Oils: Like almond extract, use lemon, orange, lime or tangerine oil in small amounts. We tend to use this most when we fall short of the required zest in a recipe. It helps boost the flavor but it can become overpowering. In general, ½ teaspoon of the stuff should be equivalent to the zest of 1 large orange or the like.

Orange Blossom or Rose Water: Both are distilled from the flower of either plant. We're not to keen on rose water but we use orange blossom water. OD has been adding a small drop of it to whipped cream and it's just fantastic. It has a lighter, fresher aroma and flavor than orange extract and lends a delicate hint rather than a wallop of orange.

Liqueurs: The drinks cabinet is one of our favorite places to look for necessary flavorings or new ideas. When we bake something coffee-flavored, we almost always add a dose of Kahlúa or other coffee liqueur. When we want a subtle variation to anything orange, we will add some Grand Marnier or Cointreau. Limoncello makes a great addition to anything lemony. Brandy, bourbon, wine, port, whiskey … you name it, we've used it. When making butterscotch recipes we'll replace the vanilla with scotch for a touch of authenticity and to help balance the sweet butterscotch. While many extracts can be hard to come by, there is always an alternative at your nearest liquor store. The good news is any of these can be enjoyed on their own as well.

Cocoa Powder: After roasting and grinding cacao beans, the cocoa butter is then removed and what's left is cocoa liquor, a dried paste of sorts, which is then ground into a fine powder. Cocoa powder contains no sugar but provides the deepest chocolate flavor to baking. Often recipes call for Dutch-process cocoa which has been treated to balance its inherent acidity. Darker than natural or pure cocoa, it will give you an even deeper flavor and color. At home Hershey's is the most popular natural cocoa and Hershey's 'Dutched' cocoa is also available. Both here and abroad we have only used Valrhona cocoa powder for its utterly superior flavor and versatility in any recipe. Natural cocoa is acidic and needs additional alkali to work its magic. That's where baking soda comes in. Dutch-process cocoa needs acid added back and for that there is baking powder.

Unsweetened Chocolate is 100% Cocoa: This is one step up from cocoa powder in that it has some of the cocoa butter added back but nothing else. No sugar. When used alone it must be melted before being added in and those recipes typically call for quite a bit of sugar. We will often use it in conjunction with other sweetened chocolates to deepen both the flavor and color. For the most part, any 85% chocolate will do since there is so little sugar in them the intensity remains intact.

Bittersweet is 70% Cocoa (on average): Like coffee and wine, chocolate is becoming increasingly exotic and nuanced. Depending on its place of origin, the way in which it was grown and its method of production, it can naturally have a wide variety of flavor. Overtone, undertone, nose, body, perfume, aftertaste, lingering notes ... all of these terms have been used when describing how a chocolate tastes. Again we use Valrhona exclusively and the variety of flavor in their chocolate can tweak recipes in a new direction: for something with nuts we would use either Tainori or Caraibe and for something with fruit we would use either Manjari or Alpaco. Cocoa solids for this type

of chocolate can be anywhere from 60 to 85%. It has more to do with your flavor preference and what you're trying to achieve with a specific recipe. Typically available in blocks or callets (oval discs shaped to promote even melting) it is produced for professional bakers because of the formats and quantities in which it is sold. However, we offer a wide variety of it in the shop for home bakers everywhere. Sometimes these chocolates are infused with additional orange or coffee flavor which are great for things like Orange Chocolate Brownies and anything mocha. The best results come from using the best ingredients you can find regardless of the brand. Green & Black's and Callebaut also make for fine baking.

Semi-sweet is 50% Cocoa (or thereabouts): As above but with less cocoa and more sugar. It's great to snack on while measuring, unlike some bittersweet chocolate which can seem like you've just sucked a lemon. This falls somewhere between milk chocolate and bittersweet and so does the range in cocoa solid percentages.

Milk Chocolate is 33% Cocoa (more or less): Again, this chocolate will vary greatly in taste depending on regional and production variations. We use milk chocolate for preparing a few batters and frostings but mostly we add it in chunks or chips to both. In the States there is something called German Sweet Chocolate. If a recipe calls for it, we use milk chocolate instead.

White Chocolate is 0% Cocoa: Not chocolate at all, rather it is cocoa butter mixed with sugar and vanilla. Some white chocolates sold in supermarkets can contain shortening in place of cocoa butter and, surprise surprise, they taste awful as a result. We melt it to add to batters or frostings and use chips to add to anything.

Chips are Chips (but sometimes nibs):
The only difference between them is size.
American chocolate chips come in two sizes:
larger than nibs (our standard) or smaller
(mini). For chips we have only ever used
Callebaut, a Belgian producer of bittersweet,
milk and white chocolate chips.

Butterscotch Chips: Some find the taste of
these too cloying, which is why we temper it
by adding Scotch to a butterscotch recipe
instead of vanilla. We melt it and substitute it
for white chocolate for a new twist on a recipe.
We also add the chips directly to cookies and
brownies or anything else we can think of.
Before we were able to source these in bulk,
we used white chocolate chips in their stead.

Peanut Butter Chips: Several manufacturers
make these but Reese's are the best. On
occasion you can also find them swirled with
chocolate. The latter can be found online
or at confectionary shops specializing in
international treats. Our suppliers don't keep
them in stock. We carry Reese's Peanut Butter
Chips in the shop but they, too, can easily be
found online.

Shredded Coconut is Thread Coconut:
This one was a hard nut to crack, no
pun intended. In America we have moist
sweetened, shredded coconut which is very
thin and tender. It is usually sold in bags but
also available in cans. We eat it straight out
of the bag before adding it to anything. It
also makes a great textural finish when you
sprinkle it on to a finished cake or cupcake.
Here in the UK we first found desiccated
coconut which is more like what we call
coconut meal. Sometimes we add this to
batters for a finer texture since it cuts more
easily when serving up a cake slice. It has
plenty of flavor but on its own it isn't very
pleasant to eat given it's quite dry. We then
discovered that if you look hard enough,

you can track down thread coconut which
is available in medium or fine thread but we
have yet to determine a real difference. For
the most part it is available either on line or
at health food stores. Each strand is thicker,
longer and drier than our shredded coconut.
It's best for adding to rustic recipes such
as granola or cookies but in cakes it just
sort of sits in the layer as opposed to being
incorporated. Because we keep a stock of
American shredded coconut in the shop we
use it instead. Toasting coconut should be
done with care. It can go from golden brown
to black in the blink of an eye. Watch it like a
hawk under the broiler/grill or in the oven.

Spices: Just a quick word about these miracle
workers: they contain unstable oils which
cause them to lose their oomph over time.
If you're not a frequent baker it's best to buy
smaller amounts as you need to keep things as
fresh and flavorful as possible. When it comes
to nutmeg, try to grate your own. Once you
do, we promise you will never go back. At long
last you will finally realize what nutmeg tastes
like. To grate it you can use a MicroPlane or a
grater but you can also find nutmeg graters
which are the best. We prefer the one made
by MicroPlane, which we were able to source
online or at a place like Lakeland.

Nuts: Like spices they, too, contain oils which
will eventually turn rancid if the nuts are kept
too long. The best way to determine this is by
eating one. It will do no harm other than to
your tastebuds. When a recipe calls for nuts
we always toast them first to bring out the
flavor. Normally we spread them on a baking
sheet and put them in a preheating oven. It
should take about 10 to 15 minutes. Less if the
oven is already hot. You will know when they're
done because they become fragrant. Some
nuts toast faster than others so just keep
an eye on the oven if you're toasting several
different types.

Dried Fruit: When using dried fruit make sure it is moist and tender. If it should dry out or become tough, let it soak in hot tap water or boiling water to soften it up. Drain it before folding into the recipe. To add another level of flavor, we soak fruit in hot tea or liqueur if we want something extra special. Often fruit is processed with apple juice to help it stay moist; sometimes you notice the flavor, sometimes you don't. When it comes to apricots we prefer unsulphured or organic ones for their flavor. They look like little brown discs but the taste is far, far better than the pretty orange ones, which are full of preservatives.

IN THE FRIDGE

Butter: Unsalted or sweet butter is the only way to go. If salt is needed you can control it yourself by adding as much or as little as you like. There is no substitute for butter, it's taste or the texture it gives. Butter-flavored shortenings are awful, though we respect their place in the Kosher kitchen where meat and dairy cannot co-exist. Room temperature or softened butter is best for creaming because it will aerate as much as possible when beaten with sugar. In a pinch, we've been known to use cold butter: dice it up and start the mixer on a very low speed to warm the butter. As it starts to soften up, you can increase the speed to begin creaming.

Lard: Virtually water-free, lard makes flakier crusts when used with butter for flavor. The former works its magic on structure while the latter just works it magic. Water affects the formation of gluten, so for lighter crusts and pastries you want to use fats with less water content. In broad strokes, butter is about 12 to 15% water depending on brand and country of origin. Lard is rendered pork fat. Depending on what area of the pig the fat comes from, it may have a slight pork taste.

The highest grade available is leaf fat or leaf lard which comes from the pig's belly near the kidneys. It has the least amount of flavor. For baking purposed that's ideal. Most likely this would be available upon request at your local butcher especially here in the UK where they tend to be more old fashioned. Alternatively, walk into just about any supermarket and you'll find it in the refrigerated section near the butter. That's what OD uses when making his pie crusts and it works beautifully.

Eggs: Since at home we typically refrigerate our eggs, we'll add them to this section. Here in London we've come to learn many people don't. We only use large eggs. Often American recipes call for extra-large eggs, which we've never even found in the UK so all our recipes have been engineered for what the hens lay on British soil.

Whole Milk or Full-fat Milk: Our milk of choice when making batters, custards, puddings, frostings, buttercreams and anything else in the kitchen. It hovers at 4% milk fat depending on the source. Organic dairy tends to be slightly richer than what you buy in the grocery store.

Buttermilk: We love this stuff. When used in baking layer cakes it adds a slight tang and notable tender crumb. It helps balance out the sweetness of the sugar. We've also found it helps prolong the life of a cake. When it comes to certain Whoopie Pies, it's the only reason we can think of why they get more moist the longer they are stored. It is widely available in most supermarkets. You can make it at home by measuring out 1 cup of whole milk (8fl oz/240 ml) and adding 1 tablespoon of either white vinegar or lemon juice. Vinegar works better for flavor but both will curdle the milk which is what you want. Otherwise, use plain yoghurt instead.

Heavy Cream is Double Cream: With a butterfat content of 36% or more it can be used as is for batters and scones or whipped into a silky smooth topping to finish a cake or dollop on to a slice of pie. Whipping cream has a butterfat content somewhere between 30 and 36%. Since we always have heavy cream on hand we don't really use whipping cream but they are, for the most part, interchangeable. American pasteurization has prolonged shelf life more so than British practices. Dairy simply doesn't have to travel as far and therefore won't sit on store shelves as long. We find all British dairy to be richer, smoother and more full-flavored than what we left behind.

Light Cream is Single Cream: We generally don't use this but sometimes it gets delivered by mistake so we find a use for it. It has a butterfat content of about 20%. Use it instead of milk in puddings and pastry creams for a thicker, richer consistency. This will not whip up like double or whipping cream because less fat means there is too little structure to build volume.

Half and Half: Often found in diners or restaurants and served with coffee more so than any other use. It seems to be an American curiosity of half whole milk and half light cream. Just so you know, this has a butterfat content of about 12%.

Sour Cream: Thick, rich, delicious and tangy. Sour cream works miracles in keeping a cake moist and tender. Plain yoghurt can be substituted for a little less tang and we've used clotted cream, mascarpone or crème fraîche for even less. Low-fat versions of each could be used with success but will not, obviously, produce the same rich results. Fat-free versions should be avoided. Coffee cakes, especially NYC Crumb Cake (page 126), use sour cream a lot. Once you've tasted and felt the difference you'll know why we go through tubs of the stuff each week.

Mascarpone: Depending on what you prefer for taste and texture, there are several options to use if you can't find mascarpone though in general it's easily found in any supermarket. Mascarpone is Italian, clotted cream is English and crème fraîche is French. We use them all. Our preference for versatile mascarpone comes down to texture: it is thicker than the other two and holds up when beaten into a frosting. Any of them can be used in a batter or dough for added moreishness. Baked into a cheesecake it makes a fantastic recipe superb.

IN THE CABINETS AND CUPBOARDS

Measuring Cups: Yes, it's true. In America we weigh many things by volume. And yes, it's also true, you can easily find a set of these lovely nesting cups at Marks & Spencer as well as other UK retailers and e-tailers. Get this … they're even calibrated in cups! Crazy we know! A typical set should include ¼ cup, ⅓ cup, ½ cup and 1 cup. Sometimes they are available in other odd increments as well. Stainless steel are the best and most durable. But we've also taken a liking to weighing our ingredients so fear not, we have provided weight equivalents both imperial and metric throughout the book so regardless of your chosen method or mood you will achieve the same results.

Measuring Spoons: Typically these come in a set of four: ¼ teaspoon, ½ teaspoon, 1 teaspoon and 1 tablespoon. For these we also prefer metal since its more durable and dry ingredients don't stick to it like they do to plastic.

Kitchen Scale: This has become a must have in our kitchen since moving to London. A scale that measures both grams and ounces is worth the investment since you will then be able to move easily between any cookbook and method. Plus, you can spend hours pressing the button to instantly convert anything. A 'tare' function is also very useful: it will zero out so you can keep adding successive ingredients in the required amount without having to move the bowl. Electric scales are far more versatile, productive and accurate than those operated by hand. If you're into antiques, by all means stick with an old-school one. They tend to be far prettier.

Oven Thermometers: With recent technology home appliances are becoming much more reliable than they used to be. Still, an oven thermometer is helpful in determining performance over time if you suspect sudden changes. Any oven will have fluctuations within it which is why we always rotate pans during oven time to ensure even baking.

Candy Thermometers are Sugar Thermometers: These are very helpful as well since they indicate the various stages in heating sugar used when making a variety of things. We prefer the ones with clamps so they can attach to the pot and keep your fingers out of harm's way. Molten sugar is not something to fuss with.

Mixing Spoons: We use both stainless steel and wooden spoons in the kitchen, depending on what's being done. Wooden spoons are fine for mixing and stirring but they are not great for ladling or portioning. That's where stainless steel spoons come in handy. Slotted spoons are helpful for scooping and draining sliced apples before you fill a pie, for example. Another key item is a flat-bottom wooden spatula or scraper. When making pudding or pastry cream this helps you to clean the bottom of the pot while you stir so that things don't get stuck down there. Spoons don't. OD will only use a wooden spoon to make his

biscuits, though why he does so remains a mystery.

Mixing Bowls: We use stainless steel bowls for their durability and versatility. Ideally we'd prefer heatproof glass but those aren't allowed in a commercial kitchen since they can shatter. Plastic and ceramic bowls are fine but they won't double as pots since they can't be heated. We melt chocolate in mixing bowls placed either in the oven or over a pot of simmering water. We don't have a microwave but you could use plastic bowls and melt chocolate in one of them just like the pros.

Rubber Spatulas: These come with short or long handles and are useful for scraping bowls, folding in ingredients, smoothing batters, cooking fillings and, of course, licking. We keep several of each to facilitate preparing a variety of things simultaneously so you don't have to clean in the middle of mixing all the time. Heatproof spatulas are widely available and the only ones we have on hand. They can be used for anything by anyone at any time, so they eliminate any guesswork. They are a bit more expensive but well worth the investment. Silicon spatulas are another possibility but, to be honest, when it comes to baking we've found silicone isn't all it's cracked up to be.

Metal or Icing Spatulas are Palette Knives: Sorry for the confusion, but we call many things spatulas. These come in all sizes and even shapes. Flat ones are good for applying frostings or smoothing batters or even scraping chilled brownies off parchment paper. Smaller ones give you better control. Offset spatulas are the ones with the kink near the handle. The bend in the metal gives you a different angle from which to work and can be very helpful when frosting the sides of a cake or cupcakes or sheet cakes left in their pans. They can allow for finer detail work if that's your thing.

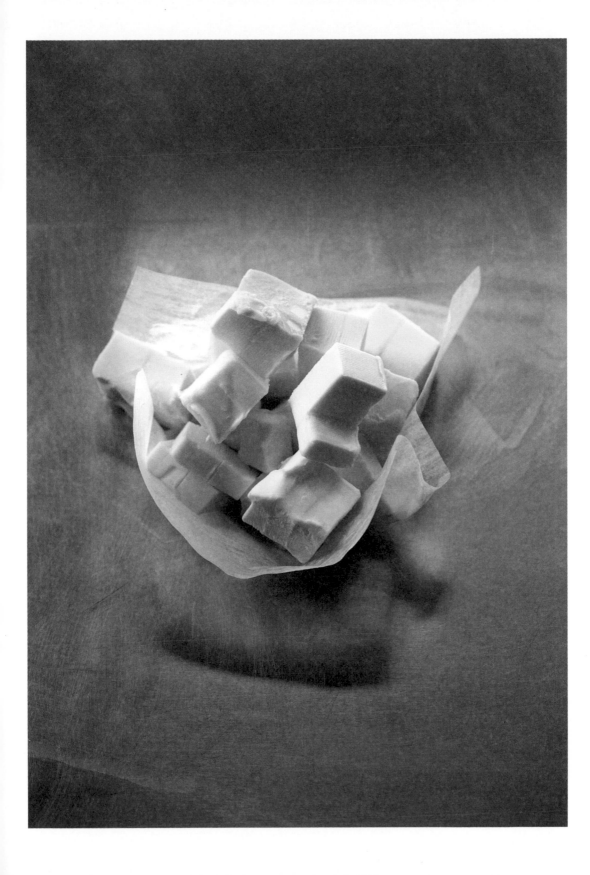

Whisks: Hand whisks are great to mix together dry ingredients or smoothing out a simple glaze. We don't sift or sieve, we place all the dry ingredients called for in a medium bowl then whisk together to aerate them and remove any clumps. When making a drizzle glaze for muffins or the like, sometimes the icing sugar is lumpy and won't smooth out. Take a whisk to it and it'll even out in no time.

Stand Mixers are Food Mixers: Since we bake only in small batches, we use the same mixers found in many home kitchens. Stand mixers are worth every penny especially in terms of time saved. Leave it to the task at hand and continue with other preparations or make a cuppa. KitchenAid is our preferred brand and they come with two bowls, lids, a whisk attachment, a paddle attachment (like a flat beater) and a dough hook. Any of the recipes included in the book can easily be prepared using a hand mixer if you have the time to slave over the mixing bowl.

Food Processor: Another time-saver to invest in. Better than a blender since it's more versatile and powerful. We use ours to make pie crust, smooth cooked fillings if they get lumpy, chop nuts (though we often place them in a plastic bag and smash them with a rolling pin), shred carrots which we do far too often and anything else. We were recently sent a replacement by Cuisinart since our original kept stalling out on us. In all our years of cooking, it is by far the best one we've had. Our mothers swear by Robot Coupe.

Rolling Pins: There is something glorious about a well-seasoned wood rolling pin. Something so immediate and low-tech. Our favorite is a simple cylinder without contour or handles. We also like the same shape in metal, since we can keep it in the freezer, which helps to keep the butter cold as you're rolling out pie crust.

Bench Scraper: This is a piece of flat metal attached to a wooden handle. Some are made entirely of metal. When rolling or kneading pastry, this is a great help in scraping the pastry off the counter to turn it or move it. It will also make cleaning up afterwards easy as pie (sorry, couldn't resist). We also use it to remove brownies from their pan to cut them. It is sturdy enough to wedge between the pan and cooled brownies. Also good for cutting scones into shapes.

Pastry Brushes: These are good to have on hand to brush the side of a pot when making caramel or to apply an egg wash to unbaked pastries, or syrups or liqueur to baked goods. This is the one thing we prefer silicone for as the natural bristles always (repeat always) come loose from the handle and end up where you don't want them to be.

Pans are Tins: Or are they? When we first got started in the shop we needed pans to fit recipes newly engineered for larger yields. We only had a few from the states and we desperately needed more. We took to the internet and found Alan Silverwood who is the premier manufacturer of UK bakeware. Dad Alan started the business in 1966 and his two sons continue the tradition to this day in the original mill building in Birmingham. The one son Simon has become a friend. But Simon has a unique way with words and he often teases us about Americana and all things political. We figured he was best suited to settle the pan/tin debate:

With regard to pans and tins, its a differentiation which is greyer (is that a word?) than John Major in a grey suit, or England at Twickenham, if you happen to watch rugby.
To be precise: Pan is a generic term for a variety of containers, some of which are related to food preparation and some not

(salt pan, etc). Tin related originally to the material a pan was made from. My dear old father used to get very hot under the collar if anyone referred to our products as tins, as we don't use tin. Fair enough, and I always try to avoid using the term in our literature. However, out in the big wide world things get stirred-up (culinary ref. V Good) and the resulting hotchpotch (there we go again) that we call English is at best imprecise, and at worst, American. As far as Joe public is concerned, there's no real difference between pan, tin and indeed in some cases, dish. To us a pan is used either on the stove or in the oven. Pots are generally kept on the stove but many are ovenproof so in they go. We don't use the term tin for baking paraphernalia.

Sheet Pans: These are rectangular with straight sides best used for brownies and some coffee cake recipes. Our recipes call for a 9 x 12 x 2in (25 x 30 x 5cm) deep pan. To us a sheet cake is a large, single-layer rectangular cake and thus the name. If we're not mistaken, in the UK they would be called a tray bake.

Cake Pans are Sandwich Tins: Layer cakes are baked in a variety of sizes and shapes. Mostly we use 9in/25cm diameter pans that are 2in/5cm deep. Most of our cakes are round though we do make the occasional square cake, also 9in/25cm. We prefer bright or dull aluminium, not dark, non-stick pans which conduct heat faster and give cakes a darker finish. We stack layers, whereas in the UK, as best we can determine, you sandwich filling.

Springform Pans: Think of these as layer cake pans but with removable sides. Many recipes suggest using these for cheesecakes because they are 3in/7.5cm tall but in our experience the crust sticks to the embossed bottom disc and makes removing the cheesecake near impossible. We use ours for one-layer 9in/25cm

desserts and tarts because we like the simple straight sides.

Loaf Pans are Loaf Tins: We use wooden moulds that come with a parchment liner, mostly because we can to easily wrap the whole lot as a gift. They are made by a company called Panabois. A simple web search will reveal several retailers. Otherwise our recipes call for 5 x 9in/25cm loaf pans.

Tube Pans: A so-called tube pan is nothing more than an angel food pan, although the latter would always have prongs sticking up from the top rim while the former might not. All tube pans have a hollow center tube allowing heated air to circulate around the pan baking the batter, in a sense, from the inside out as well as the outside in. Tube pans are available in either one piece or two. One-piece pans are akin to tall savarin moulds but with a narrower center tube. Like savarins they have a rounded bottom which, when inverted, becomes the top of the finished cake. Unlike savarins they are one continuous surface without any relief or design. Tube pans come in a variety of sizes and shapes. Bundt pans are one-piece non-stick tube pans with scalloped, ridged sides. They have a 12-cup capacity and measure 10in/15cm across by 3in/7.5cm tall. Angel food cake pans are made of aluminium with a removable center piece which includes the cylindrical open tube. They also measure 10in/15cm across but at 4in/10cm tall they are slightly deeper than Bundt pans. They, too, are rated at 12-cup capacity. One-piece aluminium tube pans are slightly smaller: 9in/25cm across and 3in/7.5cm tall. None of the recipes call for Bundt or 9in/25cm tube pans but we do use the latter in the shop.

Tart Pans are Loose-bottomed Tart Tins: Tart pans are often shallow with small scalloped sides and a removable bottom. We also use a deeper pan with larger scallops because they are visually more impressive (to us anyway) and far easier to clean with fewer scallops to navigate. You can also buy lovely ceramic tart plates which bake beautifully. They are one-piece and used as the serving dish since the tart stays in there – we like Emile Henry ones.

Muffin Pans: Standard muffin pans are also used for American cupcakes and have either 6 or 12 capacity; they measure about 2in/30cm across. Texas or jumbo muffin pans have a capacity of 6 and measure about 3in/7.5cm across. Mini muffin or cupcake pans are either 12 or 24 capacity; each cup is about 1in/2.5cm across. While silicone has been making inroads for these types of pans, we much prefer metal. In our experience, silicone clings to muffins, it stinks up the kitchen when in the oven and imparts a weird flavor. That last one might be a figment of our imagination but given the aroma coming out of the oven, it's not a stretch.

Cheesecake Pans: Maida Heatter, the legendary 'Queen of Desserts' uses these exclusively. For years we never knew what one was. These are straight-sided aluminium pans with a removable bottom, though many are one-piece. How one removes a cheesecake by inverting the pan remains a mystery to us so we only have two-piece pans. On average they are 3in/7.5cm deep but some are 4in/10cm deep. We use ours for all sorts of recipes as they have proven to be very versatile. The only trick is to wrap the base with foil before putting the pan in the oven. The base is loose enough that batter or butter from the cheesecake base will ooze out of the pan and on to the oven floor. Never a good thing.

Pie Plates are ???: Our choice for these is ceramic or glass such as Pyrex. Metal bakes fine but it makes removing a slice a bit more difficult. The smooth surface of glass or ceramic is better for sliding the goods up out of the plate. Metal is better for tarts because the removable bottom lets you slide the entire tart on to a serving plate. Pie plates that are 1in/2.5cm deep have a smooth, flat rim and are best for single-crust custard-type pies. Plates that are 2in/5cm deep have a fluted or shaped rim and are best for filled, double-crust pies. Pottery plates are prone to shattering in the oven so we avoid them pretty though they are.

Cookie Sheets are Baking Sheets: They can have a rim or not. Those with one or two rims are also called cookie sheets. We have rimmed since they are much easier to manipulate in and out of the oven plus they do double duty as pans for certain flat recipes. We use 12 x 18 x 1in/30 x 45 x 2.5cm pans with straight sides. These are sometimes referred to as half-sheet pans. It helps to have several of these on hand since it's not advisable to put batter or dough on a warm sheet pan otherwise things spread before they should.

Baking Parchment is Baking Paper: One of the best time-savers you will ever know. We line our pans with baking parchment to prevent cakes from sticking and to facilitate removing cooled items from their pans. It is an excellent natural non-stick surface for baking just about anything. Line a baking sheet with parchment before baking cookies and you won't have to clean it. Priceless. A word of caution: we learned the hard way that greaseproof paper cannot be substituted for parchment – everything adheres to it.

Cooling Racks: It helps to have a selection of these in varying shapes and sizes. Small, round ones are helpful when releasing cake layers from their pans while large, rectangular ones are good for cooling several layers or cookies. We cover a layer cake pan with a round rack, flip it to release the layer and then flip it back again on to the rectangular rack with the other layers from the same batch. Placed in a baking sheet, a rectangular rack is ideal when covering a cake with a glaze. It lets the glaze run down the sides of the cake while keeping the cake itself out of the puddle of glaze that gathers on the baking sheet.

Cake Testers are Knives: Why waste money on something you already have? A sharp, pointy paring or boning knife does the trick better than anything.

Scissors: Another sound investment. Sometimes known as kitchen shears, the best ones are those that can be separated for the most thorough cleaning. We use them to cut parchment as well as dates and other gooey things that don't take well to knives.

Graters: Easy, peasy. We think the best ones are MicroPlanes. They now make a variety of products with numerous size openings to produce any texture you need. The original, their namesake, is the finest one which makes zesting lemons surprisingly easy. The long, straight ones are best but they also come in a rounded rectangle. We find it easier to zest with longer strokes as opposed to shorter, more frantic ones. Our MicroPlane nutmeg grater is, perhaps, our favorite tool. A standard box grater will work fine for most needs but your fingertips may pay the price.

Flour Dredgers are Shakers: We keep several of these on hand all with clear labels lest they get mixed up. One has flour for dusting pans, one has icing sugar for dusting finished goods (its best not to confuse these two) one has cocoa powder for dusting chocolate goodies and one has cinnamon which lives on top of the espresso machine in the shop but we abscond with it all the time and use it for dusting things in the kitchen. We much prefer dredgers to using the fill-a-strainer-with-icing-sugar-and-knock-it with-a-spoon trick. They

are much easier to control and you don't have to fill then empty the strainer. Use what you need and you're good to go for the next time.

Scoops or Portioners: To the home baker these look like and are known as ice cream scoops, the kind with the squeezable bottom and the metal band that scrapes the inside of the scoop. To the caterer, they are known as portioners since they are calibrated for determining the number of portions per batch or recipe. They come in a wide variety of sizes and we keep several of each on hand to quickly go from one batch to the next. The average size ice cream scoop is typically enough to fill a cupcake liner correctly. Another scoop of the same size should be enough to frost the same cupcake. While you can use a spoon, these are better for consistency and speed.

Cookie Cutters: There are endless shapes and sizes to these, be they standard or more novel. We like simple things so we keep circles, squares and triangles with and without fluted edges. That said, we have a treasure trove of others in the cabinet, too.

Cake Turntable: Absolutely, without question, an indispensable bit of equipment. The best ones are the heavy, cast-iron ones which stay in place better than any. These make frosting a cake simple and quick. One hand spreads while the other hand turns and before you know it you're done. Hold a spatula in one hand and whiz the turntable with the other and, presto, you'll have a smooth finish all around the sides. We love the look of these so we also use them as serving pieces. Ateco makes the best one.

Blow Torch: You can pick these up at most kitchen or hardware stores or online. They are safe and easy to use when toasting marshmallow meringues or crème brûlée.

'AMERICAN BROWNIES? DIFFERENT? Who knew?' We get that comment a lot from customers – be they locals or fellow expats from far and wide. Apparently the difference is gooey and chewy versus cakey. To us it's really all about baking time. You can take any one of these recipes and by leaving it in the oven a few minutes longer take it from one end of the chewy scale to the other. We prefer to 'underbake' our brownies so that when you test them with a knife it will emerge with streaks of batter. A mere 5 minutes' extra baking time and those STREAKS on a tester knife will disappear. You may still have a chewy brownie but, to us, it won't seem quite so decadent. Ten minutes more and you should have just baked a cake instead. If you prefer to poke versus stab to test doneness, a brownie should not spring back when poked, rather your finger will leave a slight dent. Soon enough you will be able to tell the difference between raw batter lurking under the top crust and cooked batter that leaves a dent.

In order for brownies to set correctly, it's best to cool them for at least 4 hours in the pan before you dig in. If you just can't resist, don't be disappointed if you cut them and they come out of the pan with rough edges and crumbs and melted bits of GOO all over. This may also require licking a finger or two or three. If you're a neat freak or somehow err on the side of a more perfect presentation, chill them and they will cut into lovely perfect shapes. The beauty of the humble brownie is how simple it is to prepare and how incredibly indulgent it is to eat. For extra chewability, try replacing some or all of the sugar with soft light or dark brown sugar if the recipe doesn't already call for it.

OWIE
RONIS
R & S
B A R

SNICKERS BROWNIES

For some odd reason, here we show an almost unforeseen amount of restraint – we prefer to finish these with a thin caramel glaze as opposed to a thick, chewy layer. Not sure that how that happened, but go figure. Make a note: these are not for neat eaters (what's up with them anyway?), as the caramel oozes and squishes all about. Makes 12

INGREDIENTS

For the brownie base:

all-purpose or plain flour
8oz / 225g / 1½ cups
baking powder
¾ teaspoon
bicarbonate of soda
½ teaspoon
kosher salt
½ teaspoon
peanut butter, smooth or crunchy
6oz / 175g / ¾ cup, packed
unsalted butter, softened
4oz / 115g / ½ cup
granulated sugar
8oz / 225g / 1 cup
light brown sugar
8oz / 225g / 1 cup, packed
large eggs
3
vanilla extract
¾ teaspoon
salted peanuts
6oz / 175g / 1 cup
semi-sweet chocolate chips
9oz / 250g / 1½ cups
mini marshmallows
2oz / 50g / 1 cup

For the topping:

granulated sugar
8oz / 225g / 1 cup
heavy or double cream
4fl oz / 120ml / ½ cup
butter, unsalted or salted
2oz / 60g / ¼ cup
salted peanuts, chopped
2oz / 60g / ½ cup

Preheat the oven to 180°C/350°F/gas mark 4. Butter a pan, 12 x 9 x 2in/30 x 23 x 5cm, and line the bottom with parchment. Dust the sides with flour and tap out any excess.

Whisk together the dry brownie base ingredients in a medium bowl. Set aside. In the bowl of an electric mixer, cream the peanut butter, butter and both sugars on medium speed until smooth. Add the eggs, one at a time, beating well after each addition. Beat in the vanilla. On low speed, mix in the dry ingredients only until they are just incorporated. Remove the bowl and fold in the remaining ingredients. Spread the batter evenly in the prepared pan.

Bake for about 40 minutes, or until it is golden in color and a small knife emerges cleanish from the center. Cool to room temperature.

To make the topping, combine the sugar and 4floz/120ml/ ½ cup of water in a heavy saucepan. Whisk to dissolve the sugar and then bring to a medium simmer. As the mixture heats, brush the sides of the pan with a wet pastry brush to remove any crystals that form. Do not stir. Shake the pan to mix it, but do not stick a spoon in there and stir. Once the mixture takes on a caramel color, watch the pot closely – it will go from beautiful golden caramel to burnt mess in no time. You're aiming for a deep amber. This can take up to 20 minutes, depending on how high the heat is. We have found that the bubbling settles down and things get quiet as you near the finish line. Remove from the heat and very slowly add the cream. We pour a bit, whisk a bit and repeat, otherwise you get a face full of steam and a bubbling puddle on your stovetop. Once the mixture settles down, whisk in the butter until the caramel is creamy and smooth. Cool the caramel slightly before pouring it on top of the brownies and scattering over the peanuts.

HEPBURNS

If you read about American baking as voraciously as we do, you periodically come across brownie recipes attributed to Katharine Hepburn. It's not surprising this method is simple, direct and incredibly good. Just like the actress. Also no surprise, it is no-nonsense done stem to stern in one pot. Not a bowl. A pot. Of course. How else to do it? It is also one of the few brownie recipes which, believe it or not, uses cocoa powder instead of melted chocolate to get the most intense chocolate flavour we know. The depth of the flavour stands up well to any additions you may choose, but why mess with perfection? Like the late great, these are elegant in that down-to-earth sort of way, so it seemed only apt to name them after her. Makes 12

INGREDIENTS

all-purpose or plain flour
  4oz / 115g / ¾ cup
cinnamon
  1½ teaspoons
kosher salt
  ¾ teaspoon
unsalted butter
  12oz / 340g / 1½ cups
unsweetened cocoa powder
  7oz / 200g / 1½ cups
instant coffee granules
  2 tablespoons
caster sugar
  24oz / 675g / 3 cups
large eggs, at room temperature
  6
vanilla extract
  1 tablespoon
semi-sweet, milk or
  white choc chips
  9oz / 250g / 1½ cups
walnuts, chopped (optional)
  6oz / 175g / 1½ cups

Preheat the oven to 170°C/325°F/gas mark 3. Butter a pan, 12 x 9 x 2in/30 x 23 x 5cm, and line the bottom and 2 sides with parchment. Dust the sides with flour and tap out any excess.

In a medium bowl, whisk together the flour, cinnamon and salt. Set aside.

Place the butter in a medium-sized pot over a low heat. As it begins to melt, add in the cocoa and instant coffee granules, stirring constantly until everything is blended. Remove from the heat and, with a spatula, stir in half of the sugar at a time. Many recipes call for cooling the chocolate mixture first to prevent cooking the eggs once added, but we find that adding the sugar off the heat helps cool the mixture enough, plus the sugar starts to melt before it goes in the oven. Next add the eggs, one at a time, followed by the vanilla. Don't stir too briskly to minimize the air being incorporated into the batter. Otherwise the brownies become cakey. Add all the dry ingredients and stir until just combined. Stir in the chocolate chips and the nuts, if using. Scrape the batter into the prepared pan and smooth evenly with an offset spatula.

Bake for 20 to 25 minutes, or until a small knife emerges clean. These will have a papery, dry top crust and appear gooey underneath. Cool in the pan completely before refrigerating overnight. Because of the cocoa these tend to be richer than most brownies (if that's even possible), so a little can go a long way. We often cut these into twelve 3in/8cm squares, then cut them again into quarters.

MILE HIGH BROWNIES

We got the idea for this as we were doing our virtual state-by-state tour of
America for the London Farmers' Markets, attempting to teach locals about treats
hidden within our borders. The combination of flavors if not technique comes from
Denver, also known as the Mile High City for precisely the reason you think. Makes 12

INGREDIENTS

For the base and crumb top:

all-purpose or plain flour
  13½oz / 380g / 2½ cups

bicarbonate of soda
  1 teaspoon

kosher salt
  1 teaspoon

unsalted butter, softened
  8oz / 225g / 1 cup

light brown sugar
  16oz / 450g / 2 cups, packed

large eggs
  2

vanilla extract
  1½ teaspoons

jumbo or slow oats
  9oz / 250g / 3 cups

For the filling:

condensed milk (1 small can)
  14oz / 400g / 1¾ cups

semi-sweet chocolate chips
  12oz / 350g / 2 cups

unsalted butter
  2oz / 60g / ¼ cup

kosher salt
  ¼ teaspoon

vanilla extract
  1 teaspoon

raisins or other dried fruit
  6oz / 175g / ¾ cup

walnuts, peanuts or chef's choice
  6oz / 175g / 1 cup

bran cereal, e.g. All Bran
  3oz / 75g / 1 cup

Preheat the oven to 180°C/350°F/gas mark 4. Butter a pan,
12 x 9 x 2in/30 x 23 x 5cm, and line the bottom and 2 sides
with parchment. Dust the sides with flour and tap out
any excess.

Whisk the flour, bicarbonate of soda and salt together in
a medium bowl and set aside. In the bowl of an electric
mixer, cream the butter and sugar until evenly combined
and fluffy. One at a time, add the eggs, beating for about
a minute after adding each one. Stir in the vanilla. Slowly
add the flour mixture, followed by the oats, mixing on
low speed or by hand. Scrape the bowl as you go to mix in
anything left on the bottom. Spread and press the batter on
to the bottom of the prepared pan, making sure to set aside
3 or so cups for the crumb top.

Combine the condensed milk, chocolate chips, butter and
salt in a heatproof bowl set over simmering water. Once the
mixture is warmed through and the chocolate and butter
are melted, remove from the heat and stir in the vanilla,
dried fruit, nuts and cereal. For a more rustic texture leave
larger nut pieces. Walnut halves and whole peanuts work
just fine, but chop them if you prefer. Pour this mixture
over the batter in the pan and smooth with a spatula.
Sprinkle the remaining batter/crumbs over the chocolate
mixture evenly (or not).

Bake for 25 to 30 minutes, or until golden brown. The top
should be firm and golden. Since the chocolate filling is
still gooey, it's useless to try the knife test for doneness.
Watch for when the chocolate starts to release from the
sides of the pan and then you're done. Leave to cool
completely before removing from the pan and cutting
into 3in/8cm squares.

CHOCOLATE CHERRY CHEESECAKE BROWNIES

To nitpick, these should be called Black Forest Brownies, especially because we use
kirsch to add flavour. If that's not your thing, leave it out. Ditto the almond extract, but
really think on that one before you do. It brings out the cherry, which pairs beautifully
with chocolate, one of the few fruit/chocolate combinations we enjoy. Makes 12

INGREDIENTS

For the chocolate batter:
unsalted butter
4oz / 115g / ½ cup
semi-sweet chocolate chips
12oz / 340g / 2 cups
all-purpose or plain flour
5½oz / 160g / 1 cup
baking powder
1 teaspoon
kosher salt
½ teaspoon
large eggs
4
granulated sugar
12oz / 340g / 1½ cups
vanilla extract
2 teaspoons
almond extract
½ teaspoon
dried cherries
6oz / 175g / 1 cup

For the cream cheese topping:
unsalted butter
4oz / 115g / ½ cup
cream cheese
8oz / 225g / about 1 cup
granulated sugar
6oz / 175g / ¾ cup
large eggs
3
all-purpose or plain flour
3 tablespoons
kirsch or vanilla extract
1 tablespoon

Preheat the oven to 180°C/350°F/gas mark 4. Butter a pan,
12 x 9 x 2in/30 x 23 x 5cm, and line the bottom and 2 sides
with parchment.

In the bowl of an electric mixer, cream the butter and
cream cheese on medium speed until light and fluffy.
Reduce the speed and slowly add the sugar, eggs, flour
and vanilla, blending until just combined. You want a nice,
smooth, creamy mixture, not a frothy one. Set aside.

Melt the butter and chocolate in a heatproof bowl set over
a pan of simmering water, then remove from the heat. In
a medium bowl, whisk together the flour, baking powder
and salt. In the bowl of an electric mixer, combine the
eggs and sugar on medium speed until slightly thickened.
Reduce the speed and slowly add the dry ingredients,
mixing only until just combined. Stir in the melted
chocolate, vanilla and almond extracts.

Spread half the chocolate batter in the prepared pan and
smooth with an offset spatula. Sprinkle the cherries over
the batter evenly and press them slightly into the batter.
Pour the cream-cheese mixture over the cherries and swish
it around to distribute it evenly. Sometimes we just jiggle
the pan so the topping settles. With a small ice-cream scoop
or a tablespoon, drop the remaining batter over the cream-
cheese mixture. Using a knife, gently swirl the batter and
topping together. It's fine if cherries get dislodged. Less
swirling will, oddly enough, yield a bolder marbled effect.

Bake for 30 to 35 minutes, or until the topping is slightly
puffy and just starting to brown. A small knife will
emerge sort of clean from the center. Any streaks on the
knife should look set, as opposed to uncooked. Let cool
completely before chilling in the fridge for about 4 hours,
but preferably overnight. Cut into 3in/8cm squares.

TOFFEE WALNUT BLONDIES

OD always vetoes anything coffee. Always. In our early London days we lived in Richmond. I remember walking up the street and noticing a lumpy (but charming) cake sitting in a neighbour's front window, presumably cooling off. It struck me we had seen this cake around town many times before but never paid attention to it. Until that day. That weekend we researched yet another farmers' market and the cake was at last identified: coffee walnut. By then we knew we were diving into this baking business, so it became a mission to build up our coffee walnut repertoire. The texture is quite lush and, how do you say, moreish. We've had many folks claim that these are the best 'brownies' they've ever tasted. OD hasn't tasted a single one. Oh well. His loss. Makes 12

INGREDIENTS

all-purpose or plain flour
  10oz / 300g / 2 cups
kosher salt
  1 teaspoon
white chocolate, chips or chopped
  (for melting)
  12oz / 375g / 2 cups
unsalted butter
  8oz / 225g / 1 cup
light brown sugar
  12oz / 375g / 1½ cups, packed
instant coffee granules
  2 tablespoons
vanilla extract
  2 teaspoons
large eggs, at room temperature
  4
walnuts, chopped
  9oz / 250g / 1½ cups
white chocolate, chips or chopped
  (for folding into the batter)
  9oz / 250g / 1½ cups

Preheat the oven to 180°C/350°F/gas mark 4. Butter a pan, 12 x 9 x 2in/30 x 23 x 5cm, and line the bottom and 2 sides with parchment.

In a medium bowl, whisk together the flour and salt. Set aside.

Melt the white chocolate in a heatproof bowl set over simmering water. It's fine if there are still some unmelted bits and pieces as they will melt while the mixture cools. Remove from the heat and set aside.

In the bowl of an electric mixer, cream the butter, sugar, coffee and vanilla on high speed until light and fluffy, about 2 minutes. This does not have to be creamed as much as for cake batter. Reduce the speed and add the eggs one at a time, beating well after each addition. On low speed, add the melted chocolate until evenly distributed. Add the flour mixture stirring only until it just combined. Remove the bowl from the mixer and fold in the nuts and white chocolate chips. Pour the batter into the prepared pan.

Bake for about 25 to 30 minutes or until the top is slightly browned and the blondies begin to pull away from the sides of the pan. A small knife should emerge clean-ish from the center. White chocolate recipes have a tendency to take longer in the oven than their full-on chocolate siblings. Cool completely before refrigerating at least 4 hours, preferably overnight, the cut them into 3in/8cm squares.

GUINNESS BROWNIES

Some time during a research frenzy, this recipe turned up. Neither of us
drink much and we certainly don't drink stout. But given where we live in London,
we either pass by or smell two breweries in full gear every day. We also have a penchant
for New York tabloid gossip, where a certain heiress appears regularly. So these
seemed a no-brainer to include. The Guinness lends a deep and mysterious spicy
flavor, not to mention a unique velvety texture. Makes 12

INGREDIENTS

all-purpose or plain flour
  8oz / 225g / 1½ cups
unsweetened cocoa powder
  6oz / 175g / 1 cup + 2 tablespoons
kosher salt
  ½ teaspoon
bittersweet chocolate, chopped
  12oz / 340g / 2 cups
white chocolate, chopped
  6oz / 175g / 1 cup
unsalted butter, cut into cubes
  6oz / 175g / ¾ cup
large eggs, at room temperature
  6
granulated sugar
  12oz / 340g / 1½ cups
vanilla extract
  1 teaspoon
Guinness stout, at room
  temperature
  16fl oz / 460ml / 2 cups
semi-sweet chocolate chips
  9oz / 250g / 1½ cups

Preheat the oven to 190°C/375°F/gas mark 5. Butter a pan,
12 x 9 x 2in/30 x 23 x 5cm, and line the bottom and 2 sides
with parchment.

In a large bowl, whisk together the flour, cocoa and salt
and set aside. In a heatproof bowl set over simmering water
(also known as a double boiler), melt the dark chocolate,
white chocolate and the butter. Set aside to cool slightly.

Put the eggs and sugar into the bowl of an electric mixer
and beat on high speed until light and fluffy, about 3
minutes. The mixture will become smooth and creamy
with a pale yellow color. This is also called the 'ribbon'
stage, because when the beater is removed from the bowl
the mixture will slowly ooze in wide bands back into the
bowl as opposed to dripping in droplets. Next add the
cooled chocolate mixture and continue beating on medium
speed until thoroughly combined. Scrape the bottom of
the bowl to make sure all the egg is incorporated into the
chocolate. There should be no yellowish streaks in the batter
at this point. Reduce the speed to low, stir in the vanilla then
gradually add the flour mixture, stirring only until the white
disappears. With the mixer still on low, slowly pour in the
Guinness and continue stirring until the batter is even, with
no traces of Guinness whirling about in the bowl. Pour the
batter into the prepared pan and sprinkle the chocolate chips
evenly over the top.

Bake for 25 to 30 minutes, or until a small knife emerges
clean from the center. These have a tendency to pull away
from the sides of the pan, so don't be alarmed. They may
also shrink a bit further while cooling. Cool completely in
the pan before cutting them into 3in/8cm squares.

OATMEAL CARAMEL CRUMBLE BARS

This is one of our easiest, most satisfying recipes to make. They go together quickly and, like their crumble forebears, you can chuck just about anything into them. Everyone thinks you've been slaving away in the kitchen when, in fact, all you've done is clean out the pantry. When it comes to oatmeal we typically use a 50/50 combination of jumbo and rolled oats. We never use instant. That said, if all you have on hand is one or the other you will do just fine. Rolled oats lend a finer texture, where jumbo or old-fashioned oats also add more crunch because they don't cook down as much in the oven. As for the caramel, we prefer San Ignacio dulce de leche for this. Sometimes you can buy a thicker version akin to peanut butter, but the more widely stocked shiny, oozy one works just fine. The only difference will be how often you lick your fingers. Makes 12

INGREDIENTS

For the base:

jumbo or slow oats
3oz / 75g / 1 cup
rolled or quick oats
3oz / 75g / 1 cup
all-purpose or plain flour
8oz / 225g / 1½ cups
bicarbonate of soda
½ teaspoon
kosher salt
¼ teaspoon
light brown sugar
6oz / 175g / ¾ cup, packed
unsalted butter, melted
6oz / 175g / ¾ cup

For the filling:

dulce de leche or other
storebought caramel
12oz / 340g / 1½ cups
all-purpose or plain flour
4 tablespoons

For the topping:

pecans, chopped
4oz / 115g / 1 cup
semi-sweet chocolate chips
6oz / 175g / 1 cup

Preheat the oven to 180°C/350°F/gas mark 4. Butter a pan, 12 x 9 x 2in/30 x 23 x 5cm, and line the bottom and 2 sides with parchment. Dust the sides with flour and tap out any excess.

Combine all the base ingredients in a bowl until evenly distributed. Set aside about half the mixture, then press the rest into the bottom of the prepared pan. Bake for 10 to 12 minutes, or until a light, golden brown. Leave to cool for 10 minutes. Leave the oven turned on.

Mix together the caramel and flour for the filling and set aside.

On top of the cooled base, sprinkle the pecans and chocolate chips. Dollop and spread the caramel filling over the nuts and chips. Try to stay clear of the sides of the pan, to help prevent the bars sticking once baked. We have tried spreading the caramel over the base first, but spreading it over the nuts and chocolate chips works better for serving: the bars stay intact, and don't slip and slide. Sprinkle the reserved crumb dough over the caramel.

Bake for an additional 18 minutes or so, until golden brown. Let the bars cool completely in the pan before cutting them into 3in/8cm squares.

APRICOT BARS

Sometimes we look at brownie pans and think, 'The thought of more chocolate is exhausting,' or 'Oh no, not another blondie.' This is an odd one, only because we both recall having these as kids though neither of our mothers had a recipe. Perhaps they were the result of a Christmas cookie swap? This would fall firmly into the bar cookie category, but we bake them in the aforementioned brownie pans so here they are. Makes 12

INGREDIENTS

For the pastry crust base:
confectioner's or icing sugar
  3½oz / 90g / ½ cup
all-purpose or plain flour
  10½oz / 300g / 2 cups
unsalted butter, softened
  8oz / 225g / 1 cup

For the filling:
dried apricots
  (more will make a thicker filling)
  8oz / 225g / 1½ cups
all-purpose or plain flour
  4oz / 115g / ⅔ cup
baking powder
  1 teaspoon
kosher salt
  ½ teaspoon
ground cardamom
  ½ teaspoon
large eggs
  4
light brown sugar
  16oz / 450g / 2 cups, packed
vanilla extract
  1 teaspoon
pistachios, whole or chopped
  6oz / 175g / 1 cup

Preheat the oven to 180°C/350°F/gas mark 4. Butter a pan, 12 x 9 x 2in/30 x 23 x 5cm, and line it with parchment.

Place the dried apricots in a large saucepan. Cover with water and simmer for about 10 minutes to rehydrate them. Drain, cool and chop the apricots, then set them aside. This can easily be done in advance if the chopped apricots are kept in an airtight container.

To make the pastry crust base, on low speed combine the sugar and flour in the bowl of an electric mixer. Slowly drop in the butter and continue until the mixture appears crumbly. Dump the whole lot into the prepared pan, pressing it on to the bottom and slightly up the sides. Set the mixing bowl aside to use again, as is, for the filling. Bake for 20 to 22 minutes, until just barely browned. Remove from the oven, and let cool for at least 15 minutes.

Meanwhile, whisk together the flour, baking powder, salt and cardamom in a medium bowl and set aside. Using the bowl from the pastry crust, combine the eggs, brown sugar and vanilla on low speed until evenly incorporated. Slowly add the flour mixture and blend until it disappears. Remove the bowl from the mixer and fold in the cooled apricots and the pistachios. Pour the batter over the cooled crust and smooth if need be.

Bake the bars for another 25 to 30 minutes. Let them cool in the pan completely, then cut into squares then triangles and finish with a simple dusting of confectioner's sugar, if you like.

CoK

SMALL COOKIES ARE depressing. Simple as that. Sure, you can eat several for a tinge of satisfaction, but there is nothing quite as good as devouring a single large chewy disc paired with an ice-cold glass of milk. Like brownies, the difference between a chewy and a crisp cookie comes down to baking time. Cookies with oatmeal are 'tricky' only because they look underbaked when they actually are ready to come out of the oven. They will firm up as they cool, more so than a dough with only flour in it. DITTO for doughs with an inverted sugar like molasses, golden syrup, etc. We prefer chewier cookies, so baking times given reflect that. If you prefer crisp, crunchy treats, leave them in the oven for another 2 to 3 minutes. And if you prefer those dainty little wastes of time, simply make smaller dough balls,

making sure to adjust baking time accordingly. On average oven time will be cut in half, but that will depend on just how small your dough balls are.

For the record, these recipes are all what are referred to as 'drop cookies', meaning the dough is scooped or spooned out of the mixing bowl and 'dropped' on to the cookie sheet for baking. They are simpler, easier and more rustic than other types of cookies such as rolled (think rolling pin and cookie cutters) and refrigerated (those where the dough is made, formed into a LOG, refrigerated and then sliced before baking). That said, the refrigerator can be your friend here as well. When we make these in larger quantities we portion and refrigerate the dough balls in a sealed plastic container. As needed, we bake however many cookies we want. For thicker, chewier cookies leave the dough ball round. For crisper, flatter cookies squash the ball into something resembling a hamburger pattie. Dough balls can last in the fridge for about a week. Typically you will need another 2 to 3 minutes in the oven if you go that route. Technically speaking you can also freeze the dough balls for about 3 months. They can go into the oven STRAIGHT from the freezer, but we've found that extended baking scorches the cookies before they are done. To avoid that, you can cover them loosely with foil as they finish. And of course you could thaw them first. But for a busy, cramped kitchen such as ours, the last thing we can cope with is another step and things taking up more space than they should.

The only reason we opted for drop cookie recipes is simply to expedite transit from bowl to mouth.

CHOCOLATE SNICKERDOODLES

Classic Snickerdoodles are simple vanilla-laced sugar cookies rolled in cinnamon sugar before baking. Most recipes use some amount of shortening in addition to butter. Never fans of solid shortening, we use either sunflower or canola oil instead. Using this recipe, we've sometimes replaced the butter with peanut butter and added chocolate chips for another great variation. Here we've opted for the simple all-chocolate version using only butter. No one knows for sure where the name comes from, but most attribute the recipe to New England. It dates back to a time when baking powder wasn't yet on the market. Undoubtedly this is the reason many Snickerdoodle recipes call for cream of tartar in addition to bicarbonate of soda. In fact, the ratio shown is precisely that for baking powder: two parts tartar to one part soda. We prefer to make our own, since commercially available baking powders often contain metallic additives which, surprise surprise, impart a metallic taste. Makes about 8 large or 24 small cookies

INGREDIENTS

all-purpose or plain flour
  12oz / 340g / 2¼ cups
unsweetened cocoa powder
  2oz / 60g / ½ cup
cream of tartar
  1 teaspoon
bicarbonate of soda
  ½ teaspoon
kosher salt
  ¼ teaspoon
unsalted butter, softened
  4oz / 115g / ½ cup
granulated sugar
  12oz / 340g / 1½ cups
large eggs
  2
vanilla extract
  1 teaspoon
Cinnamon Sugar
  (page 74), for rolling

Preheat the oven to 200°C/400°F/gas mark 6. Line 2 baking sheets with baking parchment.

Whisk together the flour, cocoa, cream of tartar, bicarbonate of soda and salt in a medium bowl.

In the bowl of an electric mixer, cream the butter and sugar on medium–high speed for about 1 minute, until light and fluffy. One at a time, add the eggs, beating well after each addition. Stir in the vanilla. Scrape the bottom of the bowl and beat for another minute, until the mixture is consistent. On low speed, slowly add the dry ingredients and continue mixing only until the flour disappears. With a large ice-cream scoop, divide the dough into balls approximately 5 to 6oz (150 to 175g) each. Roll the dough balls in the cinnamon sugar and place 4 of them on the prepared baking sheets about 2in/5cm apart. With damp fingers, flatten the dough balls slightly until they are 1in/2.5cm thick.

Bake the cookies for 12 to 15 minutes, until golden brown at the edges and set in the middle. If you've refrigerated the dough, add another minute or two to the baking time. They should still feel slightly undercooked in the center, they just shouldn't look it. Don't be alarmed if they look cracked. Cool on the baking sheets for 10 minutes before transferring them to racks to cool completely.

PEANUT BUTTER COOKIES

Among the American cookie repertoire, this is the basis for an all-time favourite: a Black-eyed Susan. For those, you would take small scoops of this dough, squish a Hershey's chocolate kiss into the center of each and then pop them into the oven. It was always a real treat when they arrived in a Christmas cookie basket, because for some reason, lazy American mothers never baked them throughout the year for their ever well-behaved, appreciative children. No, we always had to wait for the other mothers to bake these. Not sure what that was all about, but somehow we survived this injustice. We've opted for another classic finish to these, as chocolate kisses aren't always on hand. And that would be the fork cross-hatch described below. *Makes about 8 large or 24 small cookies*

INGREDIENTS

all-purpose or plain flour
   11oz / 320g / 2 cups
bicarbonate of soda
   1 teaspoon
kosher salt
   1 teaspoon
unsalted butter
   8oz / 225g / 1 cup
smooth peanut butter
   (chunky is okay too)
   8oz / 225g / 1 cup
granulated sugar
   8oz / 225g / 1 cup
dark brown sugar
   8oz / 225g / 1 cup, packed
large eggs, at room temperature
   2
vanilla extract
   2 teaspoons
roasted peanuts, chopped or not
   3–4oz / 75–115g / ¾ cup
granulated sugar, for rolling

Preheat the oven to 180°C/350°F/gas mark 4. Line 2 baking sheets with baking parchment.

In a medium bowl, whisk together the flour, bicarbonate of soda and salt.

In an electric mixer, cream the butter, peanut butter and both sugars until well combined. For cookies the creaming does not have to be light and fluffy. Add the eggs, one at a time, and the vanilla and beat until smooth. On low speed, add a quarter of the flour at a time, mixing only until combined. You can either add the nuts on low speed, or remove the bowl and fold them in with a rubber spatula. Using a large ice-cream scoop, place 6 scoops of dough on each prepared baking sheet, leaving at least 2in/5cm between cookies. Each dough ball will be 4 to 5oz or roughly 115 to 150g. Using a fork with large tines, press it into the dough balls to flatten them slightly, then make a cross-hatch pattern on each one by turning the fork 90 degrees and pressing down again. Sprinkle the tops of the cookies with granulated sugar. Refrigerate the dough balls for at least 4 hours before baking – this will make them puffier as opposed to flatter.

Bake the cookies for 12 to 15 minutes, until they are golden around the edges. For a crisper cookie, leave them in the oven until golden brown all over. Cool the cookies on the baking sheets for 10 minutes before transferring them to wire racks to cool completely. With these, cookies baked for a shorter time will firm up as they cool.

NEIMAN MARCUS (NM) COOKIES

American urban legend has it that this recipe was available through the Neiman Marcus store catalogue for quite a lot of money. Other versions claim it was inadvertently added to a customer's café bill and the store refused to refund the money. Be that as it may, each year the Dallas-based store, similar to Harrods, featured these cookies in its Christmas catalogue – one that knows no bounds when it comes to unique items with hefty price tags. Apparently people fell over themselves trying to get the recipe and, supposedly, the store obliged. We've no idea if this is truly the recipe, let alone what the veracity of the story might be, but we fell across this in one of our humble community cookbooks from Arkansas (AR). One can also do a handy web search and unearth 'THE' official recipe from Neiman's website, but that version appears to be little more than a chocolate chip cookie with espresso powder chucked in. We thought it best to represent all sides of the story herein … Makes about 8 large or 24 small cookies

INGREDIENTS

all-purpose or plain flour
  10½oz / 300g / 2 cups
blended oatmeal
  (measured then blitzed to a
  fine powder in a processor)
  7½oz / 210g / 2½ cups
kosher salt
  1 teaspoon
baking powder
  1 teaspoon
bicarbonate of soda
  1 teaspoon
instant espresso powder
  1 tablespoon
unsalted butter, softened
  8oz / 225g / 1 cup
light brown sugar
  8oz / 225g / 1 cup, packed
granulated sugar
  8oz / 225g / 1 cup
large eggs
  2
vanilla extract
  1 tablespoon
semi-sweet chocolate chips
  12oz / 340g / 2 cups
chopped nuts of choice
  (NM no nuts, AR nuts)
  6oz / 175g / 1 cup

Preheat the oven to 180°C/350°F/gas mark 4. Line 2 baking sheets with baking parchment.

Whisk together the dry ingredients in a medium bowl. Using an electric mixer, cream the butter and two sugars until light and fluffyish. One at a time, add the eggs, beating well after each addition. Stir in the vanilla. Scrape the bowl and beat for another minute until the mixture is consistent. On low speed, slowly add the dry ingredients and continue mixing only until the flour disappears. Remove the bowl and fold in the chocolate chips and nuts.

With a large ice-cream scoop, divide the dough into balls approximately 5 to 6oz (150 to 175g) each. Place the balls on the prepared baking sheets about 2in/5cm apart. You will get 6 cookies per sheet. At this point you can refrigerate the dough and bake as needed.

Bake the cookies for 15 to 20 minutes, until they are golden brown at the edges and appear cooked in the middle. If you've refrigerated the dough, add 1 to 2 minutes to the baking time. They should still feel slightly undercooked in the center, they just shouldn't look it. Cool on the baking sheets for 10 minutes before transferring them to racks to cool completely.

SUGAR SAUCERS

Sometimes there's nothing better than the simplest of flavors. We both love these cookies as they are or with a simple glaze, or sprinkle demerara sugar on them for a bit of sparkle. If you add 1 tablespoon of cream of tartar to the dry ingredients and roll them in cinnamon sugar prior to baking you would have classic Snickerdoodles. With orange or lemon zest they can easily be nudged in other directions. When we lived in New York there was a little bakery, now gone, called Mary's Off Jane. She made the most incredible lime shortbread-ish cookies with a lime glaze that we devoured. These come close, but we have yet to recreate them to her standard.

Makes about 10 large or 36 small cookies

INGREDIENTS

all-purpose or plain flour
   21oz / 600g / 4 cups
bicarbonate of soda
   1 teaspoon
kosher salt
   ½ teaspoon
unsalted butter
   12oz / 340g / 1½ cups
canola oil
   4fl oz / 120ml / ½ cup
granulated sugar
   8oz / 225g / 1 cup
confectioner's or icing sugar
   7oz / 200g / 1 cup
large eggs
   2
vanilla extract
   4 teaspoons
additional granulated sugar,
   or sprinkes for rolling

Preheat the oven to 180°C/350°F/gas mark 4. Line 2 baking sheets with baking parchment.

In a medium bowl, whisk together the flour, bicarbonate of soda and salt.

In the bowl of an electric mixer, cream the butter on medium speed for about a minute. With the mixer on, slowly pour in the oil, and then add the two sugars, the eggs and the vanilla. Make sure to stir well after each addition. Slowly add the flour mixture about a quarter at a time. Mix only until the flour disappears. Don't be alarmed, as this dough is quite soft when you're done. Refrigerate for at least 1 hour or up to several days before baking.

Using a large ice-cream scoop, divide the dough into balls approximately 5 to 6oz (150–175g) each. Place 4 balls per baking sheet and stagger them so they won't spread into each other as they bake. Using your fingers, flatten the balls slightly and sprinkle each one with sugar. If glazing, leave the sprinkle off altogether. We've also just rolled the balls in granulated sugar or sprinkles before flattening them on the baking sheet.

Bake for 15 to 20 minutes, or until the edges start to turn golden. The middles will appear soft but will firm up as they cool. If you prefer crisper cookies, add another minute or two. Cool on the baking sheets for 5 minutes before transferring them to wire racks to cool.

XXX-RATED CHOCOLATE CHIP COOKIES

One of our favourite New York haunts, Mary's Off Jane (now closed) called these Chubby Hubbies. Many sources trace similar recipes back to the Soho Charcuterie, one of the first gentrified outposts in a derelict manufacturing district, which called them Chocolate Gobs. Understand that at the time the Soho section of New York City was a ghost town of run-down buildings, so the idea of anyone baking in the area, let alone to acclaim, is a bit odd. In other circles still, they could be called Chubby Husbears. We opted to renounce any affiliation and went with this simple racy moniker. Not to worry, it only refers to the three types of chocolate used. These are exclusively OD's handiwork. Makes about 8 large or 24 small cookies

INGREDIENTS

chopped pecans
 6oz / 175g / 1 cup
chopped walnuts
 6oz / 175g / 1 cup
unsalted butter, softened
 4oz / 115g / ½ cup
bitter or semi-sweet chocolate,
 chips or chunks
 6oz / 175g / 1 cup
unsweetened chocolate,
 chips or chunks
 6oz / 175g / 1 cup
all-purpose or plain flour
 2½oz / 75g / ½ cup
baking powder
 ¼ teaspoon
kosher salt
 ¼ teaspoon
large eggs, at room temperature
 3
granulated sugar
 8oz / 225g / 1 cup
vanilla extract
 1 tablespoon
semi-sweet or milk chocolate chips
 9oz / 250g / 1½ cups
mini marshmallows
 2–3oz / 60–75g / 1½ cups

Preheat the oven to 180°C/350°F/gas mark 4. Toast the nuts on baking sheets for 8 or so minutes, until aromatic. Cool completely. Line several baking sheets with parchment.

Melt the butter and both chocolates in a heatproof bowl set over a pan of simmering water. Stir occasionally to hasten melting, which will keep the mixture at the lowest temperature possible. Remove from the heat and set aside.

Whisk together the flour, baking powder and salt in a medium bowl.

In the bowl of an electric mixer, beat the eggs and sugar on medium speed until fluffy. Add the vanilla and cooled chocolate mixture. Continue beating on medium speed for about 2 minutes, until the dough is thick and glossy. Add the flour mixture and stir only until just incorporated. Fold in the toasted nuts, chocolate chips and marshmallows. Let the dough rest for 15 to 20 minutes to facilitate scooping.

With a large ice-cream scoop, drop dough balls on to the prepared baking sheets, keeping at least 2in/5cm between cookies. Stagger them so they don't morph into one giant lump when baking. Each ball of dough will be 4 to 5oz (115 to 150g). There should be no more than 6 cookies per sheet. Refrigerate for 4 hours or up to 3 days before baking.

Bake for 15 to 20 minutes, until the tops crack and become glossy. To the touch they will seem underdone. Allow the cookies to cool on the sheets for 5 to 10 minutes before removing them to wire racks to cool completely.

OATMEAL MAPLE COOKIES

Another classic favourite! As with breakfast, some like fruit in their oatmeal and others don't. We always go for a drizzle of maple syrup (okay, and a dot of butter, too). OD likes to add dried cherries or cranberries to this recipe, where I would add raisins if anything. Our reasoning here was to create a portable bowl of oatmeal you could enjoy any time, anywhere. And everyone knows how healthy oatmeal is. Makes about 8 large or 24 small cookies

INGREDIENTS

For the cookies:

all-purpose or plain flour
  8oz / 225g / 1½ cups
bicarbonate of soda
  2 teaspoons
kosher salt
  ½ teaspoon
jumbo or slow oats
  9oz / 250g / 3 cups
dried fruit of choice (optional),
  diced as required
  8oz / 225g / ¾ cup
unsalted butter, softened
  6oz / 175g / ¾ cup
pure maple syrup
  2fl oz / 60ml / ¼ cup
granulated sugar
  4oz / 115g / ½ cup
light brown sugar
  6oz / 175g / ¾ cup, packed
large eggs
  2
vanilla extract
  1½ teaspoons

For the glaze:

confectioner's or icing sugar
  6oz / 175g / 1 cup
pure maple syrup
  2fl oz / 60ml / ¼ cup
heavy or double cream
  2fl oz / 60ml / ¼ cup
kosher salt
  a pinch

Preheat the oven to 180°C/350°F/gas mark 4. Line 2 baking sheets with baking parchment.

In a medium bowl, whisk together the flour, bicarbonate of soda and salt. Add the oats and dried fruit, if using, and mix thoroughly. Set aside.

In the bowl of an electric mixer, cream the butter, maple syrup and both sugars on medium speed until well combined. Beat in the eggs, one at a time, until evenly incorporated. Stir in the vanilla. Slowly add the dry ingredients, mixing only until they disappear. Finish mixing with a rubber spatula. Using a large ice-cream scoop, place 6 scoops of dough on each prepared sheet, leaving 2in/5cm between cookies – each ball will be 5 to 6oz or 150 to 175g.

Bake the cookies for 12 to 15 minutes, or until they are golden brown. Cool on the baking sheets for 10 minutes before transferring to wire racks to cool completely.

To make the glaze, put all the ingredients into a medium bowl and whisk until smooth. You may heat the mixture gently to help remove any lumps. If it looks too thick, add another tablespoon of cream. Dip the tops of the cooled cookies into the glaze and put them back on the rack, right side up, to set the glaze, for about 30 minutes. Alternatively, use a spoon to take a scoop of icing and drizzle it on to the top of each cookie, then use the back of the spoon to smush it around.

TONGASS FOREST COOKIES

So-called because the original recipe was found while sleuthing for our virtual state-by-state baking tour of America. The Tongass Forest is America's largest national park, covering most of south-eastern Alaska just west of British Columbia and north of Washington State. Sadly, though, neither of us have been there yet. We've used any crunchy cereal in place of the Rice Krispies (even Cocoa Puffs) for variety. Butterscotch chips are widely available in the UK online, but if you can't find them or aren't in the mood for e-shopping, use white chocolate chips instead. About 8 large or 24 small cookies

INGREDIENTS

all-purpose or plain flour
10½oz / 300g / 2 cups
bicarbonate of soda
1 teaspoon
baking powder
½ teaspoon
kosher salt
½ teaspoon
shredded coconut
4oz / 115g / 1 cup
oats (slow, quick or a combo)
6oz / 175g / 2 cups
Rice Krispies cereal
2oz / 60g / 2 cups or so
butterscotch chips (optional)
6oz / 175g / 1 cup
unsalted butter, softened
8oz / 225g / 1 cup
granulated sugar
8oz / 225g / 1 cup
light brown sugar
8oz / 225g / 1 cup, packed
large eggs
2
vanilla extract
1½ teaspoons

Preheat the oven to 180°C/350°F/gas mark 4. Line 2 baking sheets with baking parchment.

Whisk together the flour, bicarbonate of soda, baking powder and salt in a medium bowl. In a large mixing bowl, combine the coconut, oats, Rice Krispies and butterscotch chips, if using. Set both aside.

In the bowl of an electric mixer, cream the butter and both sugars on medium–high speed until well combined. Reduce the speed and add the eggs, one at a time, beating well after each addition. Scrape the bottom of the bowl and mix for 1 minute. Stir in the vanilla. On low speed, add the flour mixture and stir only until it disappears. We find it best to scrape the batter into the oat mixture bowl and smush everything together with slightly floured hands. It will be thick and seemingly difficult to incorporate, but persevere. It won't take as long as you think. With a large ice-cream scoop, divide the batter into balls that are each 4 to 5oz/115 to 150g. Press them slightly, to look like hamburger patties. You can refrigerate them for a few days, freeze them for up to 3 months or bake them right away. Place 4 patties on each sheet, staggered so they don't spread into each other while baking.

Bake the cookies for 15 to 20 minutes. They may look underdone but they will firm up and become chewy once cooled. If you like crisp, crunchy cookies, bake them for another minute or two, but no more. Overdone cookies can become rock hard when cooled, so don't overdo it. These are quite soft when fresh out of the oven, so it's best to let them cool for about 10 minutes on the baking sheet before removing them to wire racks to cool completely.

NUT JOB COOKIES

Every single time these get made, anyone in or near the kitchen comes asking what smells so good. But of course any cookie baking in the oven smells good. Here it's roasting the nuts first that gets everyone's noses twitching. Invariably we end up with fewer macadamias making their way into the batter, because a warm, roasted macadamia is simply irresistible. To us, anyway. This, by far, is one of our favourite cookie recipes. About 8 large or 24 small cookies

INGREDIENTS

pecans, chopped
  12oz / 340g / 2 cups
macadamias, chopped
  6oz / 175g / 1 cup
walnuts, chopped
  6oz / 175g / 1 cup
almonds
  6oz / 175g / 1 cup
all-purpose or plain flour
  12oz / 340g / 2¼ cups
bicarbonate of soda
  1 teaspoon
kosher salt
  ¾ teaspoon
unsalted butter, softened
  8oz / 225g / 1 cup
granulated sugar
  8oz / 225g / 1 cup
light brown sugar
  8oz / 225g / 1 cup, packed
large eggs
  2
vanilla extract
  2 teaspoons
almond extract
  2 teaspoons

Preheat the oven to 180°C/350°F/gas mark 4. Line 2 baking sheets with baking parchment.

Place the nuts on 1 or 2 baking sheets in a single layer and toast in the oven for 8 to 10 minutes, until lightly browned and fragrant. Cool the nuts for at least 5 minutes.

Whisk together the flour, bicarbonate of soda and salt in a medium bowl.

In the bowl of an electric mixer, cream the butter and sugars on medium–high speed for about 1 minute, until light and fluffyish. This is not, repeat not, cake batter so there is no need to cream to the same extent. One at a time, add the eggs, beating well after each addition. Stir in the vanilla and almond extracts. Scrape the bottom of the bowl and beat for another minute, until the mixture is consistent. On low speed, add the dry ingredients and continue mixing only until the flour disappears. Stir in the nuts (or fold them in if you want an upper-arm workout).

With a large ice-cream scoop, divide the dough into balls approximately 5 to 6oz (150 to 175g) each. You can do this in advance and refrigerate the dough balls. Place the balls on the prepared sheets about 2in/5cm apart. You will get 6 cookies per sheet. With wet fingers, flatten the dough balls slightly until they are 1in/2.5cm thick.

Bake the cookies for 15 to 20 minutes, until they are golden brown at the edges and appear cooked in the middle. If you've refrigerated the dough, add another minute or two to the baking time. They should still feel slightly undercooked in the center, they just shouldn't look it. Cool on the baking sheets for 10 minutes before transferring them to racks to cool completely.

SCONES &

UH-OH. It's time for the dreaded scone v. biscuit debate. To us there is little difference between a scone and a biscuit. Wikipedia is a handy resource to illustrate the differences, slim though they are: British scones are often sweetened, but may be savory. In the US, scones are drier, larger and often sweet. The term 'biscuit' is sometimes used interchangeably. Round British scones resemble North American biscuits, but they rely on cold butter for their flaky texture, while biscuits often use animal fat or vegetable shortening and are crumbly rather than flaky. To keep the peace no matter where you reside, we offer a new term for all to share: sconebiscuit.

As for the method of consumption, in the UK scones are typically eaten as a snack with tea, while in the US they are more often than not eaten for breakfast. American scones have more inclusions (raisins, chocolate chips, nuts, etc.), and are eaten as a complete treat as opposed to being slathered with clotted cream and jam. Not that we don't, but we're trying to differentiate. If anything, US biscuits are more like UK scones: they are simpler and lend themselves to additional sweets or savories. They are also eaten as a bread and used to sop up lingering liquids, either in a bowl or on a plate. That said, nothing stops us piling sweet butter and fresh preserves on a fresh-from-the-oven biscuit (it doesn't get much better).

An American biscuit is NEVER a cookie. Cookies are cookies and nothing else. One look at a jammy dodger and we'd think 'cookie'.

Generally speaking, cookie doughs use softened butter, sometimes (though rarely) shortening and sometimes a combination of the two. Fats will almost always be creamed with sugar, so for best results they should be 'soft' and at room temperature to help incorporate them. When incorporating fats into sconebiscuit dough they should be cold and mixed in more gently to help create the desired texture once baked. With sconebiscuits, the fats used may vary. Some recipes use butter, others double cream; some eggs, some not; some a combination of them all. At home a traditional buttermilk biscuit uses ... buttermilk, in combination with lard to get its loft. Don't like lard? Can't use lard? Can't find lard? Use butter. Or vegetable shortening. A critical ingredient common to all sconebiscuits is baking powder, to HELP them rise to greater heights. If a recipe calls for bicarbonate of soda as well, it's because there's a need for extra oomph in the oven. Typically this is because something has upped the 'acid' factor, and the bicarb helps neutralize and balance the finished dough before the oven finishes the job. Buttermilk and sour cream are the usual suspects when it comes to 'acids'; cocoa is another culprit. Regardless of the ingredients, method or terminology, what you're aiming for with sconebiscuits is something crunchy on the outside, tender on the inside. Toward that end, a quick bake time and a hot oven also come in handy. As with any pastry, keeping ingredients cold before, during and, to a degree, after mixing (more on that later) will help. Reason being the combination of cold ingredients/dough in a hot oven will melt the fats and create steam at a pace that builds the light, fluffy texture you want. What you lack in technique can be offset with the help of your refrigerator. Sconebiscuits are best eaten fresh from the oven, so we have offered a few tricks to help integrate these into your schedule at a moment's notice. If you have any left over the next day, pop them into a medium oven for 5 to 10 minutes to perk them up.

Now. On to the helpful bits. Don't be put off if you've glanced at the length of this section and thought, 'Oh, crap.' We aim to inform, not intimidate. To us the best trick is understanding the reasons behind the entire process, more so than the actual manipulation of ingredients, so we err on the side of being explicit. DO NOT FRET! While reading this section may seem daunting, the techniques outlined are not complicated. We won't lie: they require some practice, but after a time or two you will get the knack. In situations like this, we remind people that brownies were, at one time, a mistake. So how bad could it possibly be? Here we go …

Before mixing the dough, we measure the dry ingredients into the bowl of an electric mixer, whisk together by hand to aerate and combine them, then pop the whole lot into the fridge for at least 30 minutes and sometimes overnight. How long is entirely up to you and your schedule. Meanwhile, we measure and dice the butter or lard, etc., and put that into the fridge. Next, we combine (if needed) any liquids, flavorings or eggs into one measuring cup. Into the fridge with that as well. If all you need is double cream, that can be measured when you mix it in, as opposed to beforehand. But if you're a sucker for preparedness, by all means go for it, just keep it chilled. Again, how long all this is kept on ice, so to speak, is up to you. When you're ready, remove the flour from the fridge and on low speed stir things up.

Get the butter or other fat from the fridge and drop it in bit by bit, and continue mixing until you see lumps and bumps ranging in size from a chickpea (or squashed chickpea as the case may be) to a petit pois and everything else in between. Here consistency is not required. Some people incorporate fat by hand, others prefer to whiz it up in a processor. With the former you rub everything between your fingers, which creates flat little SLABS (not peas), while the latter yields a more consistent texture of even crumbs. We prefer the mixer, since hot-blooded hands aren't part of the equation. Plus it's one less appliance to clean, since the same bowl can be used throughout. Regardless of technique or tool, aim to do this quickly to keep the butter lumps cold. We often stop at this point, put the flour/fat mixture back into the fridge and finish mixing the next morning. This goes to schedule and nothing else. If the kitchen

or season is particularly warm, we will also do this to help the butter firm up again.

When ready to keep going, we make a well in the bottom of the flour mixture and pour in the cold wet ingredients all at once. With a spatula or a wooden spoon, we scrape around the outside of the bowl and up from the bottom to incorporate the wet and dry ingredients. At this point we pop the bowl back on the mixer and stir on the lowest setting for 10 to 12 seconds to expedite mixing. When you look into the bowl you will see what some call 'a SHAGGY mass'. Shaggy mess is more like it. Precisely what you want. You absolutely do not want an evenly mixed, smooth dough. As you carry on, the dough will continue to be mixed and become more even. Flour a work surface and your hands, then dump the dough out of the bowl.

Quickly and gently press the dough into a flattish rectangle with your fingertips. Using the palms of your hands will warm the butter prematurely and start kneading the dough, when all you want is to mix a bit more. Kneading creates gluten, which makes a chewier sconebiscuit. Think of it as tough love: a little neglect goes a long way. Once you have a rectangle, start the folding process. Along with cold fats, creating layers within the dough builds the texture of the finished sconebiscuit. The trapped air between the folds or layer helps to create PUFF. It's best to imagine a sheet of paper that's folded into thirds before putting it in an envelope. If your rectangle is longer top to bottom, fold the bottom up onto the middle third and then fold the top onto the middle third to stack the dough. If your rectangle is longer left to right, start at either end, fold the dough up onto itself in the middle then fold it onto itself again from the opposite side. With your fingertips or a floured rolling pin, gently and quickly flatten the dough into another rectangle about the same size as before. For this we use an aluminium rolling pin that lives in the fridge, so we can work quickly and keep things cold.

Repeat this process twice more, then roll or press the dough until it is about ¾in/2cm thick.

Take any shape and size cookie cutter, flour it, then plunge it into the dough. Resist the urge to twist, as some believe this prevents sconebiscuits rising to their fullest potential. Sometimes individual scones pull away from the rectangle with each plunge and sometimes they don't. If not, nudge them out with your fingers. Once you've cut out as many shapes as possible, bunch the remaining dough together, press or roll it out again to the same thickness as before, and continue. Most but not all doughs will let themselves be balled and re-rolled. We have included only those recipes which are so forgiving. Once you're done forming your dough, place each sconebiscuit on a baking sheet lined with parchment. Rather than cutting out scones with a cutter, you can also use a SHARP knife to cut the flattened rectangle into squares or triangles, which eliminates the need for balling and re-rolling. We then brush the top of each scone with cream (any kind) or egg wash (1 egg, pinch of salt, tablespoon of water, all mixed up) to give them a golden sheen once baked. We've even used milk for this step. Then place the sheet in the fridge and let the dough rest for 20 to 30 minutes. This will relax any gluten that has built up and, surprise, surprise, let the butter firm up again. Many recipes suggest freezing the scones at this point and baking them as needed. We've tried this many a time and have come to prefer chilling them for up to 24 hours before baking. Any longer in a cold environment and they don't puff as much. We believe an extended chill lessens the potency of the baking powder. They will taste fine and crunch fine, but they will never look as glorious. If you've gotten this far and are ready to forge ahead, rest assured it will take far less time to implement what you've just read. Remember to chill yourself and your dough, work quickly and gently and to leave any Type A personality traits out of the kitchen. You will do just fine.

LEMON LAVENDER SCONES

One of our favourite combinations was discovered on a trip to the Maltings in Snape, a small village on the Alde River. In its heyday, it was the heart of the Suffolk malt industry, where barley was processed into malt for baking and beer. Amid the revitalized buildings we stumbled into a café/deli selling delicious locally produced blueberry lavender preserves. One of us loves jams, the other doesn't. But both of us couldn't get enough of it. From then on we are forever finding ways to combine these flavours. If you've a delectable jam like blueberry lavender on hand, omit the dried fruit. As for dried lavender, most specialty food shops will have this on offer, otherwise try Steenbergs Organic online. At all costs avoid lavender that hasn't been grown for consumption. It's a mouthful of awful. Makes about 8

INGREDIENTS

For the scones:

all-purpose or plain flour
  10½oz / 300g / 2 cups
granulated sugar
  2½oz / 70g / ½ cup
kosher salt
  1 teaspoon
baking powder
  1 teaspoon
bicarbonate of soda
  1 teaspoon
lemons, zest freshly grated
  2 tablespoons
dried lavender, finely chopped
  2 teaspoons
unsalted butter, cold, and diced
  4oz / 115g / ½ cup
dried blueberries (optional)
  3–4oz / 75– 115g / ½ cup
plain yoghurt
  4fl oz / 120ml / ½ cup
buttermilk, cold
  4fl oz / 120ml / ½ cup

For the icing:

confectioner's or icing sugar
  6oz / 175g / 1 cup
lemon juice, freshly squeezed
  2–3 tablespoons

Preheat the oven to 200°C/400°F/gas mark 6. Line 2 baking sheets with baking parchment.

In the bowl of an electric mixer, combine the flour, granulated sugar, salt, baking powder, bicarbonate of soda, lemon zest and 1 teaspoon of dried lavender on low speed until fragrant. Drop the cold butter into the bowl and continue mixing until coarse and crumbly. If you're using them, toss in the dried blueberries. In a large measuring jug, combine the yoghurt and buttermilk and slowly add them to the bowl. Continue mixing on low speed for another 10 to 12 seconds, until the dough comes together.

Dump the dough on to a floured surface, then pat and fold it into thirds 2 or 3 times to build up layers. Pat the dough one last time, until about 1in/2.5cm thick. Because of the yoghurt and buttermilk this particular dough will stay quite moist. Cut out as many scones as possible before pushing the dough together again to cut out the rest. Place the scones on the prepared baking sheets. Because we dip the top of each scone to cover it completely with lemon icing, we omit any egg or cream wash.

Bake for about 18 to 20 minutes, depending on size. Let them cool on the baking sheet for 10 minutes. Meanwhile, combine the confectioner's sugar, lemon juice and remaining lavender, mixing until smooth. If need be, heat the mixture slightly to smooth it out. Drizzle over the warm scones. Depending on how much liquid you add, it will be thick or thin and it's entirely up to you.

ABUELA'S HAM AND CHEESE BISCUITS

For those of you who might not know, 'abuela' is Spanish for grandmother.
In our family we also bandy it about as an equivalent to 'hey, mother-in-law.' So if you
think we've scored an old family heirloom, think again. This recipe is the one OD's mother
asks for (demands) when she visits. Typically she shares a savory secret or two,
so we're only too happy to oblige. Using this as currency we've managed to score Cuban rice
and beans, chicken and rice, and picadillo, a rather acquired taste of ground beef, olives and
capers which is a bit like chili. Our basic scone, with added grated Cheddar and diced ham,
garnered a jambalaya recipe, so it can't be all that bad. When time doesn't allow for making
grits for ham and grits biscuits (let's face it, OD refuses to make them),
we will add 2½oz/75g/½ cup of cornmeal to this for a reasonably successful version.
Let's call it a Yankee version. Makes about 8, depending on cutter

INGREDIENTS

all-purpose or plain flour
  10½oz / 300g / 2 cups
baking powder
  1 tablespoon
kosher salt
  1 teaspoon
ground white pepper
  (black is fine, but we prefer
  not to see specks)
  ½ teaspoon
sharp Cheddar, Gruyère
  or Provolone, grated
  4–6oz / 115–175g / ¾–1 cup
smoked ham, diced
  4oz / 115g / ½ cup
heavy or double cream, cold
  12fl oz / 360ml / 1½ cups
additional cream,
  for brushing the tops
additional cheese,
  for sprinkling

Preheat the oven to 200°C/400°F/gas mark 6. Line 2 baking sheets with baking parchment.

In the bowl of an electric mixer, whisk together the flour, baking powder, salt and pepper. Remove the bowl from the mixer and stir in the cheese and ham until evenly distributed. Make a well in the center of the bowl and pour in the cream. Using a large fork or a spatula, fold the dry ingredients into the cream to start blending. Return the bowl to the mixer and, on low speed, continue for another 10 to 12 seconds. Dump the shaggy mess on to a floured work surface. Pat the dough, gently kneading it, until it is 1in/2.5cm thick. Fold ⅓ over the middle ⅓ and then the remaining ⅓ over the middle again to stack the dough. Repeat this twice more to finish mixing and build up the layers. Pat the dough down to the 1in/2.5cm thickness again, then cut it into 3in/8cm squares. Place about 8 biscuits per prepared baking sheet and let them chill in the fridge for about 15 minutes. If you want, brush with additional cream and sprinkle grated cheese on top of each biscuit.

Bake for 20 to 22 minutes, or until the biscuits are golden brown and firm to the touch. These are downright scrumptious when eaten warm from the oven. You can also reheat them gently the following day, which is what Abuela does. She also freezes them, as she tends to freeze just about anything.

OATMEAL RAISIN SCONES

This is one of the few oatmeal recipes for which we prefer quick-cooking or rolled oats. Slow oats, as we like to call porridge or old-fashioned oats (the flat, oval flakes), work fine but they will give these a more nubbly, rustic texture. Another recent trick we've just come across is to blitz the oats in a processor before adding them, for a more mysterious yet lush texture. Currants work as well as raisins, as would any other dried fruit or nut. Diced fresh apple? Banana? As you wish … Makes about 8, depending on cutter

INGREDIENTS

all-purpose or plain flour
9oz / 250g / 1¾ cups
whole wheat or wholemeal flour
2½oz / 70g / ½ cup
jumbo or quick oats
2oz / 60g / ½ cup
baking powder
1 tablespoon
light brown sugar
2 tablespoons
kosher salt
½ teaspoon
unsalted butter, cold and diced
8oz / 225g / 1 cup
buttermilk, or heavy
  or double cream
2fl oz / 60ml / ¼ cup
maple syrup (real, not fake)
2fl oz / 60ml / ¼ cup
large eggs
2
dried fruit or nuts,
  chopped if need be
6oz / 175g / 1 cup
egg wash
1 egg, pinch of salt,
1 tablespoon water or milk
demerara sugar, for sprinkling

Preheat the oven to 200°C/400°F/gas mark 6. Line 2 baking sheets with baking parchment.

In the bowl of an electric mixer, whisk together the two flours, oats, baking powder, sugar and salt. Drop in the butter, piece by piece, and continue on low speed until the mixture is coarse and crumbly. Combine the buttermilk, syrup and eggs and slowly add these to the running mixer. Remove the bowl and fold in the fruit or nuts, scraping up the unloved bits lurking at the bottom of the bowl.

Dump the mixture on to a floured work surface and pat down until the dough is about 1in/2.5cm thick. This dough can be sticky, so we omit the three-fold technique for this recipe. We like to cut these into triangles but any shape will do, depending on your mood. Brush with egg wash and sprinkle the tops with demerara sugar. Place the scones on the prepared baking sheets and let them chill in the fridge for 15 minutes.

Bake for 20 to 22 minutes, until the tops are golden brown and firm. The edges should be crunchy and crisp. Prop the scones on the rim of the baking sheet to let them cool slightly before you enjoy.

APPLE CHEDDAR SCONES

For these we prefer to use applesauce or apple butter, since they pack a more concentrated apple punch that better complements sharp Cheddar. As an alternative, in the States we'd use apple cider (non-alcoholic) but in the UK we use apple juice. We won't lie, these take practice depending on how soupy or pasty your applesauce is or whether you use apple juice, hence the range in flour quantity: pasty less flour, soupy more. Once mixed, these are stickier than other scone doughs, so resist the temptation to keep mixing. Keep a quick and light touch and you will be just fine. No matter what, these always taste great. *Makes about 8, depending on cutter*

INGREDIENTS

all-purpose or plain flour
9–10oz / 250–275g / 1¾–2 cups
cornmeal, white or yellow
(use another ½ cup of flour if you prefer)
2½oz / 70g / ½ cup
granulated or light brown sugar
2 tablespoons
baking powder
1 generous tablespoon
bicarbonate of soda
¼ teaspoon
kosher salt
¼ teaspoon
buttermilk, cold
4fl oz / 120ml / ½ cup
large egg, cold
1
applesauce or apple juice, cold
2oz / 60g / ¼ cup
unsalted butter, cold and diced
4oz / 115g / ½ cup
Cheddar cheese, grated
3oz / 75g / ½ cup
medium apple,
peeled, cored and chopped
1

Preheat the oven to 200°C/400°F/gas mark 6. Line 2 baking sheets with baking parchment.

In the bowl of an electric mixer, whisk the flour, cornmeal, sugar, baking powder, bicarbonate of soda and salt. Refrigerate until needed. Measure the buttermilk into a large jug, then add the egg and applesauce or juice. Stir to combine. Refrigerate that as well. When you're ready to continue, prepare the butter, cheese and apple. Set aside.

Remove the bowl from the fridge. On low speed, add the butter piece by piece and mix until you have a crumbly mess. Take the bowl off the mixer, add the cheese and apple, stir with a large fork, then add the buttermilk mixture. Return the bowl to the mixer and continue blending for 10 to 12 seconds on low speed. Dump the mixture on to a floured surface and pat out until it is 1in/2.5cm thick. Pat and fold over in thirds 2 or 3 times, but do not press down too firmly. This will not only finish any mixing, it will also help build layers and make the scones rise while baking. Pat or roll until the dough is 1in/2.5cm thick again. Try to be quick and gentle. The more forceful you are, the tougher the scones will be. Cut into whatever shape you want, and place the scones on the prepared baking sheets. We like these to look more rustic, so we omit the egg wash or brushing them with cream at this point. Refrigerate the whole lot for 15 minutes or so, to let the dough rest and the butter chill again.

Bake for 20 to 22 minutes, or until golden and firm. If you used rimmed baking sheets, prop the scones against the rim. This will help prevent them steaming and possibly becoming smushy. You want a crunchy exterior all around.

PEACH JAM SCONES

These are, bar none, among our favourite scones. The recipe for the jam can be adapted to use any dried fruit you may prefer. Alternatively, you can use any store-bought fruit preserve as long as it is thick and full of texture, not thin and watery like jelly can be. Some might call it fruit butter. As you'll see in the Peach Jam recipe (page 194), we use plenty of bourbon, which permeates these scones and takes them to another level. If that isn't your thing, using a ready-made preserve or fruit butter easily omits the liquor. When these are in the oven everyone in the kitchen gets very impatient and clamours around the oven when they come out. Word to the wise: be as patient as possible, because biting into a hot scone indeed can be a transcendent experience unless you hit the molten jam inside. Makes about 8

INGREDIENTS

all-purpose or plain flour
21oz / 600g / 4 cups
granulated sugar, depending
on the sweetness of the jam
4–6oz / 115–175g / ½–¾ cup
baking powder
3 tablespoons
kosher salt
½ teaspoon
unsalted butter, cold and diced
8oz / 225g / 1 cup
peach jam
2½oz / 70g / ½ cup
buttermilk, cold
8–10½fl oz / 240–320ml / 1–1¼ cups

Preheat the oven to 200°C/400°F/gas mark 6. Line 2 baking sheets with baking parchment.

In the bowl of an electric mixer, whisk together the flour, sugar, baking powder and salt. Piece by piece, drop in the butter and mix on low speed until it is unevenly crumby. Remove the bowl from the mixer and stir in the peach jam, followed by the buttermilk. Once the dough starts to come together, dump it on to a floured work surface. Because of the jam swirling through the dough this is very sticky, so don't freak out. Pat the dough out as best you can (vinyl or latex gloves can help with this) until it is ¾in/2cm thick. Cut the scones into the desired shape and transfer to the prepared baking sheets. If you're looking to gild the lily, sprinkle some demerara sugar on top. We leave them as is, which is marbled-looking.

Bake the scones for 18 to 20 minutes, or until they are golden brown and firm. Because of the jam they can be bubbly and oozy and tend not to rise as much as other scones. They can sometimes even look like a real mess. But they are delicious, so who cares?

CHOCOLATE SCONES

Sometimes a simple scone or biscuit just won't do. For those moods, we offer these.

Makes about 8

INGREDIENTS

all-purpose or plain flour
9½oz / 260g / 1¾ cups

cocoa powder
1oz / 25g / ¼ cup

granulated sugar
2½oz / 70g / ½ cup

baking powder
1 tablespoon

bicarbonate of soda
¼ teaspoon

kosher salt
½ teaspoon

unsalted butter, cold and diced
6oz / 175g / ¾ cup

chocolate chips
3–4oz / 75–115g / ½ cup

heavy or double cream, cold
4fl oz / 120ml / ½ cup

large eggs, cold
2

vanilla extract
1 teaspoon

egg wash
1 egg, pinch of salt,
1 tablespoon water or milk

Preheat the oven to 200°C/400°F/gas mark 6. Line 2 baking sheets with baking parchment.

Measure the flour, cocoa, sugar, baking powder, bicarbonate of soda and salt into the bowl of an electric mixer. Stir it all together on low speed until the color is consistent. Piece by piece, add the butter and continue mixing until you have coarse, uneven crumbs. Remove the bowl from the mixer, fold in the chocolate chips and make a well in the center. Measure the cream into a large cup, add the eggs and vanilla and whisk together. All at once, pour the cream mixture into the well. Bring everything together with a large fork, spoon or spatula by scraping around the outside of the bowl and up from the bottom until the dough is almost even. Return the bowl to the mixer and stir on low speed for 10 to 12 seconds. Remember, people, shaggy mess is what you want here. Dump the dough on to a floured work surface.

Pat and fold over in thirds 2 or 3 times, but do not press down too firmly. Pat or roll one last time, until the dough is 1in/2.5cm thick. Try to be quick and gentle. Cut into whatever shape you want, and place the scones on the prepared baking sheets. Brush the top of each scone with the egg wash. Refrigerate the whole lot for 15 minutes or so, to let the dough rest and the butter chill again.

Bake for 20 to 22 minutes, or until firm. Color testing doesn't really work with these, but make sure the chocolate brown doesn't start to singe. Let them cool on a rack or propped up on the edge of the baking sheet, to keep the bottom from steaming and becoming soggy. To us these are best eaten warm, while the chocolate chips inside are still gooey. Now is also a good time to slather on your best preserves in lieu of using dried fruit inside, or a dollop of cream and some fresh raspberries.

MAPLE CORN DROP BISCUITS

If you're ever in the mood for something sconebiscuit-y but can't be bothered with the rigmarole, rest assured there is a delicious treat known as a drop biscuit. These tend toward the simpler end of the flavour spectrum, presumably because preparation is kept short and sweet. Since you're already not in the mood to make an effort, now is the time to forfeit your shape of choice. These will be quirky golden lumps of crispy dough just waiting to be paired with anything you can imagine. For a more savoury option, replace the maple syrup with extra milk and enjoy these with dinner. Chuck in some cheese and pair them with soup or stew. A little herb thrown in will quickly take them from modest to sublime. Since you're not concentrating on technique, let your mind wander and add whatever strikes your fancy. Then again, you're feeling lazy. So don't. Makes about 8

INGREDIENTS

all-purpose or plain flour
  9oz / 250g / 1 cup and 2 tablespoons
yellow cornmeal
  4oz / 115g / ½ cup
baking powder
  1 tablespoon
bicarbonate of soda
  ¼ teaspoon
kosher salt
  ½ teaspoon
granulated sugar
  2 tablespoons
unsalted butter, cold
  4oz / 115g / ½ cup
whole milk, cold
  4fl oz / 120ml / ½ cup
pure maple syrup
  2fl oz / 60ml / ¼ cup

Preheat the oven to 220°C/425°F/gas mark 7. Line several baking sheets with baking parchment.

In the bowl of an electric mixer, whisk together the flour, cornmeal, baking powder, bicarbonate of soda, salt and sugar. Slowly add the cold butter on low speed and continue stirring until you have an uneven pebble-like mixture. Remove the bowl from the mixer and make a well in the center.

In a large measuring jug, combine the milk and maple syrup. All at once, pour the liquids into the well. Using a large fork, give the bowl a few stirs and, if needed, return the bowl to the mixer and turn it on and off a few times until everything starts to come together. It should take no more than 10 seconds on low speed in order for the dough to come together. If stirring is your thing, you can easily do this by hand, since this dough is more like a thick batter. Using a large ice-cream scoop or large serving spoon, drop the dough on to the prepared baking sheets. It will spread, so be sure not to crowd the sheet. Typically we get no more than 6 per baking sheet, fewer if your sheets are smaller.

Bake the biscuits for about 15 minutes, or until they are puffy and golden. Don't expect proper-looking biscuits. These have an informal, uneven charm to them and will spread in all directions while baking. Let them cool slightly before diving in. Diving with a butter-laden fork is highly recommended. Diving with a butter-laden fork and an extra drizzle of maple syrup should be mandatory.

SOUR CREAM SPICED PECAN BISCUITS

During the winter holidays we make Spiced Pecans (see page 185) with loads of cinnamon and nutmeg. They keep well and make great gifts when you're visiting family and friends or a delicious nibble when entertaining at home. We came across a recipe for a sour cream pecan biscuit which we both liked. One day it occurred to us, why not use spiced pecans? Instead of liking, we now love these. When training new staff, a common mistake is for them to use chopped pecans instead of halves when making spiced pecans. Our trade suppliers have great-quality pecan pieces readily available, so they are always on hand in our kitchen, in case you were wondering how you get from halves to chopped so easily. It's difficult to get upset with them only because we know there will be a stash to use up in these mouthwatering treats.

Makes about 8, depending on cutter

INGREDIENTS

all-purpose or plain flour
21oz / 600g / 4 cups
baking powder
2 tablespoons
bicarbonate of soda
½ teaspoon
kosher salt
1 teaspoon
light brown sugar
4oz / 115g / ½ cup, packed
unsalted butter, cold and diced
8oz / 225g / 1 cup
sour cream, cold
8oz / 225g / 1 cup
whole milk, cold
4fl oz / 120ml / ½ cup
Spiced Pecans, finely chopped
6oz / 175g / 1 cup

Preheat the oven to 220°C/425°F/gas mark 7. Line several baking sheets with baking parchment.

In the bowl of an electric mixer, stir the flour, baking powder, bicarbonate of soda, salt and brown sugar on low speed until everything is evenly distributed. Slowly add the butter and continue on low speed until you have a pebbly mixture. Remove the bowl from the mixer, toss in the chopped pecans, then stir until the nuts are coated with flour.

In a large measuring jug, combine the sour cream and milk. Make a well in the mixing bowl, pour in the wet ingredientsand then stir with a large fork, scraping the sides and bottom, to moisten everything. Return the bowl to the mixer and pulse or stir the mixture on low speed until everything is evenly combined (absolutely no more than 10 seconds). On a floured work surface, turn out the dough and gently pat, push and/or roll it until it's ½ to ¾in/1 to 2cm high. The dough may appear not fully mixed or uneven, which is precisely how it should be. Cut out as many biscuits as you can on the first try. Gather the scraps and pat the dough out again to cut the remaining biscuits. Place the biscuits on the prepared baking sheets.

Bake the biscuits for about 15 minutes, or until they are tall, puffed and golden brown. Let them cool on a rack or propped up on the edge of the baking sheet to keep the bottom from steaming and becoming soggy.

OD'S FAMOUS BUTTERMILK BISCUITS

Here is an attempt to memorialize the collaborative process. OD has given me notes to transcribe, as he has on many an occasion. Notes including arrows here, there and everywhere, along with an odd (in every sense) diagram or two. Previous attempts have gotten me a huge 'NO NO NO' written across the draft, but I soldier on. This is also testament to the elusive nature of pastry. He won't attempt scones and I won't attempt these. I prefer the taste of these when he only uses butter, but the inclusion of lard or shortening will make for a fluffier biscuit. Don't blame me for some of the strange notations. I type it as I see it. They are, however, a true Southern American classic to serve with any meal.

Feel free to let me know how it goes (david@outsidertart.com). And since this collaboration now includes our delightful editor, Imogen, please feel free to use the aforementioned email and we'll be happy to send you a proper recipe. She was worried folks wouldn't be able to do this as written. This was included intact in the event anyone out there could empathize with my beleaguered existence. Makes about 8

INGREDIENTS

all-purpose or plain flour
10oz / 300g / 2 cups
kosher salt
½ teaspoon
baking powder
3 teaspoons
bicarbonate of soda
½ teaspoon
butter, shortening or lard, cold
2½oz / 750g / 5 tablespoons
buttermilk
8fl oz / 240ml / 1 cup

Combine all your dry. Cut in your butter. Work this similar to a crust dough so peas size chunks of butter should be visible. Make a well in the center & add buttermilk.

500 degrees F 250 degrees C oven for 8 to 10 minutes.

A little goes a long way with these so cut into 2-inch rounds or squares. (Why the hell would anyone make such a small biscuit?)

This will be a very sticky dough. Mix the bottom well.

Dump out on to a floured surface and pat into a flat 1" thick rectangle shape. Fold you left half over you right and roll out to 1" thick again. One more half fold. Roll out 1" thick again.

[Good Luck!]

Quick bread. Quick intro. Promise.

THESE LUSCIOUS LOAVES rely on leavening agents to work their magic, not yeast. No kneading, no proofing, no repeating. Just mix, bake and eat. In point of fact, muffins, scones, biscuits, coffee cakes and, to be nerdy about it, pancakes and waffles are all members of the Quick family. Baking powder is the primary force in the batter or dough and in the oven, since it works doubly hard: first it creates bubbles in the bowl when mixed with liquid and then it reacts again when exposed to heat in the oven. Since it is chemical and not organic like yeast, it is not susceptible to any variety of factors in order to get the job done. Quick breads benefit most from quick love. Most recipes call for wet ingredients to be poured all at once into dry ingredients and gently but SWIFTLY combined. You don't even have to be thorough about it. This is how a light, open texture is produced to better absorb anything you might want to schmear on. In addition to the muffin or stirring method just described, two other techniques are also used: the creaming method of beating the butter and sugar together first, adding eggs and then alternately adding dry and wet ingredients; and the scone/biscuit or pastry method, incorporating cold butter (and/or other fat) into the dry ingredients to form flakes or lumps that create steam and therefore PUFF when exposed to heat. And just one last thing to help explain why the Quick family tree has so many branches … there is a wide variety in the consistency of the dough or batter. Pouring batters used for pancakes and the like, dropping batters that produce either loaves or biscuits (we literally call them drop biscuits), and stiff dough used for other types of biscuits and scones.

So, certainly enough blather from us. Plenty of reading from you. Let's get to it.

LEMON DRIZZLE

In some small way, we'd like to think this recipe helped put us on the map. We made this for our very first farmers' market, since it can be done in advance and kept in the fridge for a week or more. We prefer to use homemade Almond Paste (page 195), since ready-made paste can have a chemical taste. There are two easy tricks to getting this 'right'. Only use granulated sugar for the drizzle and resist the urge to make it ahead of time. Once the loaf is baked, prepare the drizzle. By doing this, the granulated sugar won't dissolve and as a result the finished cake will glitter and sparkle. As it cools, the drizzle dries into a crunchy, sweet/tart, delectable crust. Be careful when drizzling: the best results come when you drizzle a hottish loaf, which is not only unpleasant to touch, but tender to manipulate. Serves 10–12

INGREDIENTS

For the loaf:

all-purpose or plain flour
4oz / 115g / ¾ cup
baking powder
½ teaspoon
kosher salt
½ teaspoon
large eggs, at room temperature
5
vanilla extract
1 teaspoon
granulated sugar
8oz / 225g / 1 cup
lemon zest, freshly grated
1 tablespoon
orange zest, freshly grated
1 tablespoon
almond paste,
   at room temperature
8oz / 225g / 1 cup
unsalted butter, softened
8oz / 225g / 1 cup

For the drizzle:

lemon juice, freshly squeezed
2oz / 60ml / ¼ cup
orange juice, freshly squeezed
2oz / 60ml / ¼ cup
granulated sugar (not caster)
8oz / 225g / 1 cup

Preheat the oven to 180°C/350°F/gas mark 4. Butter a 9 x 5in/23 x 12cm loaf pan, line the 2 long sides and bottom with baking parchment and dust with flour.

Mix together the flour, baking powder and salt in a medium bowl, using a hand whisk. In a large measuring jug, combine the eggs and vanilla and set aside. If desired, you can add additional lemon or almond extracts judiciously. Set aside.

Measure the sugar into the mixing bowl and add the lemon and orange zests. Mix on low speed until the sugar becomes fragrant and the zest is distributed. Add the almond paste and combine thoroughly. Increase the speed to medium and add the softened butter, one chunk at a time. Cream the mixture until light and fluffy, about 6 to 8 minutes. On medium–low speed, slowly pour in the egg mixture, allowing it to thoroughly incorporate before tipping in a bit more. Scrape the bowl as you go. Next add the flour mixture in small amounts, until just thoroughly combined. Finish the mixing by hand with a rubber spatula. Pour the batter into the prepared pan and smooth the top with a spatula.

Bake for 50 to 60 minutes or until golden and firm to the touch. Cool for 10 minutes or so while you make the drizzle.

Combine the drizzle ingredients in a small bowl. Carefully remove the hot loaf from the pan and place it on a wire rack set into a rimmed baking sheet. Brush the loaf entirely with the glaze – the drizzle will run off, so transfer the rack to another sheet and tip the run-off drizzle over the cake. Do this until all of it is used. Cool to room temperature.

CINNAMON LOAF

For us there is nothing more satisfying than a piece of gooey cinnamon something for breakfast. The cinnamon streusel, or swirl, runs through this loaf: sometimes it will be a thin vein imparting a whiff of cinnamon and other times it will be a moist, chewy blob your tongue will thank you for. Teamed with a cup of strong, hot coffee, this will get you started on the right foot even if you've woken up on the wrong side. One bite and all will be right in the world. At least for a few minutes, anyway. Serves 10–12

INGREDIENTS

For the cinnamon sugar:
granulated sugar
4oz / 115g / ½ cup
light brown sugar
4oz / 115g / ½ cup, packed
cinnamon
1 tablespoon
nutmeg, freshly grated
½ teaspoon

For the batter:
all-purpose or plain flour
10oz / 275g / 1¾ cups
baking powder
1 teaspoon
bicarbonate of soda
¼ teaspoon
kosher salt
¼ teaspoon
unsalted butter, softened
4oz / 115g / ½ cup
granulated sugar
6oz / 175g / ¾ cup
large eggs, at room temperature
2
vanilla extract
2 teaspoons
sour cream
8oz / 225g / 1 cup

Preheat the oven to 180°C/350°F/gas mark 4. Butter a 9 x 5in/23 x 12cm loaf pan.

Make the cinnamon sugar. Combine all the ingredients in a medium bowl. (This recipe uses about ½ this mixture, but we find it best to have more on hand and store what's left in an airtight container. It will keep indefinitely.)

In a medium bowl mix together the flour, baking powder, bicarbonate of soda and salt, using a hand whisk.

In the bowl of an electric mixer, cream the butter and sugar on medium–high speed until light and fluffy, about 6 to 8 minutes. Reduce the speed to medium and add the eggs, one at a time, beating well after each addition. Add the vanilla. On low speed, alternately add the flour mixture and sour cream in 3 or 4 additions, mixing only until just combined. Remove from the mixer and scrape the sides and bottom.

Spoon ⅓ of the batter into the prepared pan. Sprinkle ½ the cinnamon sugar on to the batter, spoon another ⅓ of the batter into the pan, sprinkle it with the remaining cinnamon and finish by spooning in the final ⅓ of the batter. Don't fret if each batter layer isn't precisely ⅓. Once everything is in the pan, take a knife and make a zig-zag line from one narrow end of the pan to the other. Only do this once. Avoid the temptation to do it again or do anything else. It will swirl just fine when baking.

Bake for 50 to 60 minutes, or until a knife emerges clean from the center. The top will be golden and because of the zig-zagging it may also be split. Cool the loaf on a wire rack for 15 minutes before releasing from the pan to cool completely.

DATE NUT BREAD

Growing up, this was a favorite after-school snack, especially when smothered with cream cheese. While the original recipe is no longer (or so Momma Lesniak says), this one comes close to recreating it one bite at a time. For all we know, mothers of a certain age all made the same recipe, taken off the back of the date package. The older we get, the more mysteries of this sort get resolved. For something less sweet but no less delicious, try it with prunes. Serves 10–12

INGREDIENTS

all-purpose or plain flour
   10½oz / 300g / 2 cups
baking powder
   2 teaspoons
kosher salt
   ½ teaspoon
unsalted butter, softened
   8oz / 225g / 1 cup
cream cheese,
   at room temperature
   4oz / 115g / ½ cup
dark brown sugar
   6oz / 175g / ¾ cup, packed
large eggs
   4
vanilla extract
   1 teaspoon
dates, pitted and chopped
   6oz / 175g / about 1 cup
walnuts, chopped
   4oz / 115g / 1 cup

Preheat the oven to 180ºC/350ºF/gas mark 4. Butter and flour a 9 x 5in/23 x 12cm loaf pan and set aside.

Mix together the flour, baking powder and salt in a medium bowl, using a hand whisk.

In the bowl of an electric mixer, cream the butter, cream cheese and sugar on medium–high speed until light and fluffy, about 5 to 6 minutes. On low speed add the eggs, one at a time, beating well after each addition. Add the vanilla. Scrape the bowl and mix for 1 minute more to incorporate any sludge that may have been lurking at the bottom. Slowly add the flour mixture and continue stirring only until just combined. Fold in the dates and nuts. Spoon the batter into the prepared pan and smooth the top with a spatula.

Bake for 50 to 60 minutes, or until the loaf is deep brown and a small knife emerges clean from the center. If tradition is any guide, this will be split on top. Cool in the pan for about 20 minutes before releasing the loaf to cool completely on a wire rack.

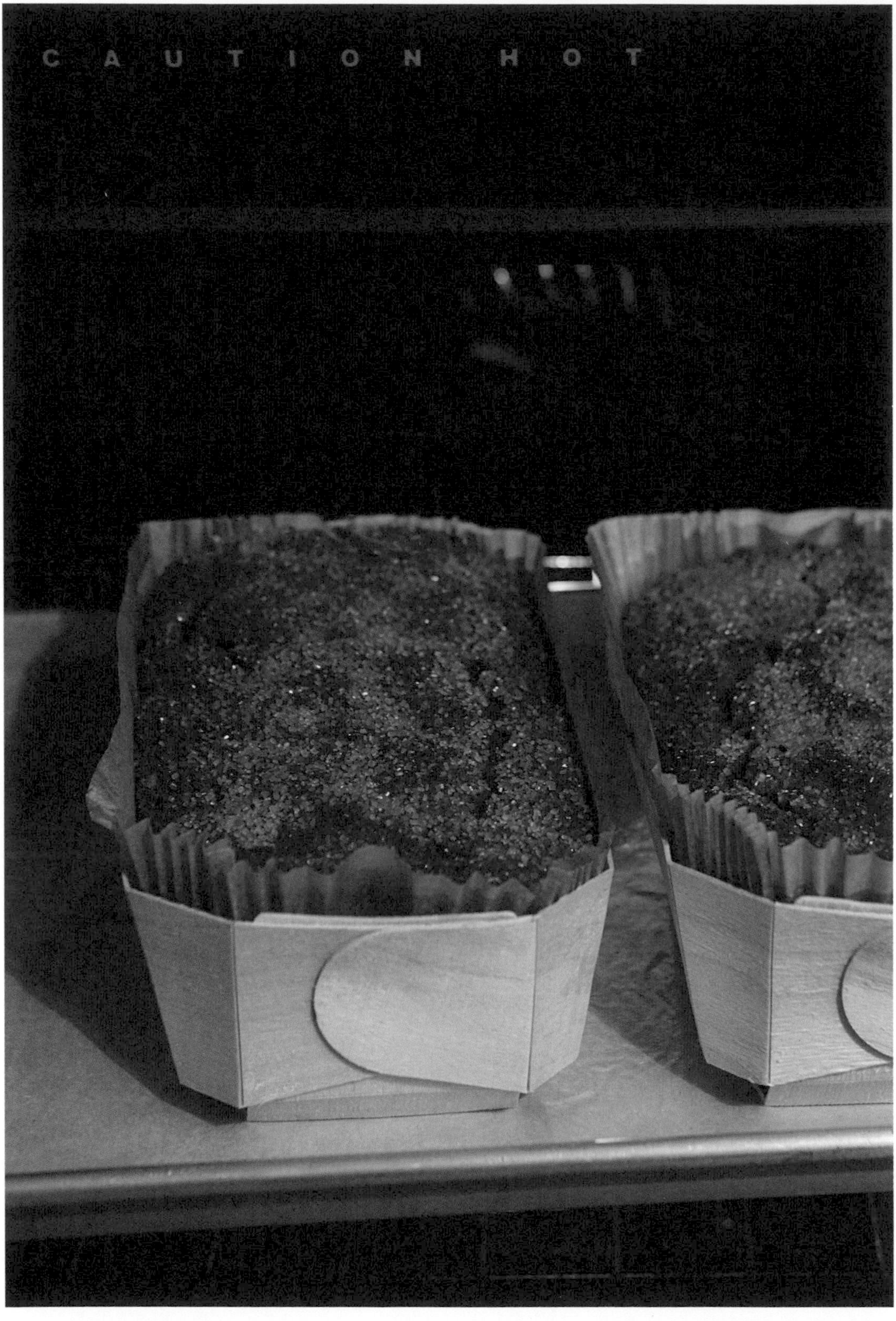
CAUTION HOT

OATMEAL IN A SLICE

This has all the goodness of a bowl of oatmeal only in a slightly different form. People can be quite specific when it comes to their morning oats, so by all means use this as a starting point if you'd prefer another combination. Sometimes we add nuts but we like it gushier so we leave them out. We've fiddled with this recipe quite a bit and our conclusion (for the moment, anyway) is that using both types of oats gives just enough structure and texture. It will come out just fine if all you have is one type. Old-fashioned or jumbo oats produce a nubbier loaf, while rolled or quick oats break down in the oven sooner so they are harder to detect in a finished slice. They produce a lovely, moist loaf without the telltale crunch of the larger oats. Serves 10–12

INGREDIENTS

canola oil or the like
  2fl oz / 60ml / ¼ cup
buttermilk
  4fl oz / 120ml / ½ cup
applesauce,
  preferably unsweetened
  10oz / 275g / 1¼ cups
large eggs
  2
all-purpose or plain flour
  5½oz / 160g / 1 cup
whole wheat or wholemeal flour
  1½oz / 40g / ¼ cup
light brown sugar
  6oz / 175g / ¾ cup, packed
baking powder
  1½ teaspoons
bicarbonate of soda
  1½ teaspoons
kosher salt
  ½ teaspoon
cinnamon
  1 teaspoon
nutmeg, freshly grated
  ¼ teaspoon
rolled or quick oats (not instant)
  2oz / 60g / ½ cup
jumbo or slow oats
  2oz / 60g / ½ cup
dark or golden raisins
  3–4oz / 85–115g / ½ cup

Preheat the oven to 180ºC/350ºF/gas mark 4. Butter a 12 x 9in/30 x 23cm loaf pan, dust with flour and line the 2 long sides and bottom with parchment.

Put the oil, buttermilk, applesauce and eggs into a large measuring jug. By doing it in this order you can measure each successive ingredient into the same jug as opposed to using several. See, the primary chemistry lesson of displacement actually did come in handy! With a small hand whisk or fork, evenly blend everything together.

In a large mixing bowl, mix together the 2 flours, sugar, baking powder, bicarbonate of soda, salt and spices. Add the oats and fruit and toss together. Make a well in the dry ingredients and, all at once, pour in the wet ingredients. Stir until everything is evenly moistened, but be careful not to overdo it. Pour the batter into the prepared pan and even the top with a spatula. Sometimes we sprinkle demerara sugar on top of the batter.

Bake for 50 to 60 minutes, or until the bread is well browned and a thin knife emerges clean from the center. Let the loaf cool for about 15 minutes before removing it from the pan to cool completely on a wire rack. If you cut into the warm loaf, your slice may be a bit crumbly; it slices better when it has a chance to cool and set completely.

BAM BREAD

At first this may seem an unlikely combination. But sweet bananas work perfectly
with tart apricots and buttery macadamias. Pecans also work well. No nuts?
Another fine option. The bran helps with rationalizing a slice of this for breakfast,
plus it adds some fiber. But when we're in the mood to call a spade a spade we chuck in
a cup of chocolate chips and dive right in. Given the wide variety of dried fruits available,
this can also be taken in a more tropical direction by replacing the apricot with
mango or pineapple. For that, might we suggest adding shredded coconut? As with
most quick breads, the possibilities are limited by imagination only.
1 large loaf, serving 10–12, depending on how thick you like your slices

INGREDIENTS

all-purpose or plain flour
  10½oz / 300g / 2 cups
baking powder
  2 teaspoons
bicarbonate of soda
  ½ teaspoon
kosher salt
  ¾ teaspoon
unsalted butter, softened
  6oz / 175g / ¾ cup
granulated sugar
  8oz / 225g / 1 cup
large eggs
  3
vanilla extract
  1 tablespoon
All Bran cereal
  3–4oz / 75–115g / 1½ cups
mashed bananas
  16oz / 450g / 2 cups
dried apricots, diced
  6oz / 175g / 1 cup
macadamia nuts, chopped
  6oz / 175g / 1 cup
bittersweet chocolate chips
  (optional)
  3–4oz / 75–115g / ½ cup

Preheat the oven to 180°C/350°F/gas mark 4. Butter a 9 x
5in/23 x 12cm loaf pan and line the bottom and 2 long sides
with baking parchment. Set aside.

Mix together the flour, baking powder, bicarbonate of soda
and salt in a medium bowl, using a hand whisk.

In the bowl of an electric mixer, cream the butter and sugar
on medium–high speed until light and fluffy. On low speed
add the eggs, one at a time, beating well after each addition.
Add the vanilla. Scrape the bowl and mix for 1 minute more
to incorporate any sludge that may have been lurking at
the bottom. Add the cereal. As it gets crunched up by the
mixer, don't worry if you end up with uneven cereal strands.
Alternately add the flour mixture and mashed bananas,
beginning and ending with the dry ingredients and mixing
only until just combined. Fold in the apricots, nuts and
optional chocolate chips. Pour the batter into the prepared
pan and smooth the top with a spatula.

Bake for 50 to 60 minutes, or until the loaf is deep brown
and a small knife emerges clean from the center. Cool in the
pan for about 20 minutes before releasing the loaf to cool
completely on a wire rack.

PENNSYLVANIA DUTCH SPICE LOAF

Here is something we unearthed recently. We thought it odd the original recipe called for shortening, since the Pennsylvania Dutch are self-sufficient. How they'd make margarine on a farm is beyond us, so we figured it was more appropriate to use butter.
It's rare that we don't garnish a slab of any quick bread with something else, but this, in all its simple glory, needs nothing but a hot, robust cup of coffee. If, like us, you think that's a whole lotta clove, venture forth and we promise you won't be disappointed.
Makes 1 large loaf, 8 to 12 slices depending on how thick the slices are

INGREDIENTS

all-purpose or plain flour
13oz / 375g / 2½ cups
bicarbonate of soda
1 teaspoon
kosher salt
½ teaspoon
cinnamon
2 teaspoons
ground cloves
1 teaspoon
ground allspice
1 teaspoon
unsalted butter, softened
8oz / 225g / 1 cup
light or dark brown sugar
16oz / 450g / 2 cups, packed
large eggs
2
buttermilk
8fl oz / 240ml / 1 cup

Preheat the oven to 150°C/300°F/gas mark 2. Butter a 12 x 9in/30 x 23cm loaf pan, line the 2 long sides and bottom with baking parchment and dust with flour.

Mix together the flour, bicarbonate of soda, salt and spices in a medium bowl, using a hand whisk.

In the bowl of an electric mixer, cream the butter and sugar for about 4 minutes. No need to get to the light and fluffy stage with this like you would for a cake. Add the eggs, one at a time, blending well after each addition. Stir in the buttermilk. Slowly add the flour mixture to the bowl, stirring only until the flour just disappears. Transfer the batter into the prepared pan.

Bake the loaf for 50 to 60 minutes, or until browned and a small knife emerges clean from the center. Let the cake cool for about 15 minutes before removing it from the pan to cool completely. The flavour will become more pronounced as the loaf mellows overnight, if you can wait that long.

ORANGE LOAF

Most simple pound cake recipes are laced with vanilla or lemon. Glazed, this makes for a great snack on its own; unglazed, it can be the foundation for an easy dessert topped with fresh fruit and whipped cream (we pile it on a plate, you trifle it in a bowl). For the latter we sometimes find lemon too assertive, so we use orange instead. For something fancier, add a tablespoon of Cointreau or Grand Marnier along with the vanilla. Note that this glaze hardens as it cools, so slice it with a serrated knife. Slightly difficult cutting but overly delicious eating. Serves 10–12

INGREDIENTS

For the loaf:

all-purpose or plain flour
  12oz / 340g / 2¼ cups
baking powder
  2¼ teaspoons
bicarbonate of soda
  ¾ teaspoon
kosher salt
  ¾ teaspoon
sour cream
  6oz / 175g / ¾ cup
vanilla extract
  1½ teaspoons
orange juice
  4 tablespoons
granulated sugar
  8oz / 225g / 1 cup
orange zest, finely grated
  (about 3 oranges)
  3 tablespoons
unsalted butter, softened
  6oz / 175g / ¾ cup
large eggs
  3

For the glaze:

confectioner's or icing sugar
  10oz / 275g / 1½ cups
fresh orange juice
  2 tablespoons

Preheat the oven to 180°C/350°F/gas mark 4. Butter a 12 x 9in/30 x 23cm loaf pan, line the 2 long sides and bottom with baking parchment and dust with flour.

Mix together the flour, baking powder, bicarbonate of soda and salt in a medium bowl, using a hand whisk. Combine the sour cream, vanilla and orange juice in a large measuring jug. Set both aside.

In the bowl of an electric mixer, combine the sugar and orange zest on low speed until fragrant. Be sure to scrape the paddle, as the zest tends to cling to it for reasons that remain unknown. Drop in the butter 1 or 2 tablespoons at a time and continue mixing until the butter is somewhat combined with the sugar. Increase the speed to medium–high and cream the mixture until it is light and fluffy, about 5 minutes. On low speed add the eggs, one at a time, making sure to beat well after each addition. Scrape up the gunk from the bottom of the bowl and mix for 1 minute more, until all is evenly combined. Alternately add the flour and sour cream mixtures, beginning and ending with the dry ingredients and mixing only until just combined. Scrape the batter into the prepared pan and smooth the top with a spatula.

Bake the loaf for 45 to 60 minutes, or until a small knife emerges clean from the center. Let it cool for about 10 minutes before releasing it from the pan. To prepare the glaze, combine the confectioner's sugar and orange juice in a small pan and bring to the boil, stirring once or twice. Simmer for 2 to 3 minutes, then remove from the heat. Using a skewer of some sort, poke holes every inch or so in the loaf, then brush/pour the glaze over. Let the loaf cool completely before slicing to serve.

GOLDEN PUMPKIN LOAF

Both of us are wild about pumpkin. Anything pumpkin. We searched high and low and toyed for hours before settling on this recipe based on one from a favorite cookbook, Greg Patent's *Baking in America*. Many pumpkin breads call for raisins, but to us their flavor gets lost amid the earthy pumpkin and spices. Cranberries persevere and lend just the right amount of tang. Nuts aren't a necessity but give a more rustic charm to a slab of this that can only be made better with a schmear of cream cheese. We thought the addition of cornmeal was a stroke of genius for added texture. Makes 1 large loaf, but we're extra greedy and not entirely sure if it gets 10 or more slices

INGREDIENTS

all-purpose or plain flour
  10½oz / 300g / 2 cups
yellow cornmeal
  4oz / 115g / ¾ cup
baking powder
  1½ teaspoons
bicarbonate of soda
  ½ teaspoon
kosher salt
  ¾ teaspoon
ground ginger
  1½ teaspoons
ground cardamom
  ½ teaspoon
nutmeg, freshly grated,
  or ground mace
  ½ teaspoon
large eggs
  3
dark brown sugar
  10oz / 275g / 1¼ cups, packed
granulated sugar
  6oz / 175g / ¾ cup
canned pumpkin purée
  12oz / 350g / 1½ cups
vanilla extract
  2 teaspoons
canola or other flavourless oil
  6 tablespoons
dried cranberries
  6oz / 175g / 1 cup
walnuts, chopped
  4oz / 115g / 1 cup

Preheat the oven to 180°C/350°F/gas mark 4. Butter a 9 x 5in/23 x 12cm loaf pan and line the 2 long sides and bottom with baking parchment.

Mix together the flour, cornmeal, baking powder, bicarbonate of soda, salt and spices in a medium bowl, using a hand whisk. Set aside.

In the bowl of an electric mixer, beat the eggs and both sugars on medium–high speed until creamy and thick, for about 3 minutes. Reduce the speed, then add the pumpkin, vanilla and oil and continue mixing until smooth. On low speed, slowly add the dry ingredients a little at a time, mixing only until the flour just disappears. Remove the bowl from the mixer, scrape the bowl up from the bottom and fold in the cranberries and walnuts. Transfer the batter into the prepared pan.

Bake for 60 to 75 minutes, or until the loaf is well browned and a small knife emerges clean from the center. Cool in the pan for about 15 minutes before releasing it to cool completely on a wire rack.

MUFFINS

MUFFINS? WHAT'S this you say? Yes, it's true. We diverge once again from British terminology. We've had many people refer to our cupcakes as muffins. We've also had a grown man comment that our muffins are formidable. One wonders how people get intimidated by baked goods, but that's another book altogether. Unless, of course, he was referring to something else entirely, in which case we have yet another book on our hands. What is useful, though, is to compare cupcakes to muffins. In general, American muffins have evolved into something larger than their cupcake cousins. Home bakers in the US often bake a batch of muffins using the same pan as that used for cupcakes (usually without any paper liners), hence they are precisely the same size as cupcakes. A single muffin would be a snack. Two or three muffins would be a meal. Bakeries and other catering kitchens typically bake a larger muffin to be eaten for breakfast. Some refer to these as Texas-sized muffins, and you can search online for Texas muffin pans. This stems from the adage 'everything's bigger in Texas', which we've found usually refers to ego and/or delusion versus something more concrete. Then again, Texas muffins give rise to Texas derrières if eaten too often. Though it is possible to find savory muffins at home, nine times out of ten they will be SWEET but not as sweet as cupcakes. They are rarely, if ever, frosted. At most, a muffin will have a drizzle or covering of a simple flavoured glaze like lemon or coffee. Since we consume them as an alternative to other breakfast meals, our muffins can be packed with nuts, fruits and fibers to tide you over until lunch. Alternatively, they can be slightly sweet, with just enough flavour and texture to nudge you out of the deepest slumber.

The preparation of muffins puts them firmly in the quick bread category, as opposed to cupcakes, which, ostensibly, are nothing more than individually portioned cakes. It should be noted that, like quick breads, muffins do not use any yeast. Muffins go together quickly and easily and are usually made shortly before they are eaten, although many muffin batters can be made the night before, refrigerated and baked the next morning or even throughout the week if you wish. Melted butter or flavorless oil such as sunflower or canola is frequently used to incorporate the fat quickly and eliminate the need for creaming butter and sugar, as with cakes. This will also produce a LIGHTER texture. For the most part a muffin will be mixed like so: combine the dry ingredients, mix in any fruit, nuts, etc., combine the wet ingredients separately (eggs, melted butter/oil, milk, vanilla and such), then quickly stir the two lots together. You don't even have to mix thoroughly. Streaks of flour are fine. Over-mixing will produce a tougher, flatter muffin. Portion the batter and pop the muffins into a hotter than usual oven to start creating the characteristic light and fluffy texture. A properly mixed muffin will be domed on top. Once you take muffins out of the oven it's best to get them out of the pan as soon as possible, otherwise they can stick. If that should happen, they can easily be coaxed out by running a small knife around the perimeter, with one last shove upward which is conveniently aimed at your mouth. Sure, you can use liners for preventing this, but at that time of morning, who can be bothered with an extra step? Plus, you'd have to peel the paper off before diving in.

TEXAS CORN CREAM MUFFINS

Here it is. An ultimate in American baking. Nothing tops a corn muffin split and pan-fried in butter. If you can't wait for that, then try these fresh from the oven with sweet butter melting down the sides and strawberry or, better yet, cranberry jam. Or just a drizzle of honey. Unbeatable. Many think these are savory. While they indeed can be steered in that direction, to us it's just a mouthful of weird. For breakfast muffins we normally leave the fresh corn out. But this recipe can also be baked in a sheet pan, in which case we'll add the corn and serve it on the side of a bowl of hot, spicy chili. Classic corn bread is always slightly sweet, so if we're eating this with savories we halve the sugar. If you omit it altogether, we'd recommend adding some grated Cheddar cheese before using it to mop the chili bowl. We've seen many a recipe which will also add in sautéed peppers, maybe some onion and even sausage. But again, to us – weird. Makes 6 large, 12 small

INGREDIENTS

all-purpose or plain flour
12½oz / 350g / 2⅓ cups
cornmeal or polenta
5½oz / 160g / 1 cup
sugar (use half if eating
  with something savory)
3oz / 175g / ⅔ cup
baking powder
4 teaspoons
kosher salt
½ teaspoon
unsalted butter,
  melted and cooled
4oz / 115g / ½ cup
heavy or double cream
16fl oz / 460ml / 2 cups
large eggs
2
fresh or canned corn or dried fruit,
  diced as needed (optional)
4oz / 115g / about 1 cup

Preheat the oven to 180°C/350°F/gas mark 4. Grease 6 jumbo or 12 standard muffin cups with melted butter or pan spray.

In a medium bowl, whisk together the flour, cornmeal, sugar, baking powder and salt.

In the bowl of an electric mixer, combine the melted butter, cream and eggs. On low speed, slowly add the flour mixture and mix just until the ingredients are combined and not lumpy. Add the corn or dried fruit if you're using it. This batter is quite thick, so don't be alarmed. Using a large ice-cream scoop or spoon, divide it evenly among the prepared cups. Alternatively, the batter can be made ahead and refrigerated in a covered container for up to 3 days. Just remember to add 3 to 5 minutes to the baking time to compensate for the chilled batter.

Bake larger muffins for 30 to 35 minutes and smaller muffins for 20 to 25 minutes, or until golden brown. Don't panic if the edges are darker than the middle. This is how a corn muffin should look. If you're prone to worry, loosely cover the muffin tray with foil to calm your nerves. The muffins should spring back when poked and a small knife should emerge clean. Let the muffins cool in the pan for 5 minutes before turning them out to cool on wire racks.

LEMON BLUEBERRY STREUSEL MUFFINS

It should be said that you can make these muffins without the streusel topping. Admittedly there are many mornings when we'd rather not bother ourselves. Sure, you'll have a lovely muffin, but the superior experience is getting a mouthful of gushy, tart fruit offset with the slightly sweet, slightly spicy crunch. Rarely can we wait until summer rolls around, so we keep a stash of frozen blueberries to satisfy the sudden urge for these. It's best to toss in the berries frozen, since they stay intact and thawing will turn them into mush as they get folded into the batter. All will taste fine, but the color tends toward a dull blue/gray, not the preferred golden with speckled blue dots. Makes 6 large, 12 small

INGREDIENTS

For the streusel:

all-purpose or plain flour
3oz / 75g / ½ cup
granulated sugar
6 tablespoons
nutmeg, freshly grated
1½ teaspoons
unsalted butter, chilled
4oz / 115g / ½ cup

For the muffins:

all-purpose or plain flour
18¾oz / 525g / 3½ cups
granulated sugar
12oz / 340g / 1½ cups
baking powder
1 tablespoon
kosher salt
1 teaspoon
unsalted butter, chilled and diced
6oz / 175g / ¾ cup
blueberries, fresh or frozen
(not thawed)
12oz / 340g / 3 cups
large eggs, at room temperature
2
vanilla extract
1 teaspoon
whole or full-fat milk
12fl oz / 350ml / 1½ cups
lemon curd
4–6oz / 115–175g / ½–¾ cup

Preheat the oven to 180°C/350°F/gas mark 4. Grease 6 jumbo or 12 standard muffin cups with melted butter or pan spray.

To make the streusel, combine the flour, sugar and nutmeg in a small bowl. Using a small fork or your fingertips, work the butter into the flour until you get small flakes and crumbs. Refrigerate until ready to use.

To make the muffins, whisk together the flour, sugar, baking powder and salt in the bowl of an electric mixer. Using a paddle attachment, cut in the butter until the mixture is crumbly. Remove the bowl from the mixer and gently toss the blueberries into the flour mixture. In a separate bowl, combine the eggs, vanilla and milk. Make a well in the middle of the dry ingredients, add the wet ingredients into the dry all at once, and fold gently with a rubber spatula until just combined. Less is definitely more at this point. The batter will be slightly stiff.

With an ice-cream scoop or spoon, divide half the batter among the prepared muffin cups. Top each with about 1 tablespoon lemon curd, then divide the remaining half of the batter among the muffin cups again. Don't worry if the curd oozes out. Sprinkle the streusel on top of the muffins and pat it gently into the batter.

Bake larger muffins for 30 to 35 minutes and smaller muffins for 25 to 30 minutes, or until the streusel is golden brown and a small knife emerges somewhat clean. You're bound to dredge up some curd on a tester knife but you don't want uncooked batter on there too. Cool in the pan for 5 to 10 minutes before removing the muffins to a wire rack until cool.

GINGER SPICE MUFFINS

Neither one of us is particularly fond of ginger. We have noticed, however, that the British public has a penchant for it. Readily available stem and candied ginger was our first clue. The second was what appears to be the ongoing tussle about what to add (or not add) to rhubarb crumble. Ginger always seems to come out on top. So we set out to make something gingery for breakfast. Since we keep stem and candied ginger in the pantry, we've been known to dice about 4oz/115g/¾ cup of either and fold it into the batter. Personally we're not yet at that level of gingerness, but we must admit that one of these, split in half and then pan-fried in butter until crispy, isn't the worst way to start a chilly morning. An added dollop of jam isn't all that bad either. Makes 6 large, 12 small

INGREDIENTS

all-purpose or plain flour
16oz / 450g / 3 cups

bicarbonate of soda
1½ teaspoons

kosher salt
½ teaspoon

ground ginger
1 tablespoon

ground allspice
½ teaspoon

nutmeg, freshly grated
½ teaspoon

unsalted butter, softened
6oz / 175g / ¾ cup

granulated sugar
6oz / 175g / ¾ cup

molasses or sorghum
(½ each of golden syrup
and treacle work, too)
6fl oz / 175ml / ¾ cup

large eggs
3

buttermilk
6fl oz / 180ml / ¾ cup

chopped stem ginger (optional)
3oz / 75g / ½ cup

Preheat the oven to 180°C/350°F/gas mark 4. Grease 6 jumbo or 12 standard muffin cups with melted butter or pan spray.

Whisk together the flour, bicarbonate of soda, salt and spices in a medium bowl.

In the bowl of an electric mixer, cream the butter and sugar until light and fluffy, about 5 minutes. Add the molasses (or alternative) and mix until evenly incorporated. One by one, add the eggs, beating well after each addition. Scrape the bottom of the bowl and mix for 1 minute more. On low speed, alternately add the flour mixture and buttermilk, beginning and ending with the dry ingredients, mixing only until just combined. Fold in the chopped stem ginger, if using, with a rubber spatula. Using a large ice-cream scoop, divide the batter evenly among the prepared cups. Each cup should be about ¾ full. Like many muffin batters, this can be kept in the refrigerator for 3 to 4 days and baked at another time.

Bake larger muffins for 30 to 35 minutes and smaller muffins for 25 to 30 minutes, or until a small knife emerges clean from the center. Let the muffins cool for about 5 minutes before releasing them from the pan. We like to finish these with a simple milk glaze spiced up with some more ground ginger, or a citrus glaze using either lemon or orange juice.

BANANA BRAN MUFFINS

For an American muffin it doesn't get more classic than this. We've seen similar recipes that fold in grated carrot and/or grated apple for something called a Rocket or Morning Glory Muffin. We've also heard anecdotes of how people have used a basic recipe such as this and tweaked it many times over until they get it just right, so don't by any means think of this as being etched in stone. No recipe is, for that matter. Let your mind wander and use this as a guide. Makes 6 large, 12 small

INGREDIENTS

all-purpose or plain flour
12oz / 340g / 2¼ cups
baking powder
1 generous teaspoon
bicarbonate of soda
½ teaspoon
kosher salt
¾ teaspoon
unprocessed wheat bran
(bran cereal will work, too)
3oz / 75g / 1½ cups
buttermilk
12fl oz / 340ml / 1½ cups
light brown sugar
4oz / 115g / ½ cup, packed
orange, zest freshly grated
1 tablespoon
unsalted butter, softened
4oz / 115g / ½ cup
large eggs, at room temperature
3
molasses or sorghum
6fl oz / 175ml / ¾ cup
vanilla extract
¾ teaspoon ·
raisins, dark or golden
8oz / 225g / 1½ cups
bananas, diced
2
walnuts, chopped
3oz / 75g / ¾ cup

Preheat the oven to 180°C/350°F/gas mark 4. Grease 6 jumbo or 12 standard muffin cups with melted butter or pan spray.

In a medium bowl, whisk together the flour, baking powder, bicarbonate of soda and salt. In a large measuring jug, combine the bran and buttermilk. Set aside.

In the bowl of an electric mixer, combine the sugar and orange zest on low speed until fragrant. Add the butter and cream everything on medium–high speed until light and fluffy, about 5 minutes. Reduce the speed to medium and add the eggs, one at a time, mixing thoroughly after each addition. Scrape the bowl, then add the molasses, vanilla and bran mixture and stir to incorporate evenly. On low speed, slowly add the flour mixture only until just combined. Less is more at this stage. Remove the bowl from the mixer and fold in the raisins, bananas and walnuts with a rubber spatula. Using an ice-cream scoop, divide the batter evenly among the muffin cups. Each cup should be almost completely full.

Bake for 30 to 35 minutes for larger muffins and 20 to 25 minutes for smaller ones, or until a small knife emerges clean. Color-checking for doneness can be tricky with these, as they start out dark and achieve their final color early on in the oven. Cool in the pan for about 5 minutes before removing the muffins to cool more on wire racks.

ALABAMA BISCUIT MUFFINS

Just when you think you've got it, when you think you've finally mastered the differences between scones, biscuits, fairy cakes, cupcakes and muffins … along comes this recipe. Sorry, folks. If these weren't one of our most popular items, one that many have asked us to share, we wouldn't be putting you through this torture. These are tossed together like OD's Famous Buttermilk Biscuits (page 69) but, rather than putting you through the paces of biscuit making, this 'shaggy mess' dough is chucked first into a greased muffin pan and then directly into the oven. Only butter is used versus a combination of butter and lard. As a result, these have a crunchy exterior and a tender but slightly dense, crumbly interior. They are fantastic as is, but you can also slather them with sweet, creamy butter and your favorite jam and rest assured you won't care about any confusion they might have caused. Makes 6 large, 12 small

INGREDIENTS

all-purpose or plain flour
20oz / 550g / 3¾ cups

granulated sugar
6 tablespoons

baking powder
1 generous tablespoon

kosher salt
1½ teaspoons

bicarbonate of soda
½ teaspoon

unsalted butter, cold and diced
8oz / 225g / 1 cup

buttermilk
12fl oz / 350ml / 1½ cups

Preheat the oven to 180°C/350°F/gas mark 4. Grease 6 jumbo or 12 standard muffin cups.

In the bowl of an electric mixer, combine the dry ingredients on low speed until evenly distributed. One tablespoon at a time, add the butter and stir until the mixture is crumbly, with pea-sized pieces scattered about. Pour in the buttermilk and stir until the dough looks evenly moistened. It might seem counter-intuitive, but the trick with this is NOT to stir until the dough comes together into a ball. If you continue mixing until the dough forms larger clumps you will end up with a tough muffin. What you should see in the bowl is various-sized lumps of butter and wet flour with slight bits of dry flour still lingering.

Remove the bowl and with a spoon or rubber spatula stir up from the bottom to incorporate any larger pockets of dry ingredients that remain. As with any muffin, complete mixing is not required. With an ice-cream scoop or large spoon (or even with your hands), divide the dough evenly among the muffin cups. Since this dough remains loose and crumbly, compress it into the scoop or in your fist and push it into the cups. If you're concerned things still look dry and powdery, top each muffin with a little butter, which will, in a sense, baste the muffin while it bakes.

Bake for 30 to 35 minutes for large muffins and 25 to 30 minutes for smaller ones, or until firm. The tops should be a darkish golden brown and they will look ruggedly lumpy. Cool in the pan for about 5 minutes before removing them.

APRICOT CARDAMOM MUFFINS

This recipe originates from one of our favourite cookbooks, Greg Patent's *Baking in America*. It caught our attention because of the fresh apricots (in our opinion at the time, better dried than fresh) and the use of cardamom, which isn't found in most American kitchens. Sometimes something might not necessarily strike your fancy but it will capture your interest, as this did ours, so we had to see for ourselves what was going on here. After one bite we decided then and there that wherever apricots go, so goes the cardamom. For our palates it's an intoxicating combination. We sometimes can't wait for fresh apricots, so we do substitute dried on occasion, but fresh is best. If you taste the fresh apricots as you're chopping them, don't be put off by any dull taste or texture. The full flavour comes out once the oven has worked its magic. Makes 6 large, 12 small

INGREDIENTS

buttermilk
12fl oz / 350ml / 1½ cups

large eggs, at room temperature
2

vanilla extract
2 teaspoons

all-purpose or plain flour
16oz / 450g / 3 cups

granulated sugar
10½oz / 300g / 1½ cups

baking powder
4 teaspoons

bicarbonate of soda
1 teaspoon

kosher salt
1 teaspoon

ground cardamom
1 teaspoon

unsalted butter, cold and diced
6oz / 175g / ¾ cup

fresh apricots, roughly chopped
12–14oz / 340–400g / 2½ cups

dried cherries, chopped
4oz / 115g / ½ cup

Preheat the oven to 190°C/375°F/gas mark 5. Grease 9 jumbo or 18 standard muffin cups with melted butter or pan spray.

In a large measuring jug, whisk together the buttermilk, eggs and vanilla.

In the bowl of an electric mixer, stir together the flour, sugar, baking powder, bicarbonate of soda, salt and cardamom on low speed until thoroughly combined. Add the cold butter and continue stirring until the mixture resembles coarse meal. All at once, add the buttermilk mixture and stir only until everything looks evenly moist but not evenly mixed. Remove the bowl from the mixer and fold in the chopped apricots and cherries. With a large ice-cream scoop, divide the batter evenly among the prepared cups until each is almost if not completely full.

Bake for about 35 minutes for larger muffins and 25 minutes for smaller ones, or until the tops are golden brown and domed and a small knife emerges clean. Cool in the pan for 5 to 10 minutes before removing the muffins to cool on a wire rack.

MIXED UP MUFFINS

Both of us love these muffins. The mere fact that OD consumes something
with dried fruit (especially prunes) is a testament to their appeal. Their texture is uniquely
satisfying given what gets tossed in, and the fruit variations are endless. More often than not we
opt for a variety in color and a balance between sweet and tart, so it's not uncommon to
find cranberries or cherries buried within. We've tried adding nuts, but prefer them without.
The maple syrup lends a little sweetness, but the fruit is what gets the job done. Semolina
would make a fine substitute if you don't care for or have cornmeal at hand. They
are a great alternative to bran muffins if you're not in the mood for a mouthful of wheatiness
but prefer a 'healthier' muffin. Makes 6 large, 12 small

INGREDIENTS

all-purpose or plain flour
  8oz / 225g / 1½ cups
whole wheat or wholemeal flour
  3oz / 75g / ½ cup
yellow cornmeal or semolina
  3oz / 75g / ½ cup
jumbo or slow oats
  1½oz / 40g / ½ cup
granulated sugar
  6 tablespoons
baking powder
  1 tablespoon
bicarbonate of soda
  ½ teaspoon
kosher salt
  ½ teaspoon
dried fruit,
  diced as needed (prunes,
  raisins, apricots, cranberries)
  6oz / 175g / 1 cup
buttermilk
  12fl oz / 350ml / 1½ cups
pure maple syrup
  4fl oz / 120ml / ½ cup
large eggs
  3
unsalted butter, melted and cooled
  6oz / 175g / ¾ cup

Preheat the oven to 200°C/400°F/gas mark 6. Grease
6 jumbo or 12 standard muffin cups with melted butter or
pan spray.

Using a large mixing bowl, whisk together the two flours,
cornmeal, oats, sugar, baking powder, bicarbonate of
soda and salt. Add the dried fruit and toss everything with
your hands to evenly distribute and coat the fruit with the
flour mix. In another bowl, whisk together the buttermilk,
maple syrup, eggs and melted butter until evenly
combined. Make a well in the center of the dry ingredients
and pour the liquid mixture into it. With a rubber spatula,
gently stir (almost fold) the wet and dry ingredients to
combine. No need to be overly thorough with this. Lumps
are fine. Using an ice-cream scoop or spoon, distribute the
batter evenly among the prepared cups. They should be
almost full.

Bake larger muffins for 30 to 35 minutes and smaller
muffins for 25 to 30 minutes, or until the tops are golden
and a small knife emerges clean from the center. Cool the
muffins in the pan for about 5 minutes before turning them
out to cool completely.

BREAKFAST PUFFS

These remind us of a favorite treat: cake donuts. Not the yeasty, light, fluffy, heavily glazed ones, but a tender, ever-so-slightly chewy, denser variation that is, for argument's sake, fried cake batter. Only, these are baked. Some people think they're donut holes. To keep our options open, instead of cinnamon sugar we sometimes use cardamom, lemon, orange or even lavender sugar. When we do opt for cinnamon we sometimes make a richer, more complex mix by adding other spices to taste. Everyone is drawn to these by their irregular lumpy appearance, glistening with a cinnamon crust. Makes 12–15 small

INGREDIENTS

For the batter:

all-purpose or plain flour
16oz / 450g / 3 cups

baking powder
1 tablespoon

kosher salt
1 teaspoon

nutmeg, freshly grated
½ teaspoon

whole or full-fat milk
8fl oz / 240ml / 1 cup

vanilla extract
1 teaspoon

unsalted butter, softened
6oz / 175g / ¾ cup

granulated sugar
8oz / 225g / 1 cup

large eggs, at room temperature
2

For the cinnamon crust:

granulated sugar
8oz / 225g / 1 cup

light brown sugar
8oz / 225g / 1 cup, packed

cinnamon
2 tablespoons

nutmeg, freshly grated
1 teaspoon

something like cardamom or cloves
¼–½ teaspoon

unsalted butter
8oz / 225g / 1 cup

Preheat the oven to 180°C/350°F/gas mark 4. Grease 12 standard muffin cups with melted butter or pan spray.

Whisk together the flour, baking powder, salt and nutmeg. In a large measuring jug, combine the milk and vanilla. Set both aside.

In the bowl of an electric mixer, cream the butter and sugar on medium speed until light and fluffy, about 5 minutes. One at a time, add the eggs, beating well after each addition. Scrape the bottom of the bowl and mix for 1 minute more. On low speed, alternately add the flour and milk mixtures, beginning and ending with the dry ingredients, mixing only until the flour disappears. Using an ice-cream scoop or a spoon, divide the batter equally among the prepared cups. Each cup should be ¾ full or so.

Bake the muffins for 25 to 30 minutes, or until a small knife emerges clean from the center. These are not much to look at when they're done baking but they should appear a pale, almost dull yellow. While they bake, combine all the dry ingredients for the cinnamon crust in a medium bowl. In a medium pan, melt the butter. We've found it's easier to use larger bowls and more butter than is necessary since it facilitates dunking and rolling. Once the muffins are done, let them cool in the pan for about 5 minutes, then remove them from the pan and immediately roll them in melted butter followed by a roll in the cinnamon sugar. Completely coat the outside of each muffin. If they cool too much, the cinnamon crust will not stick to the muffin. It helps to keep one hand in the wet, melted butter and one hand in the dry cinnamon sugar, otherwise everything gets a bit slushy.

WHEN FIRST we started it took very little time for us to reach a mutual decision: by no means would we focus on the almighty cupcake. Like many, our New York lives were Magnolia-centric (as in Magnolia Bakery, the headquarters of cupcake domination), but we had no desire to create yet another iteration of a cupcake shop. To us they all look the same and, alas, taste the same, so let's be honest, just how clever can a cupcake be? Could we really set ourselves apart by doing what many already were? After exhaustive research far and wide (by then we were doubly wide after tasting so many), we thought the cupcake had had its time in the spotlight. Not that we were willing to forgo them, but we knew there was far more to AMERICAN baking than a dollop of batter baked in a paper cup. Oh, and how cute those damn cups can be. Instead we thought we'd appeal to the kid in all of us as opposed to just kids. We thought we'd bake from a more adult point of view. Let's call it a man's point of view. There is something to be said about how satisfying and nostalgic devouring a cupcake

can be, but all the fuss can be off-putting. At least to us.

First we put cupcakes where they more rightfully belong: alongside the rest of our baking repertoire, not on top of the heap. Sometimes a cupcake will HIT the spot. For us, most times it won't. Next we decided to tempt more grown-up palates with flavors and combinations that might seem familiar but are not exact replicas from your fifth birthday party. Sure, there is a simple joy in eating precisely what you remember, but by the time your fourth decade comes around that experience can be sickening. We had many cravings, but sprinkles wasn't one of them. We did, however, enjoy packing as much flavor as possible into a simple, pleated paper liner to evoke a memory but appeal to a more experienced set of taste-buds.

The final puzzle piece was committing to a size and shape that meant something to us. These were our memories, after all. Little did

we know how difficult that would be here in the UK. We quickly learned the difference between the smaller fairy cake, the medium British cupcake, a 'large' American cupcake and another item that requires a liner or case but which we have yet to see in person: some call it a muffin, some a bun. Not a squat, domed muffin small or large and clearly a descendant of the aforementioned three, but some odd flat DISC thing for which one can find ample liners if not the actual item. Don't even get us started on the Muffin vs. Cupcake battle. After much perseverance and perspiration and perhaps a few failed experiments, we finally learned what to ask for: 'muffin' cases (or baking cases or bun cases or cupcake cases, etc., etc., etc.) that are 2 x 1¾in or 50 x 44mm. They fit our pans, accommodate our recipes and, most important, satisfy our stomachs. After much trial and error we found these elusive pleated paper cups at Lakeland online (at the time a London store didn't exist) and by keeping an eye out for Wilton products in any kitchen store.

And just a quick word of distinction about finishing … we've gathered thus far that fairy cakes are iced, flat on top and almost sweet in appearance, with precious embellishments and designs to admire. Cupcakes are more typically frosted with buttercream and can be, though they are not always, finished with additional DECORATION, be it the dreaded sprinkles, nuts, or pieces of candy stuck in the frosting. We also like to fold things into frostings to give them a lumpy, almost mysterious texture, since you can't quite make out what's in there but you know something good lurks within. Cupcakes are infinitely more informal, rustic-looking creatures and may as well come with an audio loop playing 'dig in' over and over. Fairy cakes should come with a sign that says 'hands off'. Mmmmm. Yummy.

COCONUT MILK CUPCAKES

From what we can tell, coconut is sort of a love/hate thing in the UK. We both love it paired with either lemon or chocolate. Toasting the coconut will intensify the flavour and lend a nutty hint. Skip it if you don't have the time. You won't be disappointed. The almond extract isn't essential. For years we made coconut cakes without it until one day we came across a recipe that used it plus vanilla extract. So we tried it. And never turned back. If you're opting to go in a lime or rum direction (or mango or other tropical fruit), we suggest leaving the almond out. But that's our palates, not yours. Coconut milk is easily found in larger grocery stores, mixed in with Thai or Indian ingredients. Makes 12

INGREDIENTS

sweetened shredded coconut
(thread or desiccated also work)
4oz / 115g / 1 cup
coconut milk
8fl oz / 240ml / 1 cup
egg whites
5
almond extract
1 teaspoon
vanilla extract
1 teaspoon
all-purpose or plain flour
12oz / 340g / 2¼ cups
granulated sugar
12oz / 340g / 1½ cups
baking powder
4 teaspoons
kosher salt
1 teaspoon
unsalted butter, softened
8oz / 225g / 1 cup

Preheat the oven to 170°C/325°F/gas mark 3. Line 12-ish muffin cups with paper liners.

Spread the shredded coconut evenly on a baking sheet and toast for 5 to 6 minutes, tossing it midway through to make sure it browns evenly. Use a bit of caution, since a slight brown hue can go to a dark black hue in no time. Remove from the oven and either leave to cool on the pan or transfer to a sheet of wax paper.

In a medium bowl, whisk together the coconut milk, egg whites and almond and vanilla extracts.

Sift the flour, sugar, baking powder and salt into the bowl of a stand mixer. Add the toasted coconut and mix on low speed to combine. Scatter the butter over the flour and mix on low speed until the mixture is coarse and crumbly, as if making scones, for about 2 minutes. Add half the coconut milk mixture and mix on medium speed for about 1 minute. Scrape down the bowl and repeat until all is incorporated. Using a large spoon or an ice-cream scoop, fill each cup with batter until about ⅔ full.

Bake for 20 to 25 minutes, or until a knife inserted comes out clean and the tops are golden brown. Be sure to check several cupcakes per tray to ensure all are done. It's best to rotate the pans front to back, top to bottom, about ⅔ of the way through. Cool in the pan for about 10 minutes before removing them to finish cooling on wire racks.

CRANBERRY CUPCAKES

Come fall in the States, we trot out our cranberry recipes, since fresh ones become available in preparation for Thanksgiving. Here we've learned to stock up the season before by chucking bags of them into the freezer. Or wait longer for when they appear in time for Christmas. Occasionally, if you look hard and long enough, you will find frozen cranberries in the larger supermarkets prior to the holidays. The zippy tang of the cranberries pairs well with an orange glaze or orange buttercream. Makes 12

INGREDIENTS

all-purpose or plain flour
  13½oz / 380g / 2½ cups
baking powder
  1 teaspoon
bicarbonate of soda
  ½ teaspoon
kosher salt
  ½ teaspoon
cinnamon
  2 teaspoons
nutmeg, freshly ground
  ½ teaspoon
large eggs
  4
granulated sugar
  16oz / 450g / 2 cups
canola or other flavorless oil
  8fl oz / 240ml / 1 cup
vanilla extract
  2 teaspoons
orange zest, freshly grated
  2 teaspoons
sour cream
  8oz / 225g / 1 cup
fresh or frozen cranberries,
  finely chopped
  12oz / 340g / 2 cups

Preheat the oven to 180°C/350°F/gas mark 4. Line 12-ish muffin cups with paper liners.

In a medium bowl, whisk together the flour, baking powder, bicarbonate of soda, salt and spices. In the bowl of an electric mixer, beat the eggs and sugar until the mixture thickens and lightens, about 2 to 4 minutes. Scrape as you go, to check if any of the eggs are sitting at the bottom of the bowl not cooperating. On low speed, add the oil, vanilla and orange zest. Alternately add the flour mixture and sour cream on low speed in 3 to 4 additions, beginning and ending with the dry ingredients. Stir only until you still see traces of flour streaked through the batter. Remove the bowl from the mixer, add the cranberries, then fold with a rubber spatula to incorporate and finish the mixing. Using a spoon or ice-cream scoop, fill each prepared cup with batter until about ⅔ full.

Bake for 20 to 25 minutes, or until a knife inserted comes out clean and the tops are golden brown. Be sure to check several cupcakes per tray to ensure all are done. It's best to rotate the pans front to back, top to bottom, about ⅔ of the way through. Cool in the pan for about 10 minutes before removing them to cool completely on wire racks.

MILK CHOCOLATE CUPCAKES

This recipe dates back to when evaporated milk first came on the market. Unlike condensed milk, which is sweetened, evaporated milk has been heat-treated to reduce the water content and thereby prolong shelf life. In this recipe the evaporated milk is mixed with water to 'reconstitute' it, although many recipes use it straight out of the can. If your pantry is bare but your fridge is well stocked, you can replace all the liquids called for with full-fat milk. Alternatively, you can substitute the quantity of evaporated milk with single or whipping cream. In fact, there isn't really a variation that won't work. The texture will be ever so slightly different. Don't be afraid to experiment and find one that suits. This is a favorite among kids who like their chocolate milky and sweet. We found that out the hard way … we baked a chocolate birthday cake for one of our nieces then smothered it with M&Ms of various sizes (the precursor to our Smartie cake). Her favorite. Or so we thought. After one bite she proclaimed in monotone, 'This isn't chocolate.' To fix her wagon and that of others, this should do the trick. Makes 12

INGREDIENTS

all-purpose or plain flour
 13½oz / 380g / 2½ cups
baking powder
 1 tablespoon
kosher salt
 ½ teaspoon
evaporated milk
 8fl oz / 240ml / 1 cup
cold water
 4fl oz / 120ml / ½ cup
vanilla extract
 1½ teaspoons
unsalted butter, softened
 6oz / 175g / ¾ cup
granulated sugar
 12oz / 340g / 1½ cups
large eggs
 3
milk chocolate, chips
 melted and cooled
 6oz / 175g / 1 cup

Preheat the oven to 180°C/350°F/gas mark 4. Line about 12 cupcake cups with paper liners.

Mix together the flour, baking powder and salt in a medium bowl, using a hand whisk. In a large measuring jug, combine the evaporated milk, water and vanilla. Set both aside.

In the bowl of an electric mixer fitted with a whisk, cream the butter and sugar on medium–high speed until light and fluffy. Reduce the speed and add the eggs, one at a time, beating well after each addition. Scrape the bottom of the bowl, add the melted chocolate and stir on low speed until evenly combined. Alternately add the flour and milk mixtures in 3 to 4 additions. Begin and end with the dry ingredients and mix only until the flour just disappears. Using a large spoon or ice-cream scoop, divide the batter evenly among the prepared cups. Each cup should be ¾ full.

Bake for 20 to 25 minutes, or until a small knife emerges clean. Let the cupcakes rest in the pan for about 5 minutes before removing them to cool completely on wire racks.

CHOCOLATE CHIP CUPCAKES

Simply put, these are our favorite cupcakes. They are quite unusual to prepare but, fear not, they are simple to do. They are moist, chewy, absolutely loaded with chocolate chips and last for quite some time due to the sour cream. They are one of the few cupcakes we make that come out flat. Perfect for dipping in a chocolate fudge glaze. To keep things interesting we add nuts from time to time. They, too, are delicious but we both prefer the chew factor to be uninterrupted by crunch. Up to you. We like to finish them with a Dark Chocolate Glaze (page 193). Makes 12

INGREDIENTS

all-purpose or plain flour
6oz / 175g / 1½ cups
light brown sugar
12oz / 340g / 1½ cups, packed
bicarbonate of soda
¾ teaspoon
butter, chilled and diced
4oz / 115g / ½ cup
large egg
1
vanilla extract
1 teaspoon
sour cream
6oz / 175g / ¾ cup
whole milk
3 tablespoons
semi-sweet chocolate chips
9oz / 250g / 1½ cups
pecan pieces (optional)
4oz / 115g / 1 cup

Preheat the oven to 170°C/325°F/gas mark 3. Line 12-ish cupcake cups with paper liners.

Into the bowl of an electric mixer, measure the flour, sugar and bicarbonate of soda. Mix on low speed until well blended. Add the butter about a tablespoon at a time, and continue on low speed for about 2 minutes, or until the mixture resembles coarse meal. Don't worry if some of the flour hasn't been incorporated with the butter yet. Add the egg and vanilla and blend thoroughly. Stir in the sour cream and milk until the batter looks even. You may still see lumps of butter. Don't worry. This batter is very forgiving. Unlike other cupcake batters which are thick and almost pasty, this is more liquid, like pancake batter. Remove the bowl from the mixer and fold in the chocolate chips and, if using, the nuts. Using a large spoon or ice-cream scoop, place one slightly heaped scoop of batter in each cup until about ¾ full.

Bake for about 25 minutes, or until the tops feel firm and a small knife emerges clean from the center. Cool the cupcakes on wire racks for about 10 minutes.

WHITE CHOCOLATE RASPBERRY CUPCAKES

This recipe reads and prepares like a brownie recipe but bakes out to be our preferred white chocolate cupcake. The batter is quite liquid in the end, which we can never figure out, since brownie batter never is. If you have finicky eaters who moan about not liking white chocolate but appreciate being indulged, use this recipe and simply call it vanilla. They will be none the wiser and you'll come out looking like a baking genius. The raspberries are optional but we recommend them for an added treat. Makes 12

INGREDIENTS

all-purpose or plain flour
  5½oz / 160g / 1 cup
baking powder
  1 teaspoon
kosher salt
  ¼ teaspoon
white chocolate,
  chopped, or chips
  9oz / 250g / 1½ cups
unsalted butter
  8oz / 225g / 1 cup
granulated sugar
  12oz / 340g / 1½ cups
vanilla extract
  2 teaspoons
large eggs, at room temperature
  6
dried raspberries
  6oz / 175g / 1 cup

Preheat the oven to 180°C/350°F/gas mark 4. Line about 12 cupcake cups with paper liners.

In a medium bowl, whisk together the flour, baking powder and salt. Set aside.

In the bowl of an electric mixer, melt the white chocolate and butter over a pan of simmering water, stirring often, until both are almost completely melted. Remove from the heat and let any lumps finish melting. Stir in the sugar and let the mixture cool for about 5 to 10 minutes. Add the vanilla and beat with a paddle attachment on medium speed for about 3 minutes. One at a time, add the eggs, beating well after each addition. Reduce the speed and add the flour mixture gradually, mixing only until it disappears.

With the raspberries you have several options: you can either fold them into the batter, in which case they will sink to the bottom when baked; you can dust them with flour, which should help them stay afloat, or you can fill the cupcake liners with the batter and then drop the raspberries into each cup. Use a large ice-cream scoop to portion out the batter until each cup is about ⅔ full. Given how liquid the batter is this, it can be a messy proposition. Nowadays some mixers have a pour spout built into the bowl, which would be ideal here. We have also used a ladle instead of a scoop.

Bake for 20 to 25 minutes, or until a small knife emerges clean. Rotate the pan about ⅔ of the way through for even baking. These can be quite fragile, so let them cool in the pan a little while longer than usual, about 15 minutes, before removing them to cool completely on wire racks.

AH, THE whoopie pie. So much has been said on these shores about these delectable, portable cakes. We're always amused when local 'experts' opine or, worse, when we the national press touts grocery-chain versions as being the best. In a way, it's almost as if we came along and told you all a thing or two about making Victoria Sponge. It's simply not in our DNA. So might we politely request you leave this one to those who know? Those who were weaned on them? Those with whoopie cream coursing through their veins?

In terms of spirit, it doesn't get much better than these. Cupcakes get so dolled up it's easy to lose track of what you're eating. It's no FUN biting into a big glob of decoration when all you really want is to taste what's in your mouth. Sure, everyone eats with their eyes first, but one bite in and you can't deny your taste buds have taken over – and not always for the better. With whoopies, they tell it like it is. Pictures of glazed whoopies are circulating of late, but the true, genuine rendition gets straight to the point. Cake. Filling. Eat Me. No need for a knife. Or plate. Or fork. Pick it up. Dig in. Done.

Legend has it whoopie pies originated in Amish country back home. That could mean anywhere from Philadelphia, down to Kentucky and over to Ohio. Not really the East Coast, not really the Midwest, not really the South, but somewhere in the middle. The Amish are very simple people; they are a self-sufficient, faith-based community living off the LAND and eschewing modern conveniences and technologies. Horse-drawn carriages are the preferred means of transit and any contact with the outside world is done through a liaison. In the kitchen, nothing gets complicated. In a way, the most intricate technique is canning, since they put up all sorts of produce to get through winter. Nothing goes to waste, as they are far too frugal. And that gets us to whoopie pies. For it is believed that after putting a cake in the oven, a woman

PIES

Whoopies are always uneven, rustic-looking lumps of baked batter sandwiched together with a filling. In point of fact, Classic Whoopie Cream (see page 120) is nothing more than Italian meringue: heated sugar and egg whites beaten into a GOOEY cloud with soft butter whipped in. Nowadays the short-cut version would be a so-called American buttercream with marshmallow crème folded in at the end. At the shop we import a ready-made American product called Fluff – a spreadable marshmallow crème available in vanilla, strawberry and raspberry. Three variations right off the bat! Using the basic whoopie cream recipes included here, you can easily fold in additional ingredients to change the texture and flavor. Nuts. No nuts. Candy. Chocolate chips. Butterscotch chips. Peanut butter chips. Dried fruits. Coconut. Candied orange peel. You name it. Add two or three different things, if you like. The list is as endless as your imagination. Once your filling is ready, put a large dollop on one whoopie pie and then squeeze and squish the filling using another whoopie pie. Twist slightly to get better adhesion between the two halves. The filling should OOZE slightly out the sides. If you need to embellish, roll the oozed filling in sprinkles or chopped nuts or some other crumbly texture to add color, crunch, or both. To increase your repertoire, use any cake frosting or buttercream as a filling.

dolloped leftover batter on to a baking sheet and popped it in the oven alongside her cake. Once cooled she used some frosting to sandwich two of these 'cake cookies' together, wrapped them up and hid them in her children's lunch boxes. Upon digging in for their noontime repast, the kids found the SURPRISE, squealed 'whoopie', and thus a legend was born. Alternate stories posit whoopies originated in Maine, but that story is far too boring so we stick by this one. Although, in Maine they have access to the world at large, so it's entirely possible that is how whoopies made their way across America. Horses couldn't deliver all over, so someone had to.

For the record, we offer up classic whoopie pies, but, having grown up with modern conveniences, we also include a few versions to tempt more sophisticated taste buds. We often hear people moan 'ohmygod' when they bite into one of our whoopies, but it doesn't exactly roll off the tongue. So while we may have taken a few liberties with these American classics and have come close to coining a new name, we prefer to pay homage to their humble roots and simply call them whoopies.

CARROT WHOOPIES

We have a love/hate relationship with carrot cake. There are only so many times you can make it and only so many variations on what shape it takes – be it layers, cupcakes or bundts. But we get endless requests for it and we are only too happy to oblige. So to keep things interesting in the kitchen, we concocted this recipe to add to our ever-expanding carrot repertoire. We'll leave you to debate the cake-to-filling ratio ... *Makes about 15*

INGREDIENTS

all-purpose or plain flour
 10½oz / 300g / 2 cups
wholemeal or whole wheat flour
 2½ oz / 75g / ½ cup
baking powder
 1¼ teaspoons
bicarbonate of soda
 1¼ teaspoons
kosher salt
 ½ teaspoon
cinnamon
 2 teaspoons
nutmeg, freshly grated
 ½ teaspoon
quick oats
 8oz / 225g / 2½ cups
grated carrots
 14–16oz / 400–450g / about 2 cups
dried cranberries
 6oz / 175g / 1 cup
golden raisins
 6oz / 175g / 1 cup
pecans, chopped
 4oz / 115g / 1 cup
unsalted butter, softened
 10oz / 275g / 1¼ cups
light or dark brown sugar
 10oz / 275g / 1¼ cups, packed
granulated sugar
 6oz / 175g / ¾ cups
large eggs
 3
vanilla extract
 1 teaspoon

Preheat the oven to 180°C/350°F/gas mark 4. Line 2 baking sheets with baking parchment.

In a medium bowl, whisk together the 2 flours, baking powder, bicarbonate of soda, salt, spices and oats. In a separate bowl, combine the grated carrots, dried fruit and nuts. Toss it all with 1 to 2 tablespoons of the flour mixture. Set both aside.

Using an electric mixer, cream the butter and 2 sugars on medium–high speed until creamy, about 4 to 5 minutes. One at a time, add the eggs on medium speed, beating well after each addition. Stir in the vanilla. Reduce the speed again to low and add the flour mixture, 5oz/150g/1 cup at a time, mixing only until just combined. Remove the bowl from the mixer and fold in the carrot mixture with a large rubber spatula. With a large ice-cream scoop, place scoops of batter on the prepared sheets about 3in/7.5cm apart.

Bake for 10 to 12 minutes or until the cakes spring back a little when poked. The whoopies will be puffed and set but still soft to the touch. Cool on the sheets for about 10 minutes before removing to cool completely on wire racks.

These are best with Cream Cheese Mascarpone Frosting (page 186).

OATMEAL WHOOPIES

A childhood favorite among many Americans is something called an Oatmeal Cream, which is a standard-sized cookie sandwich with a chewy vanilla-cream filling. It's almost an oatmeal version of an Oreo. One of our favourites bakes is an Oatmeal Layer Cake made with an unusually large amount of nutmeg. Here you can go either way: if you use the nutmeg it will permeate the kitchen as you're baking as well as every bite you take. A reminder that when baking anything oatmeal, don't overdo it; these whoopies will be done after the cooking time given here even though they appear otherwise. They will firm up as they cool. Don't be alarmed with the cooled whoopie, either. It will be firmer, almost crisp and unlike any other whoopie you bake. Most likely you'll curse us and wonder why we had you make a batch of oatmeal cookies. Patience, people; once you fill these with Cream Cheese Mascarpone (page 186) each half will absorb moisture from the filling and soften up into one delicious bite after another. If you're a fan of all things oatmeal raisin, you can add 6oz/175g/1 cup of raisins to either the batter or the filling for another great version. Makes about 15

INGREDIENTS

all-purpose or plain flour
  10 ½oz / 300g / 2 cups
baking powder
  1 teaspoon
bicarbonate of soda
  2 teaspoons
kosher salt
  ½ teaspoon
cinnamon or nutmeg
  1 teaspoon
quick-cooking oatmeal
  6oz / 175g / 2 cups
unsalted butter, softened
  6oz / 175g / ¾ cup
light brown sugar
  16oz / 450g / 2 cups, packed
large eggs
  2
boiling water
  2fl oz / 60ml / ¼ cup

Preheat the oven to 180°C/350°F/gas mark 4. Line 2 baking sheets with baking parchment.

In a medium bowl, whisk together the flour, baking powder, bicarbonate of soda, salt and cinnamon or nutmeg. Stir in the oatmeal. Set both aside.

Using an electric mixer, cream the butter and sugar until light and fluffy, about 6 to 8 minutes. One at a time, add the eggs on medium speed, beating well after each addition. Reduce the speed again to low and add the dry ingredients, a little at a time, only until just combined. Add the boiling water and stir evenly into the batter. Using a large ice-cream scoop, place scoops of batter on the prepared sheets about 3in/7.5cm apart. Chill for a minimum of 2 hours for optimal puff.

Bake for 15 to 18 minutes or until the whoopies have puffed and seem to be set. If they still look moist in the middle, leave them in for another minute, tops two. Cool on the sheets for about 10 minutes before removing to cool completely on wire racks.

RED VELVET WHOOPIES

Red Velvet Cake is a unique creation from the American South. Deep red inside, the outside is frosted with white cream cheese frosting to conceal the goodness stacked within. Not much to look at, it's always a crowd-pleaser once the slicing begins. Years of trying and researching only revealed seemingly complicated recipes, though, to be honest, they weren't; they just had more steps than seemed necessary. Several, in fact. A virtual no-no in any busy kitchen. Some had you make a cocoa powder paste, some had you mixing vinegar and bicarb either before or after the batter was mixed. Some mixed in boiling water at the last second and rushing to the oven. Some had you doing it all. Blah, blah, blah. One day we turned things upside down and combined ingredients like we would any other cake. Dry here, wet there. We also ditched the vinegar and hot water. This is our one conceit when it comes to food color, since it's the only way to achieve the desired results; natural or organic coloring yields a brown mahogany while old-fashioned coloring gives the classic red mahogany we prefer. We've introduced orange zest to mask the aftertaste any food coloring imparts. While the quantities of bicarbonate of soda and salt might seem alarming, they are the reason the crumb is so soft and why it's called velvet in the first place. Makes about 15

INGREDIENTS

all-purpose or plain flour
  21½oz / 600g / 4 cups
bicarbonate of soda
  2 teaspoons
baking powder
  ½ teaspoon
kosher salt
  2 teaspoons
unsweetened cocoa powder
  4 tablespoons
buttermilk, at room temperature
  8fl oz / 240ml / 1 cup
red food coloring
  3 tablespoons
vanilla extract
  2 teaspoons
caster sugar
  (this gets you the velvet finish)
  16oz / 450g / 2 cups
orange zest, freshly grated
  1 tablespoon
unsalted butter, softened
  8oz / 225g / 1 cup
large eggs
  2

Preheat the oven to 180°C/350°F/gas mark 4. Line 2 baking sheets with baking parchment.

Whisk together the flour, bicarbonate of soda, baking powder, salt and cocoa in a medium bowl. Pour the buttermilk into a large, glass measuring jug then add the food coloring and vanilla. With a fork or small whisk, mix together the liquids until the color is consistent.

In the bowl of an electric mixer, combine the sugar and zest on low speed until fragrant and the zest gets pulverized. (Grinding the zest releases oil, which yields better flavour than just dumping the zest in.) Slowly add the butter and, on medium–high speed, cream until light and fluffy, about 5 to 6 minutes. Turn the speed down a notch and mix in the eggs one at a time, beating thoroughly before adding the next egg. Lower the speed again and alternately add the flour–cocoa and buttermilk mixtures in 3 to 4 additions. Scrape the sides of the bowl to ensure complete mixing and consistent color throughout the batter. With a large ice-cream scoop, place scoops of batter on the prepared sheets 3in/7.5cm apart.

Bake for 15 to 16 minutes or until the whoopies spring back when poked. Cool on the sheets for about 10 minutes before removing them to cool completely on wire racks.

VANILLA WHOOPIES

When you're in the mood for something simple and sweet but not chocolate,
give these a whirl. If you still need a fix, you can add 8oz/225g/1 cup of mini chocolate chips
into the batter. If you need a fix and are feeling adventurous, make a batch of
Classic Whoopies as well, then take one Classic (chocolate for those who jumped to this page)
and one Vanilla and sandwich them with whatever you choose.

In New York there is a hometown treat available in any deli or from any corner coffee
cart called a Black and White: a large, spongy, vaguely vanilla cookie that is finished on one
half with white icing (presumably vanilla) and on the other with black-ish icing (presumably
chocolate). Neither of us care for them. To us, you may as well just eat a sponge (as in kitchen-
sink sponge). But a Half & Half Whoopie reminds us of home, only a whole lot better. You can
also use this as one half of the batter needed for OD's Marbled Whoopies, as mentioned earlier
in this chapter. On their own these are delicious, but nothing bores us personally more than
vanilla vanilla. Makes about 15

INGREDIENTS

all-purpose or plain flour
20oz / 575g / 3¾ cups
bicarbonate of soda
2¼ teaspoons
kosher salt
½ teaspoon
buttermilk
8fl oz / 240ml / 1 cup
vanilla extract
2 teaspoons
unsalted butter, softened
6oz / 175g / ¾ cup
granulated sugar
10oz / 280g / 1¼ cups
large eggs
3

Preheat the oven to 180°C/350°F/gas mark 4. Line two
baking sheets with baking parchment.

In a medium bowl, whisk together the flour, bicarbonate
of soda and salt. In a large, glass measuring jug, combine
the buttermilk and vanilla. Set both aside.

Using an electric mixer, cream the butter and sugar until
light and fluffy, about 6 to 8 minutes. One at a time,
add the eggs on medium speed, beating well after each
addition. Reduce the speed again to low and alternately
add the flour and buttermilk mixtures, beginning and
ending with the dry ingredients and mixing only until just
combined. With a large ice-cream scoop, place scoops of
batter on the prepared sheets about 3in/7.5cm apart.

Bake for 15 to 18 minutes or until the whoopies spring
back when poked (ever so slightly less if you've flattened
the batter). They will be puffed and set but still soft to
the touch. Cool on the sheets for about 10 minutes before
removing to cool completely on wire racks.

CLASSIC WHOOPIES

Here it is folks. The one. The only. Very little beats biting into one of these chewy chocolate chunks with slightly salty Classic Whoopie Cream oozing out and possibly landing on your shirt. Many recipes call for shortening instead of or in addition to butter, but we prefer the all-butter version. Classic Whoopies, like many other whoopie recipes, use brown sugar to increase the chewiness, and buttermilk to maintain a moist crumb. By no means should they be light and fluffy. When OD is in one of his fancy moods, he makes a batch of these, a batch of Vanilla or Red Velvet Whoopies and then stirs the two batters together partially to make Marbled Whoopies. Once baked they maintain the streaked, marbelized look of the batter and take on a more formal look. It is no secret we take many liberties with our recipes and leave out or toss in any number of things to suit our moods. It's interesting to note, though, we never mess with this one. Makes about 15

INGREDIENTS

all-purpose or plain flour
  21½oz / 600g / 4 cups
cocoa powder
  5½oz / 150g / 1½ cups
bicarbonate of soda
  2 teaspoons
kosher salt
  1 teaspoon
buttermilk
  16fl oz / 480ml / 2 cups
vanilla extract
  2 teaspoons
unsalted butter
  8oz / 225g / 1 cup
light brown sugar
  16oz / 450g / 2 cups, packed
large eggs
  2

Preheat the oven to 180°C/350°F/gas mark 4. Line 2 baking sheets with baking parchment.

In a medium bowl, whisk together the flour, cocoa, bicarbonate of soda and salt. In a large, glass measuring jug, combine the buttermilk and vanilla. Set both aside.

Using an electric mixer, cream the butter and brown sugar until light and fluffy, about 6 to 8 minutes. One at a time, add the eggs on medium speed, beating well after each addition. Reduce the speed again to low and alternately add the flour and buttermilk mixtures, beginning and ending with the dry ingredients and mixing only until just combined. With a large ice-cream scoop, place scoops of batter on the prepared sheets about 3in/7.5cm apart. If you like a flatter saucer shape, wet the back of a spoon and slightly smush the batter ball so it resembles a hamburger patty.

Bake for 15 to 18 minutes or until the cakes spring back when poked (ever so slightly less if you've flattened the batter). Cool on the sheets for about 10 minutes before removing to cool completely on wire racks.

PUMPKIN WHOOPIES

We once did a TV segment for *Market Kitchen* about traditional Thanksgiving treats.
Of course pumpkin pie was discussed, including a beautiful sample of same that OD had
prepared. Before even going near it, one of the presenters proclaimed it 'vile'. We both had the
same reaction: we were on national TV with a vile pie … not great publicity. Only later did we
learn the presenter didn't care for pumpkin in any form, sweet or savory.
A little white lie of being allergic to it wouldn't have killed her – though we wanted to.
So from that point forward we set out to sway the court of UK public opinion to our side
of the pond, one slice/whoopie/cupcake at a time. Makes about 15

INGREDIENTS

all-purpose or plain flour
11oz / 320g / 2¼ cups
baking powder
½ teaspoon
bicarbonate of soda
1 teaspoon
cream of tartar
1 teaspoons
cinnamon
1½ teaspoons
ground ginger and allspice
¾ teaspoon
mace
½ teaspoon
ground cloves or cardamom
¼ teaspoon
rolled or quick oats
2oz / 60g / about ¾ cup
unsalted butter, softened
4oz / 115g / ½ cup
canola or sunflower oil
4fl oz / 120ml / ½ cup
light or dark brown sugar
10oz / 280g / 1¼ cups, packed
large egg
1
pumpkin purée, 1 small can
8oz / 225g / about 1 cup
vanilla extract
1½ teaspoons
dried cranberries (optional)
3oz / 90g / ½ cup or so

Preheat the oven to 180°C/350°F/gas mark 4. Line 2 baking
sheets with baking parchment.

In a medium bowl, whisk together the flour, baking
powder, bicarbonate of soda, cream of tartar and spices
until thoroughly combined. Stir in the oats until evenly
distributed. In the bowl of an electric mixer, combine the
butter, oil and sugar. Start on low speed so the oil doesn't
splosh around too much, then, as things start coming
together, increase the speed and mix until creamy. One
at a time, add in the egg, beating well after each addition.
Stir in the pumpkin and vanilla. On low speed, slowly
add in the flour mixture and continue stirring only until
it disappears. Remove the bowl and fold in the dried
cranberries, if using, with a rubber spatula. Using a large
ice-cream scoop, place mounds of batter on the prepared
sheets about 3in/7.5cm apart.

Bake for 10 to 12 minutes or until the cakes spring back a
little when poked. The whoopies will be puffed and set
but still soft to the touch. Cool on the sheets for about 10
minutes before removing to cool completely on wire racks.

BANANA NUT OR BANOFFEE WHOOPIES

If you're in the mood for something banana, try these. They go together more like a traditional banana cake which uses mashed bananas, as opposed to our other option, which would be to fold in diced bananas toward the end of mixing Vanilla or Classic Whoopies. If you opt for adding chocolate chips and nuts, these can be filled with just about anything vanilla-y, chocolate-y and/or cream cheese-y. Try adding a dash of rum and some coconut for something more tropical. We've opted for all-purpose (plain) flour here, but you can substitute part of it with whole wheat for a more earthy flavour.

For the Banoffee version, Gloria (the winner of the Great Oatmeal Terminology Debate) omits the nuts (the chocolate chips are still being debated) and puts a dollop of dulce de leche on one cooled whoopie before using Classic Whoopie Cream (page 122) to sandwich it together with another. For Elvis Whoopies (see opposite) we omit the nuts, use our Southern Peanut Butter Frosting (page 188) and finish with crumbled, crisp bacon and a drizzle of honey – the King's favourite combination. Makes about 15

INGREDIENTS

all-purpose or plain flour
  10½oz / 300g / 2 cups
bicarbonate of soda
  1 teaspoon
kosher salt
  ½ teaspoon
unsalted butter, softened
  4oz / 115g / ½ cup
light brown sugar
  4oz / 115g / ½ cup, packed
granulated sugar
  2oz / 60g / ¼ cup
large eggs
  2
vanilla extract
  1 teaspoon
mashed bananas, about 2
  8oz / 225g / about 1 cup
chocolate chips (optional)
  6oz / 175g / 1 cups
pecans, chopped (optional)
  3oz / 90g / ½ cup

Preheat the oven to 180°C/350°F/gas mark 4. Line 2 baking sheets with baking parchment.

In a medium bowl, whisk together the flour, bicarbonate of soda and salt.

Using an electric mixer, cream the butter and both sugars until light and fluffy, about 4 to 5 minutes. One at a time, add the eggs on medium speed, beating well after each addition. Stir in the vanilla. Reduce the speed again to low and alternately add the flour mixture and mashed bananas, beginning and ending with the dry ingredients and mixing only until just combined. Remove the bowl from the mixer and fold in the chocolate chips and nuts, if you're using them. (We're always trying to use up bananas, so we've even folded in diced bananas at this point for added taste and texture.) With an ice-cream scoop, place scoops of batter on the prepared sheets, about 3in/7.5cm apart. We get about 8 to 9 batter blobs per tray.

Bake for 10 to 12 minutes or until the whoopies spring back a little when poked. They should be puffed and set but still soft to the touch. Cool on the sheets for about 10 minutes before removing to cool completely on wire racks. Once cool, fill with the cream/buttercream/frosting of your choosing.

SHOO FLY WHOOPIES

The ultimate in Amish-ness! We figured there must be a way to combine two of the most unique Amish treats into one: Shoo Fly and Whoopie Pies. Shoo Fly Pie is a molasses custard pie akin to a treacle tart but with a flour and sugar crumb topping. The more traditional version uses sorghum which we import for our use and to sell in the shop. When we're going for the whole shebang, we squish the finished whoopie enough so the cream oozes out and then roll it in crushed Graham crackers or digestive crumbs to mimic Shoo Fly crumbs – though these are great as is.

The coffee brings out the spices more than adding a flavor of its own. We use either instant coffee, instant espresso or brewed coffee – never brewed espresso, since that tips the scale into coffee-tasting territory. For a spirited Rumshpringa version, we add 1 to 2 tablespoons Bourbon or brandy. Rumshpringa, for those new to Amish custom, is akin to a gap year. Teenagers take a year (sometimes longer) to explore life outside their realm. It is their chance to live in the modern world with all its temptations there for the taking. The Amish don't drink, so this is the only chance they have to imbibe. When time is up they need to decide: either return to the fold or stay on the outside. It's a one-way ticket, however. Whichever path is chosen, they can never go back. Once you make these, though, you can and will go back for more. Makes about 12

INGREDIENTS

all-purpose or plain flour
22oz / 650g / 4½ cups
bicarbonate of soda
2 teaspoons
kosher salt
1 teaspoon
cinnamon
1 teaspoon
ground ginger
1 teaspoon
unsalted butter, softened
4oz / 115g / ½ cup
canola or flavorless oil
4fl oz / 120ml / ½ cup
granulated sugar
8oz / 225g / 1 cup
large eggs
2
sorghum or molasses
8fl oz / 240ml / 1 cup
hot coffee (filter or instant)
8fl oz / 240ml / 1 cup

Preheat the oven to 180°C/350°F/gas mark 4. Line several baking sheets with baking parchment.

In a large bowl, whisk together the flour, bicarbonate of soda, salt and spices. Set aside.

In the bowl of an electric mixer, cream the butter, oil and sugar until light and fluffy. Add the eggs, one at a time, beating well after each addition. Stir in the molasses. Beginning and ending with the dry ingredients, alternately add the flour mixture and hot coffee in 2 to 3 additions. Scrape the bottom of the bowl and mix for 1 minute more. Refrigerate the batter for about 4 hours. Using a large ice-cream scoop, place scoops of batter on the prepared sheet, about 3in/7.5cm apart.

Bake for 15 to 18 minutes or until the cakes spring back when poked. Cool on the sheets for about 10 minutes before removing to cool completely on wire racks.

CLASSIC/CARAMEL WHOOPIE CREAM

INGREDIENTS

large egg whites
  6
granulated sugar
  (use dark brown sugar
  for a caramel whoopie cream)
  12oz / 340g / 1½ cups
unsalted butter, softened
  16oz / 450g / 2 cups
vanilla extract
  1½ teaspoons
kosher salt
  ½ teaspoon

Combine the egg whites and sugar in the bowl of an electric mixer. Place the bowl over simmering water and whisk continuously until the sugar is dissolved and the mixture is hot to the touch, about 7 minutes. Remove the bowl from the heat and whisk on high speed until thick and shiny. The bowl should be cool to the touch.

Reduce the speed to medium and drop in the butter a bit at a time – the mixture will go through several textures, so soldier on. Next, add in the vanilla and salt. If the mixture looks curdled or lumpy simply continue to whisk. Whisk or beat on high speed for another minute or so until you have a silky smooth filling. The best way to test is to plunge your finger through the middle of the bowl, whirl it around a bit then lick it. No lumps, you're good to go. At this point, we sometimes fold in chocolate chips, nuts, diced dried fruit – or sometimes all three.

CHOCOLATE WHOOPIE CREAM

INGREDIENTS

unsweetened cocoa powder
  4oz / 115g / 1 cup
confectioner's or icing sugar
  20–24oz / 550–675g / 4–5 cups
whole milk
  6 tablespoons
unsalted butter, softened
  12oz / 340g / 1½ cups
vanilla extract
  1½ teaspoons
kosher salt
  large dash
Fluff marshmallow crème
  4 cups

Start by preparing a chocolate buttercream. In the bowl of an electric mixer, whisk together the cocoa powder and half the icing sugar on low speed until evenly combined. Slowly add the milk and continue mixing until you have a thick paste. Bit by bit, drop in the softened butter. Stir in the vanilla and salt. Increase the speed and continue creaming until the mixture evens out. Add in the remaining icing sugar and cream until smooth. Unlike a typical buttercream used for finishing layer cakes, this mixture will be stiffer at this stage, but the addition of the marshmallow crème will loosen it up.

Reduce the speed to low, stir in the marshmallow crème and beat for another 4 to 5 minutes or until the filling is smooth and fluffy. If things are looking soupy, slowly add more icing sugar, a little at a time, until the filling firms up and becomes fluffy. Again, if the mood strikes, now is the time to fold anything you wish into the finished filling such as chocolate chips, chopped nuts or diced dried fruit.

JAM WHOOPIE CREAM

INGREDIENTS

large egg whites
6
granulated or caster sugar
12oz / 340g / 1½ cups
unsalted butter, softened
16oz / 450g / 2 cups
vanilla extract
1½ teaspoons
kosher salt
½ teaspoon
thick jam of your choice
¼ cup

Combine the egg whites and sugar in the bowl of an electric mixer. Place the bowl over simmering water and whisk continuously until the sugar is dissolved and the mixture is hot to the touch – about 7 minutes. Remove the bowl from the heat and whisk on high speed until thick and shiny. The bowl should be cool to the touch.

Reduce the speed to medium and drop in the butter a bit at a time – the mixture will go through several textures, so soldier on. Next, add in the vanilla and salt. If the mixture looks curdled or lumpy simply continue to whisk. Whisk/beat on high speed for another minute or so until you have a silky smooth filling. The best way to test for that is to plunge your finger through the middle of the bowl, whirl it around a bit then lick it. No lumps, you're good to go. At this point you can also add diced dried fruit that suits the jam.

ORANGE CREAM FILLING

INGREDIENTS

unsalted butter, softened
6oz / 175g / ¾ cup
sour cream
4oz / 115g / ½ cup
vanilla extract
1½ teaspoons
kosher salt
¾ teaspoon
lemon juice, freshly squeezed
1 tablespoon
orange zest, freshly grated
1 tablespoon
confectioner's or icing sugar
54oz / 1.5kg / 9 cups

This filling is sort of like a quick and easy curd without all that pesky cooking. It's also similar to an orange buttercream (go figure), so if you don't have these ingredients on hand you can handily substitute one for the other. Because of the sour cream, this has a silkier, curd-like finish as opposed to the slightly crystallized texture of buttercream. Back home, a classic summer treat is a Creamsicle: an orange ice lolly on the outside with creamy vanilla frozen custard on the inside, all sitting on a wooden stick. We use this with our standard Vanilla Whoopie Pie recipe to create Creamsicle Whoopies.

Cream the butter until light and fluffy. Add in the sour cream, vanilla, salt, lemon juice and orange zest. Continue mixing until evenly combined. Slowly add in the sugar, about 7oz/200g/1 cup at a time, and beat until you have a smooth, even consistency. If after mixing you have something that looks soupy, don't despair; the cream should stay in the refrigerator until needed, and it will set up as it chills.

SNACK

THESE ARE the quickest way to separate pats from expats. Better known to us and many as coffee cakes, here in the UK most people think they contain coffee in one form or another. Not so (for the most part, anyway). Rather, they get their name from the style and preferred method of eating, namely over coffee. They can also be called breakfast or snacking cakes, since they aren't as SWEET as layer cakes, offering just the right amount of indulgence with half or less of the guilt. In the States, even to this day, it isn't uncommon to welcome neighbors or simply reconnect with them by bringing over a coffee cake and sitting down to a cuppa and a slice-a. Coffee cake's kissing cousin is tea loaf. Do any or all of them contain tea? We think not.

All these recipes are baked in a rectangular pan measuring 9 x 12in and 2in tall, or roughly 23 x 30 by 5cm. We bake some recipes in the same pan to produce a so-called sheet cake, which is nothing more than a one-layer cake finished with frosting. To the best of our knowledge many Brits call that a tray bake. These are not those. Rather they are, ostensibly, finished when they go into the oven. Many have a streusel or SWIRL running through them. Some have streusel strewn on top. And yet others have a crumb or crumble topping. Like their quick-bread kin, they are meant to be a more expeditious way to enjoy the fruit of your labor. Or the fruit of the season. And quite possibly, both.

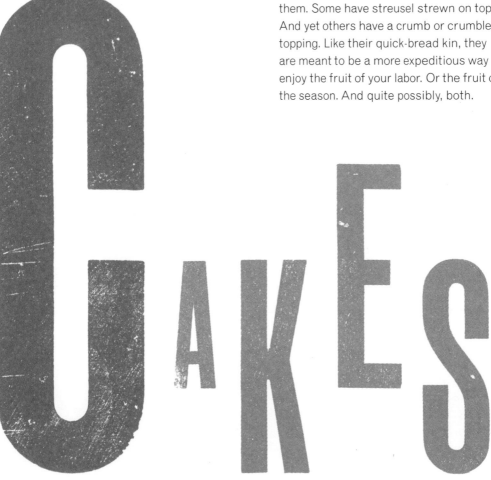

CAKES

BIPARTISAN CAKE

This recipe was conceived the week Barack Obama took office, and evolved from an Alaskan recipe. At the time Obama's preference for caramel apple cake was getting a lot of press, and we were inspired to combine the two. While we prefer to forget the chapter of American politics which brought Sarah Palin to the podium blowing smoke from her imaginary toy gun fingers, we hope in some small way this celebrates both sides of the coin. Maybe one day vying political parties across the globe can see we are all in this together and unite for the common good. At the very least, we can debate over a slice of this delicious cake. 12 portions

INGREDIENTS

For the caramel apple filling:

unsalted butter
2oz / 60g / ¼ cup

tart apples, peeled, cored and cut into ½in/1cm cubes
4

light or dark brown sugar
4oz / 115g / ½ cup, packed

For the batter and crumbs:

all-purpose or plain flour
21oz / 600g / 4 cups

granulated sugar
18oz / 500g / 2¼ cups

baking powder
2 teaspoons

bicarbonate of soda
1 teaspoon

kosher salt
2 teaspoons

cinnamon
1½ tablespoons

buttermilk
12fl oz / 350ml / 1½ cups

large eggs
2

vanilla extract
2 teaspoons

unsalted butter, softened
10oz / 275g / 1¼ cups

walnuts or pecans, chopped
8oz / 225g / 2 cups

dark brown sugar
8oz / 225g / 1 cup, packed

Preheat the oven to 180°C/350°F/gas mark 4. Butter a pan, 12 x 9 x 2in/30 x 23 x 5cm, and line the bottom with baking parchment. Dust the sides with flour and tap out any excess.

To make the filling, melt the butter in a large non-stick frying pan until foamy. Dump in the apples and sauté over a high heat for 5 minutes, stirring often. The apples should be brown on the outside but remain squishy inside. Remove from the heat and sprinkle in the brown sugar. Toss gently until evenly glazed. Leave to cool in the pan.

To make the batter and crumbs, whisk together the dry ingredients in the bowl of an electric mixer. In another bowl, combine the buttermilk, eggs and vanilla. Into the flour mixture, slowly add the softened butter and combine on low speed until you have a coarse, crumby mixture. Remove 2 cups of the crumbs, combine this with the nuts and brown sugar and set aside. Make a well in the dry ingredients and, all at once, pour in the wet ingredients. Mix thoroughly on low speed until the batter loosens up and the lumps disappear. Once the batter is mixed, fold in the caramel apples along with whatever delicious goo is left in the pan. Spread the finished batter in the prepared pan and smooth with a small spatula. Take handfuls of the nut mixture, clump it in your fist and sprinkle the crumbs over the batter. Liberally.

Bake the cake for 60 to 75 minutes, or until a small knife emerges cleanish from the center. If you hit an apple, the knife will be a bit smudged. Cover the cake loosely with foil about halfway through to prevent the nuts scorching. Let the cake cool completely in the pan. We remove the whole lot from the pan before cutting it into squares. This would be great with a little caramel or simple glaze drizzled over it.

BLUEBERRY SOUR CREAM COFFEE CAKE

Blueberries and sour cream is as classic a combination as you're gonna get for an American coffee cake. This is tart, tangy, sweet and most definitely moreish. Any whole, dark berry would work, but you may need to adjust the sugar slightly to compensate for a more tart or less ripe berry. In that regard, blueberries are far more predictable.

12 portions if cut into 3in/8cm squares

INGREDIENTS

For the crumb top:

all-purpose or plain flour
5½oz / 160g / 1 cup
granulated sugar
8oz / 225g / 1 cup
unsalted butter, softened
6oz / 175g / ¾ cup

For the batter:

all-purpose or plain flour
16oz / 450g / 3 cups
baking powder
1½ teaspoons
bicarbonate of soda
1½ teaspoons
kosher salt
½ teaspoon
unsalted butter, softened
12oz / 340g / 1½ cups
granulated sugar
12oz / 340g / 1½ cups
large eggs
3
vanilla extract
1½ teaspoons
sour cream
12oz / 340g / 12oz
blueberries
12oz / 340g / 3 cups

Preheat the oven to 190°C/375°F/gas mark 5. Butter a pan, 12 x 9 x 2in/30 x 23 x 5cm, and line the bottom with baking parchment. Dust the sides with flour and tap out any excess.

To make the crumbs, combine all the ingredients in the bowl of an electric mixer on low speed until you get coarse crumbs. Transfer the crumbs to another bowl but do not clean the mixer bowl. Set the crumbs aside if you're using them right away, or refrigerate until needed.

To make the batter, mix together the flour, baking powder, bicarbonate of soda and salt in a medium bowl, using a hand whisk. Set aside.

Using the mixer bowl you used for the crumbs, cream the butter and sugar on medium–high speed until light and fluffy, about 6 to 8 minutes. Reduce the speed to medium and add the eggs, one at a time, beating well after each addition. Stir in the vanilla. On low speed, alternately add the flour mixture and sour cream in 2 to 3 additions, beginning and ending with the dry ingredients and mixing only until just combined. Gently fold in the blueberries. Spread the batter evenly in the prepared pan, then generously sprinkle the crumbs over the batter and gently pat them into place.

Bake the cake for 60 to 75 minutes, or until a small knife emerges clean from the center. Let the cake cool completely in the pan on a wire rack. Once cooled, drizzle the cake with a simple lemon glaze. Or not.

PEANUT BUTTER CRUNCH CAKE

This falls more on the side of a snack cake than one for breakfast. Then again, you'd be surprised how many customers ask for this to start their day. Smooth peanut butter makes for a better squidge factor, but if you want more texture use crunchy and/or scatter some chopped peanuts on to the swirl as you layer the batter in the pan. Adult palates tend to prefer semi-sweet chocolate for this, where kids favour milk chocolate. Either works well, just know your audience. 12 portions if cut into 3in/8cm squares

INGREDIENTS

For the chocolate/peanut swirl:
semi-sweet chocolate chips
12oz / 340g / 2 cups
smooth peanut butter
4oz / 115g / ½ cup

For the crumbs and batter:
all-purpose or plain flour
16oz / 450g / 3 cups
light brown sugar
16oz / 450g / 2 cups, packed
unsalted butter, softened
8oz / 225g / 1 cup
smooth peanut butter
8oz / 225g / 1 cup
large eggs
4
whole or full-fat milk
8fl oz / 240ml / 1 cup
vanilla extract
2 teaspoons
baking powder
1 teaspoon
bicarbonate of soda
1 teaspoon
kosher salt
½ teaspoon

Preheat the oven to 180°C/350°F/gas mark 4. Butter a pan, 12 x 9 x 2in/30 x 23 x 5cm, and line the bottom with baking parchment. Dust the sides with flour and tap out any excess.

To make the swirl, melt the chocolate and peanut butter in a small saucepan over a gentle heat, stirring often until evenly combined and smooth. Set aside to cool slightly.

For the crumbs and batter, combine the flour, sugar, butter and peanut butter in the bowl of an electric mixer and mix on low speed until coarse crumbs form. Tightly pack 3 cups of the mixture and set aside for the crumb topping. Continue by adding the eggs to the bowl, one at a time, followed by the milk, vanilla, baking powder, bicarbonate of soda and salt. Beat on medium speed for 2 to 3 minutes, until everything comes together in a smooth batter. Spread half the batter in the prepared pan. Drizzle half the chocolate mixture over the batter, then cover it with the remaining batter followed by the remaining chocolate. Scatter the crumb mixture over the top and gently press the crumbs into the chocolate/peanut swirl.

Bake the cake for 50 to 60 minutes, or until a small knife emerges clean from the center. Cover the cake loosely during baking if the crumbs look like they are scorching. Let the cake cool in the pan before cutting into squares.

NYC CRUMB CAKE

If you grew up in or around New York City, numerous bakeries had crumb cake on offer. In our family, if Dad went to the bakery, you knew what was in store when he got home. The only thing you didn't know was if he got one with icing sugar or glaze. Diplomat that he is, he alternated, since no one could agree which was best. Glazed is the answer. The original recipe may come from Drake's in Brooklyn. If this sounds familiar to some, it should – it gave rise to the now mass-produced round snack cake with the crumb topping. *12 portions*

INGREDIENTS

For the crumbs:

unsalted butter
8oz / 225g / 1 cup

plain or all-purpose flour
13½oz / 380g / 2½ cups

dark brown sugar
8oz / 225g / 1 cup, packed

light brown sugar
4oz / 115g / ½ cup, packed

cinnamon
2 tablespoons

kosher salt
½ teaspoon

vanilla extract
1½ teaspoons

For the batter:

all-purpose or plain flour
18¾oz / 525g / 3½ cups

baking powder
1 teaspoon

bicarbonate of soda
½ teaspoon

kosher salt
1 teaspoon

unsalted butter, softened
8oz / 225g / 1 cup

caster sugar (for a lighter crumb)
12oz / 340g / 1½ cups

large eggs
3

vanilla extract
1½ teaspoons

sour cream
12 oz / 340g / 1½ cups

Preheat the oven to 180°C/350°F/gas mark 4. Butter a pan, 12 x 9 x 2in/30 x 23 x 5cm, and line the bottom with baking parchment. Dust the sides with flour and tap out any excess.

To make the crumbs, melt the butter in the bowl of an electric mixer over simmering water, then leave to cool for 5 minutes. Add the remaining ingredients and gently stir on low speed until the mixture becomes coarse and crumby. Try not to over-mix, as this will make tough crumbs. Set aside.

To make the batter, whisk together the flour, baking powder, bicarbonate of soda and salt in a medium bowl. Using an electric mixer, cream the butter and sugar until light and fluffy, about 6 to 8 minutes. Add the eggs, one at a time, beating well after each addition. Stir in the vanilla. On low speed, alternately add the flour mixture and sour cream, beginning and ending with the dry ingredients. Mix only until just combined. Spread the batter in the prepared pan and smooth with a spatula. This batter is on the thick side, so it needs to be nudged into the corners and evened out. Grab a handful of the crumb mixture and squeeze it. Break larger clumps into smaller ones as you scatter over the batter. There will be assorted-sized crumbs, which is precisely what you want. Make sure they are evenly distributed and completely cover the batter. It will seem like a lot of crumbs, but it is a crumb cake after all. Gently pat the crumbs into the batter.

Bake for 45 to 60 minutes, or until golden brown, domed on top and starting to pull away from the sides of the pan. The cake may test done sooner than it is, so make sure the middle starts to dome. Cover loosely with foil if the crumbs get too dark. Cool in the pan completely. We smother the warm cake with an icing sugar, milk and vanilla glaze that settles into all the nooks and crannies. Or dust with icing sugar.

KUNEGUNDA'S CAKE

This reminds us of something Grandma would make, using her special touch with dough. The kind of thing she would share if only she could remember. Exact amounts, that is. Most likely she's done it so often she can't recall how much of this and that is needed. She simply knows. Since the Polish grandmother in our family baked exactly like that, it seemed fitting to name it in her honor. We've made this numerous times without the applesauce/apple butter and it's delicious, but the added depth in flavor makes it all the more so. This falls smack between an apple pie and an apple cake. Made like a pie, eats like a cake. 12 portions

INGREDIENTS

For the dough:

unsalted butter
8oz / 225g / 1 cup

granulated sugar
8oz / 225g / 1 cup

large eggs
2

baking powder
1 tablespoon

kosher salt
½ teaspoon

lemon, juice of
1

all-purpose or plain flour
18¾oz / 525g / 3½ cups

For the filling:

large apples (Bramley size)
5–6

lemon juice
1 tablespoon

granulated sugar
(depending on the
apples and your preference)
4–6 tablespoons

cinnamon
1½ teaspoons

dark or golden raisins (optional)
6oz / 175g / 1 cup

thick applesauce or
apple butter (optional)
6–8oz / 175–225g / ¾–1 cup

To make the dough, cream the butter and sugar until smooth. Add the eggs and beat until fluffy. On low speed, add the baking powder and salt. Pour in the lemon juice but don't panic if it looks curdled. Gradually add the flour and mix until the dough starts to come away from the sides of the bowl. Dump the dough on a work surface, pat into a ball, and divide in half. Shape each half into a rectangle, wrap it in clingfilm and refrigerate for at least 2 hours.

To make the filling, peel and core the apples and cut them into ¼in/½cm thick slices. Toss the sliced apples in a bowl with the lemon juice, sugar, cinnamon and raisins, if using.

Preheat the oven to 190°C/375°F/gas mark 5. Butter a pan, 12 x 9 x 2in/30 x 23 x 5cm, and line the bottom with parchment. Flour the sides, tapping out any excess.

Roll out half the dough on a floured surface until a little larger than the pan in all directions. Transfer the dough to the pan and pat into place. It should come slightly up the sides. Don't worry about patching the dough, it will bake together and seal itself. If you're using applesauce or apple butter, thinly spread it over the bottom, followed by the apple filling. Roll out the remaining dough as before, and cover the filling with it. Tuck the edges down toward the upturned portion of the bottom dough. In theory the top and bottom will bake together. Brush the top of the dough with water or double cream and sprinkle with granulated sugar. Cut some air vents into the top dough.

Bake for 60 to 75 minutes, or until the dough is golden brown and the juices are bubbling up through the vents. Cool on a wire rack before cutting into nice thick wedges.

NUTMEG COFFEE CAKE

Hailing from the Garden State of New Jersey, where some of the best,
most handsome expat bakers in London come from, this simple cake is a must. It goes
together quickly and in a slightly unusual manner. The ingredients are almost unimpressive
but the result, we can assure you, is not. It is one of those things where the whole is well
more than the sum of its parts. Silky smooth with a gooey, chewy crust of sorts.
Though we've never tried, it would be fantastic with a dollop of sweet whipped cream
and fresh berries on top. *12 portions if cut into 3in/8cm squares*

INGREDIENTS

light brown sugar
32oz / 900g / 4 cups, packed
plain or all-purpose flour
21oz / 600g / 4 cups
unsalted butter, softened
16oz / 450g / 2 cups
large eggs
2
freshly grated nutmeg
2 teaspoons
sour cream
16oz / 450g / 2 cups
bicarbonate of soda
2 teaspoons
walnuts or pecans,
  chopped (optional)
4oz / 115g / 1 cup

Preheat the oven to 180°C/350°F/gas mark 4. Butter a pan,
12 x 9 x 2in/30 x 23 x 5cm, and line the bottom with baking
parchment. Dust the sides with flour and tap out any excess.

Put the sugar, flour and butter into the bowl of an electric
mixer. On low speed, blend until you have a bowl of coarse,
uneven crumbs. Remove half the mixture and scatter the
crumbs over the bottom of the prepared pan. Add the
remaining ingredients, apart from the nuts, to the bowl and,
on low speed again, slowly blend everything together until
smooth. You may see small lumps within the batter and
that's fine. Pour the batter over the crumbs in the pan and
sprinkle with chopped nuts if desired.

Bake the cake for 45 to 60 minutes, or until golden brown,
puffed and slightly firm to the touch. Cool the cake in the
pan for 15 to 20 minutes. If you eat this cake warm it is utterly
delicious, but be careful because the melted sugar 'crust' will
be warmer than the cake itself.

BUTTERSCOTCH PECAN CRUMB CAKE

A customer brought her mother, who was visiting from Glasgow, into the shop. Mom pleaded with daughter to ask if we could ship this cake to Scotland. Slightly embarrassed by the mother's request (who hasn't been there?), the daughter obliged and so did we, knowing this was a sturdy keeper. We figured this was a good candidate to survive the inconsistent Royal Mail. Thankfully we were right. A few words about the sugars: the crumb uses light brown, since it naturally darkens in the oven; the batter uses dark brown for flavor and granulated to lighten the texture. It's by no means necessary, just our preference. 12 portions

INGREDIENTS

For the crumbs:

unsalted butter, softened
8oz / 225g / 1 cup

all-purpose or plain flour
13½oz / 380g / 2½ cups

light brown sugar
12oz / 340g / 1½ cups, packed

kosher salt
½ teaspoon

For the batter:

all-purpose or plain flour
18¾oz / 525g / 3½ cups

baking powder
1½ teaspoons

bicarbonate of soda
1½ teaspoons

kosher salt
¾ teaspoon

buttermilk
16fl oz / 460ml / 2 cups

vanilla extract
1½ teaspoons

unsalted butter, softened
6oz / 175g / ¾ cup

dark brown sugar
8oz / 225g / 1 cup, packed

granulated sugar
6oz / 175g / ¾ cup

large eggs
4

pecans, chopped
12oz / 340g / 2 cups

Preheat the oven to 180°C/350°F/gas mark 4. Butter a pan, 12 x 9 x 2in/30 x 23 x 5cm, and line the bottom with baking parchment. Dust the sides with flour and tap out any excess.

To make the crumbs, combine all the ingredients in an electric mixer on low speed until you get coarse crumbs. Transfer to another bowl so you can re-use the one from the mixer. Set aside or refrigerate until needed.

To make the batter, mix together the flour, baking powder, bicarbonate of soda and salt in a medium bowl, using a hand whisk. In a large measuring jug, combine the buttermilk and vanilla. Set both aside.

In the bowl of an electric mixer, cream the butter and 2 sugars on medium–high speed until light and fluffy, about 6 to 8 minutes. Reduce the speed to medium and add the eggs, 1 or 2 at a time, beating well after each addition. On low speed alternately add the flour and buttermilk mixtures in 2 to 3 additions, beginning and ending with the dry ingredients and mixing only until just combined. Fold in the chopped pecans. Spread the batter evenly in the prepared pan. Take a fistful of crumbs, clench them and then scatter them over the batter. Press them gently into the batter (or not, it's your call).

Bake the cake for 45 to 60 minutes, or until a small knife emerges clean from the center. Cover the cake loosely with foil if it looks as though the crumbs are browning too much. Let the cake cool completely in the pan set on a wire rack before turning it out to cut into portions.

RHUBARB STRAWBERRY COFFEE CAKE

This may look complicated, but it's not. Simply follow each step for an amazing combination of crunch and squidge. The addition of strawberries has converted rhubarb detractors into lovers. If only everything were that simple … Makes 12 portions, if cut into 3in/8cm squares

INGREDIENTS

For the streusel top:

all-purpose or plain flour
5½oz / 160g / 1 cup
granulated sugar
8oz / 225g / 1 cup
unsalted butter, softened
6oz / 175g / ¾ cup

For the filling:

rhubarb, cut into 1in/2.5cm dice
16oz / 450g / 3 cups
fresh strawberries,
   roughly chopped
16oz / 450g / 3 cup
water or orange juice
4fl oz / 120ml / ½ cup
granulated sugar
8oz / 225g / 1 cup
cornflour
4 tablespoons

For the batter:

all-purpose or plain flour
16oz / 450g / 3 cups
granulated sugar
8oz / 225g / 1 cup, packed
baking powder
1 teaspoon
bicarbonate of soda
1 teaspoon
kosher salt
1 teaspoon
cold unsalted butter, diced
8oz / 225g / 1 cup
buttermilk
8fl oz/ 240ml / 1 cup
large eggs
2

Preheat the oven to 180°C/350°F/gas mark 4. Butter a pan, 12 x 9 x 2in/30 x 23 x 5cm, and line the bottom with baking parchment. Dust the sides with flour and tap out any excess.

First make the streusel top. Combine the flour, sugar and butter in the bowl of an electric mixer. Mix until you have pea-sized crumb. Cover, chill and set aside.

Place the rhubarb, strawberries and liquid in a heavy-bottomed pan over medium heat for about 5 minutes, until the fruit begins to soften. Combine the sugar and cornflour and add to the pan. Stir and continue heating for 5 to 10 minutes, until bubbly and thick. Watch carefully – this sticks to the bottom of the pan, so make sure to stir continuously with a flat, wood or rubber spatula. Set aside to cool.

For the batter, measure the dry ingredients into the bowl of an electric mixer and stir it all together on low speed. Add the butter bit by bit until the mixture gets crumbly, as it would for scones. Combine the wet ingredients in a separate bowl, then slowly add to the mixer just until everything is consistently moist. Spread half the batter in the prepared pan, followed by the rhubarb filling. If desired, sprinkle with sliced almonds to cover the rhubarb mixture. Dollop the remaining batter over the filling and smooth as best you can. Sprinkle the streusel over the batter in various-sized clumps.

Bake for 40 to 50 minutes, until firmish. The filling will stick to a tester knife, so check the batter for doneness as best you can. Leave to cool completely in the pan. Because of the rhubarb filling, this needs to set longer than most cakes before cutting.

COUNTLESS TIMES PEOPLE have asked us if these cakes are panettone.

No.

Final answer.

Panettone are yeast breads that are, indeed, of a similar size. People also confuse these with Madeira cakes, which, believe it or not, remain a mystery to us as we've never baked one. These recipes have traditional pound-cake roots: one pound each of flour, sugar, butter and eggs. No yeast in sight. They are also known as Bundt cakes because of the pan used – which, more often than not, has an ornate cast design so the batter bakes into all the NOOKS and crannies. In theory they are beautiful, but in practice we got tired of the batter sticking to the pan and scraping out baked-on chunks of cake. Don't even get us started on cleaning the damned things! True, these recipes can be baked off in two 9 x 5in/23 x 12cm loaf tins, but we have opted for the 10in/25cm tube for ease of use, not to mention reliability, in the oven. Plus we like the simple appearance.

A so-called tube pan is nothing more than an angel food pan, although the latter would always have prongs sticking up from the top rim while the former might not. Tube pans are available in either one piece or two. One-piece pans are akin to tall savarin moulds, but with a narrower center tube. Like savarins, they have a rounded bottom which, when inverted, becomes the top of the finished cake. Unlike savarins they are one continuous surface without any relief or design. BUNDT pans are non-stick (not really) with the characteristic color and feel of any non-stick pan, while rum baba or kugelhopf pans were traditionally copper. All have either a simple or an ornate textured surface that leaves its imprint on the finished cake – just not the tube pan.

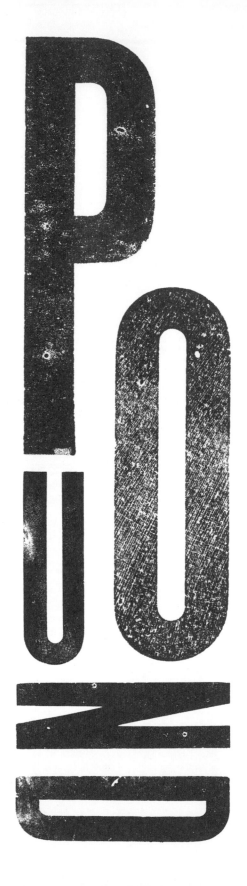

CAKES

Two-piece pans have a removable center tube connected to a flat base. The sides are also flat but slightly tapered. One-piece pans create a slightly rounded appearance while two-piece pans create a more angular/straight look. You can bake a pound cake in an angel food pan but not the other way around, because angel food cakes (aka chiffon cakes) need to be inverted the minute they come out of the oven so they don't collapse while cooling. Not so these sturdy DEVILS. Be it a Bundt or tube pan, the batter wraps around the cylindrical tube in the center, so that while baking the heat circulates up and through the tube and the cake bakes from the outside in as well as the inside out. This sets the structure of the cake relatively quickly and creates the impressive height characteristic of these beauties.

In some parts of the US these are also called slicing cakes. In either loaf or tube form they often include, or are drenched with, some booze to help them keep longer — as if the amount of butter or oil or sour cream hasn't already gotten the job done. That said, one of our favourites, Orange Date Pound Cake, is saturated with an orange glaze and it's been known to last about a month, hard though it was to put that to the test. Any of these recipes make a great addition to holiday fare, so when unexpected guests POP in there is always something to nosh on; a thin slice of rich deliciousness to share in the spirit of the occasion. Of course, that doesn't stop us from baking them throughout the year, too, to enjoy for breakfast, a snack or dessert. Certain recipes are enjoyed all day long, but we probably shouldn't admit that. On the other hand, a simple vanilla-laced pound cake, such as Trisha's Two Cents or Sand Torte, is a great staple which can easily be garnished with fresh fruit and whipped cream for a simple classic dessert any time of the year.

BABKA

Babka is a funny thing. It has two very different versions – both originated in Eastern Europe – one complicated, one not so much. Polish babka uses yeast, Russian doesn't; the former resembles a panettone, where the latter is baked as a rectangular loaf. When we moved to London, our Polish friend, Joanna, shared her mother's recipes for three varying degrees of cholesterol-laden babka – one using 24 egg yolks. It's rich. In the Lesniak household, Polish heritage dictated babka was baked for Easter. Its light crumb with bits of raisins and zest was the perfect introduction to spring. In New York, almost any Jewish deli sells a mangled-looking loaf (it felt like a brick), but the scent was intoxicating and it was difficult not to eat the whole thing in one. We've opted for a hybrid, using a Russian-style batter but baking it in a tube pan as you would the Polish dough. It's a classic sour-cream coffee cake with a chocolate, nut and raisin streusel running through layers of batter. Serves 12–16

INGREDIENTS

For the streusel:
granulated sugar
6oz / 175g / ¾ cup
chopped nuts of choice (optional)
4oz / 115g / ¾ cup
semi-sweet chocolate chips
4oz / 115g / ⅔ cup
raisins or currants
3oz / 75g / ½ cup
ground cinnamon
1 tablespoon

For the batter:
all-purpose or plain flour
16oz / 450g / 3 cups
baking powder
1½ teaspoons
kosher salt
¾ teaspoon
granulated sugar
16oz / 450g / 2 cups
unsalted butter, softened
12oz / 340g / 1½ cups
large eggs
3
vanilla extract
2 teaspoons
sour cream
12oz / 340g / 1½ cups

Preheat the oven to 180°C/350°F/gas mark 4. Butter a 10in/25cm tube pan, line the bottom with baking parchment, dust the sides and tube with flour and tap out any excess.

Start by combining all the streusel ingredients in a medium bowl. In a separate bowl, whisk together the flour, baking powder and salt. Set both aside.

In the bowl of an electric mixer, on low speed, combine the sugar the butter, then increase the speed and cream until light and fluffy, about 5 to 6 minutes. Reduce the speed to medium and add the eggs, one at a time, beating well after each addition. Scrape the bottom of the bowl, add the vanilla and mix for 1 minute more. Alternately add the sour cream and flour mixture in 3 to 4 additions, beginning and ending with the dry ingredients. Mix only until just combined. Spread ⅓ of the batter into the prepared pan then sprinkle ½ the streusel mix over it. Spread another ⅓ of the batter on top, followed by the remaining streusel and then the final ⅓ of the batter.

Bake for 75 to 90 minutes, or until a small knife emerges clean from the center. The streusel might erupt from the center, but that's to be expected. Cool the cake on a wire rack for about 15 minutes before releasing it to cool completely.

BANANA BOURBON POUND CAKE

It seems everyone and their mother has a recipe for a banana sour-cream cake
of some kind or another. Us too. (Just check the Layer Cake chapter on page 166 …)
The sour cream lends just enough tang to the otherwise sweet banana. Clotted cream or
yoghurt would also do the trick. For something really special though, try it with bourbon. The
bad bits bake off, leaving a heady aroma that permeates every last bite. For added indulgence fit
for any celebration, we've added nuts and raisins as well – about 6oz/175g/1 cup each. However,
we prefer this less ostentatious, elegant version. When it comes to baking with bananas, for the
best flavor use the darkest, ripest ones you can find. Serves 12–16

INGREDIENTS

all-purpose or plain flour
   21oz / 600g / 4 cups
baking powder
   2 teaspoons
bourbon or whole milk
   4fl oz / 120ml / ½ cup
sour cream
   4oz / 115g / ½ cup
vanilla extract
   2 teaspoons
granulated sugar
   24oz / 675g / 3 cups
orange or lemon zest,
   freshly grated
   2 tablespoons
unsalted butter, softened
   16oz / 450g / 2 cups
ripe bananas, roughly chopped
   about 3
large eggs
   6

Preheat the oven to 180°C/350°F/gas mark 4. Butter
a 10in/25cm tube pan, line the bottom with baking
parchment, dust the sides and tube with flour and tap
out any excess.

Whisk together the flour and baking powder in a medium
bowl. In a large, glass measuring jug, combine the bourbon
or milk, sour cream and vanilla. Set both aside.

In the bowl of an electric mixer fitted with a paddle,
combine the sugar and lemon/orange zest on low speed
until fragrant. Slowly add in the butter and increase the
speed to medium–high, creaming until light and fluffy,
about 6 to 8 minutes. Reduce the speed, add the bananas,
and stir until the fruit is mashed up and evenly distributed.
Next, add in the eggs, one at a time, beating well after
each addition. Scrape the bottom of the bowl and beat for
another minute or so until you have an even consistency.
On a low speed, alternately add the flour and sour cream
mixtures in 3 or 4 additions, beginning and ending with
the dry ingredients and mixing only until just combined.
(If you've opted for adding nuts and raisins too, fold
them in at this point.) Pour the batter into the prepared
pan and smooth the top with the back of a spoon or
small offset spatula.

Bake for 60 to 75 minutes or until a small knife emerges
clean from the center. Let the cake cool in the pan for
15 minutes or so before turning it out to cool completely.
Finish simply with a dusting of powdered sugar.

MOM'S APPLE CAKE

This is a great, virtually no-fail introduction to making pound cakes.
Momma Lesniak would make this cake just to have on hand – not that it lasted for long.
It's very easy to whip up, since it can be done in a single bowl, even without appliances.
Reason being, canola oil (called rapeseed oil in the UK) eliminates the need for creaming
butter. One word of caution: when layering the apples, try not to let them touch
the sides of the pan. They will stick to the pan, and while the cake will release after baking,
it might take some effort – and no primer recipe should be difficult. At home this was
always served with a lemon sauce, and the combination is out of this world. It's interesting
to note that, to date, only this recipe has been handed down; the lemon sauce remains a
mystery. We make do in the meantime by garnishing a slice of this with a dollop of lemon
curd. Another interesting fact … Mom's notes say this is great with fresh peaches though
there is no family memory of same. Serves 12–16

INGREDIENTS

For the filling:

apples, peeled,
  cored and thinly sliced
  about 6 large or 4 giant Braeburns
granulated or light brown sugar
  6–8 tablespoons
cinnamon
  5–6 teaspoons
orange zest, freshly grated
  1 teaspoon

For the batter:

all-purpose or plain flour
  16oz / 450g / 3 cups
granulated sugar
  16oz / 450g / 2 cups
baking powder
  1 tablespoon
kosher salt
  1 teaspoon
canola or other flavorless oil
  8fl oz / 240ml / 1 cup
large eggs at room temperature
  4
orange juice, freshly squeezed
  2fl oz / 60ml / ¼ cup
vanilla extract
  1 tablespoon

Preheat the oven to 190°C/375°F/gas mark 5. Generously
butter a 10in/25cm tube pan, no smaller, line the bottom with
baking parchment and dust the sides and tube with flour.

Combine the apples, sugar, cinnamon and orange zest.
Set aside to macerate.

Whisk together all the dry ingredients in a medium bowl. In a
separate bowl, combine the oil, eggs, orange juice and vanilla.
Slowly pour the wet ingredients into the dry and combine.

Spoon ⅓ of the batter into the prepared pan. Arrange ½ the
apples around the tube, being careful not to the let them touch
the sides of the pan. If the apples look dry, or simply because
you'd like to, sprinkle some of the juice from the macerated
apples over those in the pan – but by no means use more than
2fl oz/60ml/¼ cup of the reserved juice. Spoon another ⅓ of
the batter into the pan and arrange the remaining apples on
top in a ring again. Top the apples with the remaining batter.

Bake for about 60 to 90 minutes, or until a knife inserted into
the center emerges clean. If the cake is browning too quickly,
cover the top loosely with aluminium foil. Let cool for about
30 minutes before unmoulding from the pan. Sometimes we
take the reserved juice from the macerated apples, reduce it by
simmering for 10 or so minutes, then spoon the warm syrup
over a slice of cake. Add a dollop of cream or ice cream and
it will make you forget all about that missing lemon sauce.

BOULDER BUNDT CAKE

This evolved from an internet search for Colorado recipes. It landed me on a website for The Kitchen, in Boulder, an upscale-looking bistro with that earthy artisanal feel that makes food look yummy even if it isn't (no offense to them). The original recipe was for a Mocha Pound Cake, but OD doesn't like coffee in any way, shape or form. As with any internet search, tangents led me astray to an idea for a toffee version using butterscotch chips and I knew then OD would take the bait. We've also made an equally delicious alternative in which we've substituted white chocolate chips for the butterscotch. And here we are, with gratitude to the folks in Boulder. Serves 12–16

INGREDIENTS

all-purpose or plain flour
  24oz / 675g / 4½ cups
bicarbonate of soda
  ¾ teaspoon
kosher salt
  ½ teaspoon
butterscotch chips
  12oz / 340g / 2 cups
instant coffee granules or
  espresso powder for extra kick
  4 tablespoons
water
  4fl oz / 120ml / ½ cup
unsalted butter, softened
  12oz / 340g / 1½ cups
granulated sugar
  18oz / 500g / 2¼ cups
large eggs
  6
Kahlúa or Scotch
  1 tablespoon
coffee extract
  1 teaspoon
buttermilk
  8fl oz / 240ml / 1 cup
pecans or walnuts,
  chopped (optional)
  6oz / 175g / 1 cup

Preheat the oven to 180°C/350°F/gas mark 4. Generously butter a 10in/25cm tube pan, line the bottom with baking parchment and dust with flour.

Whisk together the flour, bicarbonate of soda and salt in a medium bowl. Combine the butterscotch chips, coffee powder and water in a heatproof bowl set over a pan of simmering water. Stir until smooth, remove from the heat and let cool. Set both aside.

In the bowl of an electric mixer, cream the butter and sugar on medium–high speed until light and fluffy. Scrape the bowl and stir in the cooled butterscotch mixture until well combined. Add the eggs, one at a time, beating well after each addition, followed by the liqueur or coffee extract. On low speed, alternately add the flour mixture and buttermilk in 3 to 4 additions. Begin and end with the dry ingredients and mix only until the flour disappears. Remove the bowl from the mixer and finish mixing with a rubber spatula, if need be. Fold in the chopped nuts now, if you've chosen to add them. Pour the batter into the prepared pan and smooth the top with the back of a spoon or a small offset spatula.

Bake the cake for 75 to 90 minutes, or until a small knife emerges clean from the center. Let the cake cool in the pan for about 10 minutes before turning it out to cool completely.

BRITISH EVACUATION CAKE

We believe this is the mother of all carrot cakes. Supposedly it was served in
New York City to celebrate British Evacuation Day way back in 1783. For us it is the preferred
carrot experience, unsullied by any gooey frosting. If you really must have a dollop of
something, slice the cake thin and schmear it with cream cheese. Then again, you can always
schmear some on a thick slab of it, too. Historically, the cooled cake was brushed all over with
vermouth and then finished with a drizzle made from 4oz/115g/1 cup icing sugar, 2 tablespoons
buttermilk or double cream and 1 teaspoon rum. Serves 12–16

INGREDIENTS

For the cake:

all-purpose or plain flour
  10oz / 300g / 2 cups
whole wheat or wholemeal flour
  5½oz / 150g / 1 cup
baking powder
  2 teaspoons
bicarbonate of soda
  2 teaspoons
cinnamon
  2 teaspoons
nutmeg, freshly grated
  1 teaspoon
walnuts or pecans, chopped
  6oz / 170g / 1 cup
dark or golden raisins or sultanas
  4–6oz / 115–170g / ⅔–1 cup
dried cranberries
  4–6oz / 115–170g / ⅔–1 cup
grated carrots
  16oz / 450g / about 2 cups
granulated sugar
  8oz / 225g / 1 cup
light brown sugar
  6oz / 175g / ¾ cup, packed
canola or vegetable oil
  8fl oz / 240ml / 1 cup
large eggs
  5
vanilla extract
  1 teaspoon

Preheat the oven to 160°C/325°F/gas mark 3. Butter
a 10in/25cm tube pan, line the bottom with baking
parchment, dust the sides and tube with flour and tap
out any excess.

In a medium bowl, whisk together the dry ingredients.
In a separate bowl, combine the nuts, dried fruits, carrots
and a few tablespoons of the flour mixture. The best way
to do this is with your fingers as opposed to any utensil –
the latter tends to send things flying, no matter how hard
you try not to. Using an electric mixer, beat the sugars,
oil, eggs and vanilla on medium speed until light and
creamy. Reduce the speed to low and add the flour mixture
2½oz/70g/½ cup at a time only until just combined.
Remove the bowl from the mixer and fold in the carrots,
nuts and fruit. Scrape the batter into the prepared pan.

Bake for 75 to 90 minutes or until a small knife emerges
clean from the center. Cool the cake in the pan for
30 minutes or so before turning it out onto a wire rack to
cool completely. If you're in the mood for authenticity,
once the cake is cool, finish the cake using the original
glaze as mentioned above.

ORANGE DATE POUND CAKE

Many recipes from the Southern US for cakes similar to this use orange gummy slices. Odd, was very much our reaction. Then again, many folks from those parts start their day with a can of soda. A certain author being one of them… We (okay, the other certain author) decided to make a more sophisticated version by using the best candied orange peel we could find to add a slight bitterness and balance out the sweetness of the dates. This is our version of Christmas fruit cake, and one of us has been known to wholly enjoy a taste of this unearthed sometime in mid-January. Proof positive that use-by dates mean absolutely nothing.

INGREDIENTS

For the cake:

all-purpose or plain flour
200z / 550g / 3¾ cups
bicarbonate of soda
1 teaspoon
kosher salt
½ teaspoon
candied orange peel
6oz / 175g / 1 cup
pecans, toasted and chopped
6oz / 175g / 1 cup
dates, pitted and chopped
8oz / 225g / 1¼ cups
shredded coconut
6oz / 175g / 1½ cups
unsalted butter, softened
8oz / 225g / 1 cup
granulated sugar
16oz / 450g / 2 cups
large eggs
4
buttermilk
4fl oz / 120ml / ½ cup

For the glaze:

icing sugar
12oz / 340g / 2 cups
orange juice
8fl oz / 240ml / 1 cup
orange zest, freshly grated
1 tablespoon

Preheat the oven to 150°C/300°F/gas mark 2. Butter a 10in/25cm tube pan, line the bottom with parchment, dust the sides and tube with flour and tap out any excess.

In a medium bowl, whisk together the flour, bicarbonate of soda and salt. In another bowl, combine the peel, nuts, dates and coconut and toss with 2 tablespooons of the flour mixture, making sure to separate the chopped dates.

In the bowl of an electric mixer, cream the butter and sugar on medium–high speed until light and fluffy, about 6 to 8 minutes. Reduce the speed to low and add the eggs, one at a time, beating well after each addition. Scrape the bottom of the bowl and mix for 1 minute more to incorporate any slush at the bottom. There should be no lumps in the batter at this point. Still on low speed, alternately add the flour mixture and buttermilk in 2 to 3 additions, beginning and ending with the flour mixture and stirring only until just combined. Remove the bowl from the mixer and fold in the date/nut mixture. Pour the batter into the pan and smooth the top with a small spatula.

Bake the cake for 1¼ to 2 hours or until it is golden brown and a small knife emerges clean from the center. Remove the cake from the oven and place it on a wire rack that has been set on to a baking sheet. Combine the ingredients for the glaze and pour all of it over the hot cake. Should any glaze seep out of the pan bottom, drizzle it back on to the cake, repeating as necessary until all the glaze has soaked in. Let the cake cool completely in the pan.

FRESH FRUIT 'COFFEE' CAKE

Many pound cakes include dried fruit and nuts, which help them keep for longer periods. Ditto with any booze or sugar glaze. But we're not always in the mood for all that, nor are we in the mood to limit our intake, so we devised this recipe to easily accommodate any fresh fruit. Now we can enjoy the simplicity of pound cake regardless of the season. Like OD's marriage pies, we also combine any fresh fruits we think go well together. Peach and raspberry make for a fantastic finish to a summer picnic. Serves 12–16

INGREDIENTS

all-purpose or plain flour
24oz / 675g / 4½ cups
bicarbonate of soda
2¼ teaspoons
kosher salt
1 teaspoon
buttermilk, at room temperature
20fl oz / 600ml / 2¼ cups
vanilla extract or Grand Marnier
2 teaspoons
ripe berries (or fruit of choice
cut into ½in/1cm dice)
12oz / 340g / about 2 cups
unsalted butter, softened
10oz / 275g / 1¼ cups
granulated sugar
12oz / 340g / 1½ cups
light brown sugar
6oz / 175g / ¾ cup, packed
large eggs, at room temperature
3

Preheat the oven to 180°C/350°F/gas mark 4. Butter a 10in/25cm tube pan, line the bottom with baking parchment, dust the sides with flour and tap out any excess.

In a medium bowl, whisk together the flour, bicarbonate of soda and salt. In a large, glass measuring jug, combine the buttermilk and vanilla or Grand Marnier. In yet another bowl, toss the fruit with 1oz/25g/¼ cup of the flour mixture, to prevent it sinking to the bottom while baking. Set all the bowls aside.

In the bowl of an electric mixer fitted with a paddle attachment, cream the butter and both sugars on medium–high speed until light and fluffy, about 6 to 8 minutes. Reduce the speed to medium and add the eggs, one at a time, making sure to incorporate each egg fully before adding the next. As always, scrape the bowl as needed along the way. On a low speed, alternately add the flour and buttermilk mixtures in 3 to 4 additions, mixing only until just combined. Remove the bowl from the mixer and fold in the fresh fruit with a rubber spatula. Spoon the batter into the prepared pan and smooth the top as necessary.

Bake for about 90 minutes or until the top is golden brown and a small knife emerges clean. If need be, cover the cake loosely with foil to prevent over-browning. Cool the cake in the pan for 45 minutes before releasing it. While this may seem too long a cooling period, this allows the fruit juices to set within the cake to prevent it falling apart when you release it from the pan.

Finish this either with a simple lemon glaze (page 148) or a dusting of icing sugar.

SAND TORTE POUND CAKE

During our cake-by-cake tour of America, we came across this recipe in a cookbook from Alabama. As we blogged about our journey (we never actually left London), we ended up crediting this one to Arizona since you can't find too many recipes in the desert. So we figured: sand, desert – Arizona. But, of course! We prefer oranges over lemons and Cointreau over rum to keep things lighter and more focused on the texture, which is unique among pound cakes. If you prefer, replace the liqueur with orange or lemon juice. We've made it with all sorts of extracts and liqueurs, with and without the zest, so this recipe is more open-ended for you to devise your favorite combination. This is fantastic served with blueberries and a small-ish bit of whipped cream. Serves 12–16

INGREDIENTS

all-purpose or plain flour
10oz / 300g / 2 cups
cornstarch or cornflour
10oz / 300g / 2 cups
baking powder
1 teaspoon
granulated sugar
16oz / 900g / 4 cups
orange or lemon zest,
freshly grated
2 tablespoons
unsalted butter, softened
16oz / 450g / 2 cups
large eggs
8
Cointreau, rum or cognac
3–4 tablespoons
orange blossom water
(optional)
a dash

Preheat the oven to 180°C/350°F/gas mark 4. Generously butter a 10in/25cm tube pan, no smaller, line the bottom with baking parchment and dust with flour.

Whisk together the flour, cornstarch or cornflour and baking powder in a medium bowl. Be sure there are no lumps left, since cornstarch tends to clump things up. Set aside.

In the bowl of an electric mixer fitted with a paddle, combine the sugar and zest on low speed until fragrant. Add the butter 1 tablespoon at a time, and once all the butter is in the bowl, gradually increase the speed to medium–high and cream the mixture until light and fluffy, about 6 to 8 minutes. Reduce the speed to low and add the eggs, one at a time, beating for about 1 minute after each addition. Scrape the bowl as needed to incorporate any gunk (a highly technical term only the pros use) left at the bottom of the bowl. Next, stir in the Cointreau. (At this point we sometimes add a dash of orange blossom water, depending on how much zest the orange produced. We've even made this cake without any zest and relied on 1 teaspoon orange blossom water to get us through.) Gradually add the dry ingredients, about 2oz/60g/½ cup at a time, mixing only until just combined. Pour the batter into the prepared pan and smooth the top with a small spatula.

Bake the cake for 45 to 60 minutes, or until golden brown and a small knife emerges clean from the center. Let the cake cool for about 15 minutes in the pan before releasing it to cool completely.

TRISHA'S TWO CENTS

This recipe comes from OD's side of the family – his sister-in-law, to be precise. Trisha grew up in the mossy depths of Louisiana bayou country, and according to her this recipe has been a closely guarded family secret. Don't tell her, but our research has turned up a similar cake that comes from Dallas, so we're led to believe there are more recipes of this ilk from that neck of the woods, mossy or otherwise. Every year Trisha makes this for Christmas, and since the holidays are all about family and tradition we give you this recipe more or less intact as it was given to us. She likes to bake this in a flat, Christmas-tree-shaped pan, which for our tastes is a bit much. Otherwise, it's verbatim. Being an attorney, I'm sure Trisha will have a thing or two to say about our version. You'll note the lack of raising agent here, which is true to original pound-cake heritage. Serves 12–16

INGREDIENTS

For the cake:

unsalted butter, softened
12oz / 340g / 1½ cups
cream cheese, softened
12oz / 340g / about 3 cups
kosher salt
½ teaspoon
granulated sugar
24oz / 675g / 3 cups
all-purpose or plain flour
16oz / 450g / 3 cups
large eggs
6
vanilla extract
2 teaspoons

For the glaze:

cold water
2fl oz / 60ml / ¼ cup
rum
2fl oz / 60ml / ¼ cup
sugar
2oz / 60g / ¼ cup
unsalted butter
4oz / 115g / ½ cup
pecans, chopped (optional)
4oz / 115g / 1 cup

Preheat the oven to 180°C/350°F/gas mark 4. Butter a 10in/25cm tube pan, line the bottom with baking parchment, dust the sides and tube with flour and tap out any excess.

Cream the butter and cream cheese until light and cream-colored. Add the salt and sugar and whip it well. Add 2 eggs with 5oz/150g/1 cup flour. Mix. Add 2 more eggs and another 5oz/150g/1 cup flour, then add the remaining flour and eggs. Mix in the vanilla. Pour the batter into the prepared pan and smooth the top with a small spatula.

Bake for 75 to 90 minutes. While Trisha doesn't mention this part, we will: cool the cake completely in the pan set on a wire rack.

To make the glaze, blend all the ingredients and bring them to a boil in a small pan. Simmer for about 4 minutes and add pecans if desired. Pour over the pound cake. Dust with confectioners' sugar before serving, if you like.

CHEESE CAKES

WITHIN THE PANTHEON of all things dessert, cheesecakes occupy a highly esteemed spot. It's a bit odd, given that they're some of the easiest things to throw together and lend themselves to endless permutation. For such little effort they sure can pack an incredibly elegant punch. Presumably this is why they are so revered. American cheesecake recipes call for both set and baked variations. Our preference is for the latter, since, to us, the texture and ultimate flavor is far superior. Set cheesecakes often appear to be little more than frosting on a cookie. Plus, there's no need for the occasional gelatine gimmickry.

Baked cheesecakes (many refer to them as New York cheesecakes) have a way of intimidating people, but they shouldn't. True, they are a bit more pernickety while in the oven, but getting the hang of them is no big deal. A cheesecake is done baking when it appears 'set', but that does not, repeat not, mean firm. Unbaked cheesecake batter sloshes in the pan. Fully baked batter stops sloshing and WIGGLES as one. Some batters are lighter than others and puff like a soufflé then settle down as they cool, often creating a higher rim and a flat, sunken middle. Others won't budge but they will solidify in the oven. Finished textures vary from light and almost fluffy to dense and almost chewy. Under-baked cheesecakes wiggle at the perimeter but slosh in the middle and need more oven time to cohere. A mere 5 or 10 minutes more usually does the trick. Over-baked cheesecakes stopped wiggling long ago and, more often than not, will crack on top. Sometimes you'll end up with a pretty deep crevasse up there. Even then, there is absolutely no reason to despair.

There's no telling how many Michelin-starred cheesecakes crack on top, but we venture a guess that it's far more than you realize. How better to explain the myriad choices of toppings? It can't possibly all be down to taste. As we all know, concealer can work miracles and it's no different in the kitchen.

When it comes to ingredients, cheesecakes quite possibly keep dairy suppliers in business. There is no getting around the fact that these are RICH. We embrace this truth, use full-fat everything and suggest portion-control for those misguided few who cling to the belief that dessert is not calorie-centric. Watching your waist? Don't eat it. Simple. That said, you can easily make substitutions based on availability or preference. Sour cream, mascarpone, clotted cream, crème fraîche and Greek yoghurt, to name a few, can be used interchangeably. Tangy or creamy? You decide. We encourage you to experiment and find what appeals most to your taste-buds.

Just one quick 'technical' note. Cheesecakes are a bit like cats. They have a mind of their own and don't like to be messed with. Once out of the oven, ignore them until they are completely and utterly at room temperature before chilling them in the refrigerator. If they need a little extra LOVE, they will tell you in the form of a crack where there wasn't one and then you can caress with a topping as you see fit.

If you're still unsure, all (repeat, ALL) questions should be directed to OD at: info@outsidertart.com. He's the undisputed cheesecake king.

RED VELVET CHEESECAKE

There appears to be an incessant fascination with red velvet. To be honest, churning out cupcakes, layers and Red Velvet Whoopies gets tiresome. But we soldier on. OD took it upon himself to devise this glorious recipe in a pre-emptive strike. It was only a matter of time before someone walked in asking for this. So here you go. We've had British red velvet 'experts' complain this isn't right, given the orange zest. But OD's heirloom red-velvet recipes have always included it. The best advice is never to mess with OD's family. Serves 10–12

INGREDIENTS

For the cookie base:

all-purpose or plain flour
5½oz / 160g / 1 cup
unsweetened cocoa powder
4 tablespoons
granulated sugar
6 tablespoons
baking powder
¾ teaspoon
kosher salt
¼ teaspoon
unsalted butter, softened
4oz / 115g / ½ cup
large egg yolks, lightly beaten
2

For the batter:

white chocolate
16oz / 450g / about 3 cups
light brown sugar
4oz / 115g / ½ cup, packed
orange zest, freshly grated
1 tablespoon
cream cheese, softened
32oz / 900g / about 8 cups
unsalted butter, softened
4oz / 115g / ½ cup
unsweetened cocoa powder
3 tablespoons
red food coloring
4fl oz / 120ml / ½ cup
large eggs
4
vanilla extract
1 tablespoon

Preheat the oven to 150°C/300°F/gas mark 2. Butter a round cheesecake pan with a removable bottom, 9 x 3in/ 23 x 8cm. Wrap the bottom of the pan and up the sides with foil. Or use a 9in/23cm diameter springform pan.

For the base, combine the flour, cocoa, sugar, baking powder and salt in the bowl of an electric mixer. Add the butter and stir on low speed until crumbly. Stir in the egg yolks until well incorporated – it will still be crumbly. Press into the prepared pan and pat firmly into the bottom and slightly up the sides. Pierce the surface with a fork in several places. Bake for 15 to 20 minutes, or until the crust is firm. Leave to cool.

For the batter, slowly melt the chocolate in a bowl set over a pan of simmering water, then remove from the heat to cool. In the bowl of an electric mixer, combine the sugar and zest until fragrant. Add the cream cheese, butter and cocoa, then increase the speed and cream until it is light. Stir in the food coloring and mix until the color is evenly distributed. On low speed add the eggs, one at a time, beating well after each addition. Stir in the cooled chocolate, then the vanilla. Remove from the mixer and finish mixing with a rubber spatula, scraping up from the bottom to ensure it is evenly mixed. There should be no streaks of color visible. Pour the batter on the cooled crust and shake the pan gently to even it.

Bake for 45 to 60 minutes or until set. It usually rises evenly and cracks around the edges. Cover loosely with foil if it browns too quickly. If the middle wiggles separately from the perimeter when you shake the pan, it needs 5 to 10 minutes more. All cheesecakes set as they cool, which can take a while. Leave to cool completely in the pan on a wire rack before refrigerating for at least 4 hours, preferably overnight. Frost with Cream Cheese Mascarpone Frosting (page 186)

BANANAS FOSTER CHEESECAKE

As always there is much debate about the roots of any recipe, fact or fiction. Truth is Bananas Foster was created in New Orleans at the world-famous Brennan's restaurant around 1950. Truth and New Orleans don't often appear in the same sentence, so get it while you can. Upon arriving in London, we discovered banoffee pie. Regardless of countless enquiries, the be-all-and-end-all banoffee recipe eludes us. We're starting to think it's a figment of the British imagination. Still, the two are somewhat distant relatives, with unique tics depending on who's stirring the pot. It became our mission to unite these two classics. If you disagree with our suggestions (no doubt enthusiasts of either will do so vehemently), kindly refrain from tossing spatulas in our direction and add whatever you want. Just keep the custard intact and you'll be fine. For Bananas Foster, Americans use Nilla Wafers which are available in the UK. Banoffee, as we understand it, uses a digestive cookie crust. Serves 10–12

INGREDIENTS

For the cookie crust:

cookie crumbs
10oz / 160g / 1¾cups

light or dark brown sugar
2oz / 60g / ¼ cup, packed

unsalted butter, melted
3oz / 80g / 1/3 cup

For the custard:

cream cheese
16oz / 450g / about 4 cups

mascarpone
8oz / 225g / 1 cup

large eggs, at room temperature
6

light or dark brown sugar
8oz / 225g / 1 cup, packed

mashed banana (about 4 bananas)
16oz / 450g / about 2 cups

cinnamon
1½ teaspoons

light or dark rum
2 tablespoons

For the caramel topping:

unsalted butter
4oz / 115g / ½ cup

light or dark brown sugar
8oz / 225g / 1 cup, packed

Preheat the oven to 180°C/350°F/gas mark 4. Butter a round cheesecake pan with a removable bottom, 9 x 3in/23 x 8cm. Wrap the bottom of the pan and partly up the sides with foil. Or use a 9in/23cm diameter springform pan.

To make the crust, combine all the ingredients in a bowl until evenly moist. Press the mixture into the bottom of the pan and part-way up the sides. Bake for about 10 to 15 minutes, until lightly toasted. Leave to cool completely.

To make the custard, beat the cream cheese and mascarpone in an electric mixer on medium speed until smooth. Reduce the speed and add the eggs, one at a time, beating well after each addition. Add the sugar, banana, cinnamon and rum. Mix slowly but thoroughly until evenly incorporated. Pour the batter on to the crust and smooth with an offset spatula.

Bake for about 50 to 60 minutes, or until the edge begins to pull away from the sides of the pan. It should wiggle as one, not appear as though custard is sloshing around underneath the surface. Look for a wiggle like set gelatine, not a rolling undulation. Remove the cheesecake from the oven and leave to cool completely on a wire rack. Once at room temperature, cover and refrigerate overnight before finishing.

For the topping, melt the butter in a small saucepan over low heat. Add the sugar and stir continuously until the sugar dissolves and you have a smooth, even consistency. Pour over the cheesecake and refrigerate until ready to serve.

PUMPKIN CHEESECAKE

Though we can never figure out why come Thanksgiving, people always ask about pumpkin pie alternatives, so we do our best to oblige. OD has toyed endlessly with this recipe, finally settling on the combination and amount of spice. Should you disagree, bear in mind that pumpkin is quite a strong flavor and can stand up to more spice than you'd think. The bourbon can be left out if need be, but we highly recommend it to round out the flavors and add warmth. It's not unusual for us to have a stash of our cranberry compote lying around during the holidays, so we've spread a layer of it on top of the cooled crust before pouring in the batter – just because we can. Serves 10–12

INGREDIENTS

For the ginger snap crust:

Ginger Snap or Gingernut crumbs
8oz / 225g / 2 cups
light brown sugar
2oz / 60g / ¼ cup, packed
unsalted butter, melted
2oz / 170g / ¼ cup
pinch of kosher salt

For the cheesecake:

cream cheese
16oz / 450g / about 4 cups
light or dark brown sugar
8oz / 225g / 1 cup, packed
large eggs, at room temperature
5
pumpkin purée, 2 small cans
16oz / 450g / 2 cups
cinnamon
1½ teaspoons
ground cloves, ginger and mace
¼ teaspoon each
vanilla extract
½ teaspoon
Bourbon or brandy
2fl oz / 60ml / ¼ cup

For the topping:

sour cream
16oz / 450g / 2 cups
granulated sugar
2oz / 60g / ¼ cup

Preheat the oven to 180°C/350°F/gas mark 4. Butter a round cheesecake or springform pan with a removable bottom, 9 x 3in/ 23 x 8cm. Wrap the bottom of the pan and partly up the sides with aluminium foil. As an alternative, use a 9in/23cm diameter springform pan.

To make the crust, combine all the ingredients in a bowl until evenly moist. Press the mixture into the bottom of the pan and part way up the sides. Bake for about 10 to 15 minutes, until lightly toasted. Leave to cool completely.

To make the filling, beat the cream cheese and sugar in an electric mixer on medium speed until smooth. Add the eggs, one at a time, beating well after each addition. Add the pumpkin purée, spices, vanilla and Bourbon. Mix slowly but thoroughly until evenly incorporated. Pour the batter on to the cooled crust and smooth with a small spatula.

Bake the cheesecake for about 50 to 60 minutes, or until the edge begins to pull away from the sides of the pan. Remove from the oven and increase the temperature to 200°C/400°F/gas mark 6. Whisk together the sour cream and sugar. Splosh in some more Bourbon or brandy if you're so inclined. Spread the mixture over the hot cheesecake, return the pan to the oven and bake for about 10 minutes longer, to set the topping. Remove the cheesecake from the oven and leave to cool completely on a wire rack. Once at room temperature, cover and refrigerate overnight before serving.

BLACK AND WHITE (OR NOT) CHEESECAKE

Sorry, we can never make it as simple as black and white, now can we? As the name implies, this marbled recipe is incredibly versatile. At the very least it's three recipes in one, and that's without any personal touches thrown in. If you're feeling industrious, opt for the black and white version for a truly spectacular show-stopping dessert. Not in the mood for a little extra prep work? Then use only one type of chocolate for both amounts specified. Or, as we like to say, double down. It doesn't get much richer than this, so be forewarned, a little goes a long way when serving. Or not. This is one big cheesecake, so it should easily serve upwards of 12

INGREDIENTS

For the cookie base:

all-purpose or plain flour
  5½oz / 160g / 1 cup
unsweetened cocoa powder
  4 tablespoons
granulated sugar
  6 tablespoons
baking powder
  ¾ teaspoon
unsalted butter, softened
  4oz / 115g / ½ cup
large egg yolks, lightly beaten
  2

For the batters:

cream cheese
  32oz / 900g / about 8 cups
granulated sugar
  10oz / 280g / 1¼ cups
cornflour
  3 tablespoons
kosher salt
  ¼ teaspoon
large eggs
  5
sour cream
  8oz / 225g / 1 cup
vanilla extract
  2 teaspoons
heavy or double cream
  8fl oz / 240ml / 1 cup
semi-sweet and white chocolate chips
  8oz / 225g / about 1½ cups each

Preheat the oven to 180°C/350°F/gas mark 4. Butter a round cheesecake pan with a removable bottom, 9 x 3in/ 23 x 8cm. Wrap the bottom and partly up the sides with foil.

For the base, combine the flour, cocoa, sugar and baking powder in the bowl of an electric mixer. Add the butter and stir on low speed until crumbly. Stir in the egg yolks until well incorporated – it will still be crumbly. Press into the prepared pan and pat firmly into the bottom and slightly up the sides. Pierce the surface with a fork in several places. Bake for 15 to 20 minutes, or until the crust is firm. Leave to cool.

For the batters, beat the cream cheese on medium speed until smooth. Whisk together the sugar, cornflour and salt in a bowl, then gradually add to the cream cheese. On low speed, add the eggs, one at a time, beating well after each addition. Add the sour cream, vanilla and cream. For the black and white version, split the batter into 2 containers. Melt each chocolate separately. Combine the semi-sweet chocolate with half the batter and the white chocolate with the other half. Pour half of the 'black' batter on to the crust. Hold the 'white' batter 12in/30cm above the pan and pour directly into the center of the black batter. Pouring from a distance causes the batter to push toward the edge. Repeat. For all-black or all-white versions, combine the melted chocolate of choice with the batter and pour on to the crust.

Bake for 60 minutes, or until set – it usually rises evenly and cracks around the edges. Cover loosely with foil if it browns too quickly. The middle will appear jiggly, but get jiggy with it and trust it is done – it will set as it cools. Cool completely in the pan before refrigerating for at least 4 hours, preferably overnight.

PRALINE CHEESECAKE

Anyone who's ever travelled through the American South has most likely stumbled upon an amorphous blob of creamy, fudgy praline. Heat butter, brown sugar and cream (sometimes buttermilk) until thick, fold in pecan halves and spoon blobs on to parchment for cooling. That's all there is to it. As if they weren't rich enough, we figured why not whip up a simple cheesecake base upon which to rest a praline. For this we like to use our Spiced Pecans (page 185), but most traditional Southern pralines use plain pecan halves. Serves 10–12

INGREDIENTS

For the crust:

unsalted butter, softened
4oz / 115g / ½ cup
granulated sugar
6oz / 175g / ¾ cup
all-purpose or plain flour
6 tablespoons
Spiced Pecans, finely chopped
9oz / 250g / 1½ cups

For the cheesecake:

cream cheese, softened
32oz / 900g / about 8 cups
light brown sugar
12oz / 340g / 1½ cups, packed
kosher salt
½ teaspoon
large eggs, at room temperature
4
vanilla extract
2 teaspoons
sour cream
10oz / 275g / 1¼ cups

For the praline top:

unsalted butter, softened
2oz / 60g / ¼ cup
heavy or double cream
2fl oz / 60ml / ¼ cup
light or dark brown sugar
8oz / 225g / 1 cup, packed
pecan halves
6oz / 175g / 1 cup
a pinch of kosher salt

Preheat the oven to 180°C/350°F/gas mark 4. Butter a round cheesecake pan with a removable bottom, 9 x 3in/ 23 x 8cm. Wrap the bottom and partly up the sides with foil. Or use a 9in/23cm diameter springform pan.

For the crust, combine all the ingredients in a medium bowl and stir. This can also be done in an electric mixer on low speed. Unlike other nut crusts, we like this one to have chunkier bits rather than processing everything into meal. Press the mixture into the prepared pan and partially up the sides. Refrigerate while preparing the filling.

In the bowl of an electric mixer, beat the cream cheese at medium speed until light, about 4 minutes. Add the sugar and salt and mix for another 4 minutes or so. Next add the eggs one at a time, beating well after each addition, followed by the vanilla. Reduce the speed to low and stir in the sour cream. Pour the batter into the prepared pan.

Bake for about 50 to 60 minutes, or until set. The cake usually rises evenly and cracks around the edges. Cover loosely with foil if it appears to be browning too quickly. The middle will no doubt appear to wiggle, but trust that it is done. It should wiggle as one piece, not be sloshing under the surface. Leave to cool completely in the pan.

For the topping, combine all the ingredients except the pecans in a small saucepan over low heat. Stirring continuously, heat the mixture until the sugar dissolves. Remove from the heat, stir in the pecans, then do your best to pour the mixture over the cheesecake. You may need to nudge the nuts a little to get them into place. They don't always cooperate when poured. Let the praline cool to room temperature before chilling until ready to serve.

CHERRY ALMOND CHEESECAKE

During Outsider Tart's infancy, OD was still running Gaydar Radio. A business trip took us to Portland, Oregon. As is OD's way, he planned a route from San Francisco to Seattle to Portland and a few points in between. All based on bakeries he read about. Business took all of one afternoon. Otherwise we ate and drove our way up and down the Pacific north-west. Macrina Bakery was a Seattle stop because his sister, Nen, gave us their cookbook. To this day we're convinced she had no idea what it was. She never cooks, let alone bakes. Macrina's delicious cherry almond scone inspired this recipe. To our delight, UK suppliers have dried cherries from Washington state or Michigan, two of the best locales for all things cherry. They are plump, tender and just the right amount of tart. Serves 10–12

INGREDIENTS

For the crust:

almonds, toasted
  6oz / 175g / 1 cup
light brown sugar
  2oz / 60g / ¼ cup, packed
all-purpose or plain flour
  5½oz / 160g / 1 cup
kosher salt
  ¼ teaspoon
unsalted butter, cold and diced
  4oz / 115g / ½ cup
large egg yolk
  1

For the cheesecake:

dried cherries
  9oz / 250g / 1½ cups
lime zest, freshly grated
  1 teaspoon
cream cheese
  24oz / 675g / about 6 cups
sour cream
  4oz / 115g / ½ cup
light brown sugar
  6oz / 175g / ¾ cup, packed
large eggs
  4
vanilla extract
  1 teaspoon
kirsch (optional)
  1 teaspoon

Preheat the oven to 180°C/350°F/gas mark 4. Butter a round cheesecake pan with a removable bottom, 9 x 3in/23 x 8cm. Wrap the bottom and partly up the sides with foil.

In a small bowl cover the cherries with boiling water and leave to steep for 15 minutes. Pour the cherries, their liquid and the lime zest into a food processor and whiz to a purée.

To make the crust, combine the nuts, sugar, flour and salt in a food processor and pulse until the nuts are finely ground. Add the butter and pulse until you have coarse crumbs. Add the yolk and pulse just until the dough clumps up. Press the dough into the prepared pan and partially up the sides. Pierce the surface with a fork in several places. Bake for about 20 minutes, or until golden brown. Let cool.

To continue with the filling, beat the cream cheese, sour cream and brown sugar in an electric mixer until smooth. On low speed, add the eggs, one at a time, beating well after each addition, followed by the vanilla, kirsch and the cherry purée. Mix slowly but thoroughly until evenly incorporated. Pour the batter on to the crust and gently shake the pan to settle it.

Bake for about 50 to 60 minutes, or until the edge begins to pull away from the sides of the pan. There will be a wiggle to the top of your cheesecake but the movement should be as one, and not looking as if underneath the surface the custard is sloshing around. So look for a wiggle like set gelatine, not a rolling undulation. Remove the cheesecake from the oven and leave to cool completely on a wire rack. Once at room temperature, cover and refrigerate overnight.

CLOTTED CREAM CHEESECAKE

When in Rome … OK, so we're in the United Kingdom. So we figured we may as well see what's in the local fridge and have a go at it. Clotted cream is, without a doubt, uniquely British. To our palates it's richer and smoother than sour cream, without the tang. Perfect for cheesecake. For a coffee-infused variation, add a shot or two of Kahlúa to the batter as well. If you don't want the alcohol but still want the coffee flavor, dissolve 3 tablespoons of instant espresso powder in 3 tablespoons of hot water, cool slightly, then add to the cheesecake batter. Both is good, too. Either way, you might want to omit the zest. Then again, espresso is often served with a twist of lemon in some parts of the world … Serves 10–12 with ease

INGREDIENTS

For the crust:

Graham cracker
  or digestive crumbs
  8oz / 225g / 2 cups
light brown sugar
  2oz / 60g / ¼ cup, packed
unsalted butter, melted
  2oz / 60g / ¼ cup
kosher salt
  a pinch

For the batter:

heavy or double cream
  2fl oz / 60ml / ¼ cup
vanilla extract
  1 tablespoon
granulated sugar
  10oz / 275g / 1¼ cups
orange or lemon zest,
  freshly grated
  (optional but delicious)
  1 tablespoon
cream cheese
  24oz / 675g / about 6 cups
clotted cream
  12oz / 340g / about 1½ cups
large eggs
  5
large egg yolk
  1

Preheat the oven to 170°C/325°F/gas mark 3. Butter a round cheesecake pan with a removable bottom, 9 x 3in/23 x 8cm. Wrap the bottom of the pan and partly up the sides with aluminium foil. As an alternative, use a 9in/23cm diameter springform pan.

Combine the cracker crumbs, sugar, melted butter and salt, then press the mixture firmly into the bottom of the pan and partially up the sides. Bake the crust for about 10 minutes, until it is set and slightly browned. Allow to cool before filling.

Pour the cream into a measuring jug, add the vanilla and combine. Set aside.

In the bowl of an electric mixer, combine the sugar with the zest if using and mix until the sugar is fragrant. Add the cream cheese and clotted cream and beat on medium speed for 4 to 6 minutes, or until the mixture is creamy and there are no lumps visible. Add the eggs and yolk one at a time, making sure each one is incorporated before adding the next. On low speed, pour in the cream mixture and continue mixing for about another minute, until well combined. Pour the batter into the prepared crust.

Bake for about 50 to 60 minutes. The center will appear very jiggly but will set as it cools. Cool completely on a wire rack before releasing it from the pan. Don't despair if the top has cracked, as the 'damage' can easily be covered up with either a white chocolate frosting or a chocolate glaze or some other finish to your liking.

RICOTTA TART

Based on a traditional Italian dessert, this recipe lends itself to all sorts of improvisation. It all depends on your mood and that of anyone who deserves a slice. Sometimes we dress it up with nothing more than a cup of chocolate chips and candied orange peel, and sometimes we just chuck in some dried fruit without poaching it. Because of the ricotta, this doesn't rise like other cheesecakes; rather, it solidifies in the oven, but the cheese lends its unique and rustic charm in terms of texture. The cinnamon makes this sublime. Serves 12–16

INGREDIENTS

For the filling (optional):

dried cherries
  9oz / 250g / 1½ cups
golden raisins
  9oz / 250g / 1½ cups
dark rum (optional)
  12fl oz / 350ml / 1½ cups

For the base:

all-purpose or plain flour
  5½oz / 160g / 1 cup
unsweetened cocoa powder
  4 tablespoons
granulated sugar
  6 tablespoons
baking powder
  ¾ teaspoon
unsalted butter, softened
  4oz / 115g / ½ cup
large egg yolks, lightly beaten
  2

For the cheesecake:

whole-milk ricotta
  48oz / 1.35kg / about 6 cups
granulated sugar
  8oz / 225g / 1 cup
large eggs, at room temperature
  8
Cointreau
  3 tablespoons
vanilla extract
  2 teaspoons
cinnamon
  1 teaspoon

Place the fruit, rum and enough water to cover in a medium saucepan and bring to the boil. Cook over a medium–high heat, stirring as needed, until the liquid evaporates, about 10 minutes. Drain if necessary and cool to room temperature.

Preheat the oven to 180°C/350°F/gas mark 4. Butter a round cheesecake pan, 12 x 3in/30 x 8cm.

For the base, combine the flour, cocoa, sugar and baking powder in the bowl of an electric mixer. Add the butter and stir on low speed until crumbly. Stir in the egg yolks until well incorporated – it will still be crumbly. Press into the prepared pan and pat firmly into the bottom and slightly up the sides. Pierce the surface with a fork in several places. Bake for 15 to 20 minutes, or until the crust is firm. Leave to cool.

In the bowl of an electric mixer on low speed, beat the ricotta until smooth, about a minute or two. Stir in the sugar and then the eggs, one at a time. Stir in the Cointreau, vanilla and ½ teaspoon of the cinnamon. Scatter the filling over the crust, then pour the ricotta mixture over the fruit. Even it out by rotating and jiggling the pan. This is thicker than other cheesecake batters, so you may need to smooth it with a small offset spatula. Sprinkle the remaining cinnamon on top, using a small fine-mesh strainer: put the cinnamon in it and tap the handle so the 'dust' gets distributed as evenly as possible.

Bake for about 45 minutes, or until the cheesecake is well browned and slightly puffed. It may not puff evenly but it should appear firm except in the very center, where it may seem slightly soft. If it is firm in the center, don't worry about it. This is not a jiggler like other cheesecakes. As it cools, the surface will even out. Once the cheesecake is at room temperature, wrap it in clingfilm and refrigerate overnight.

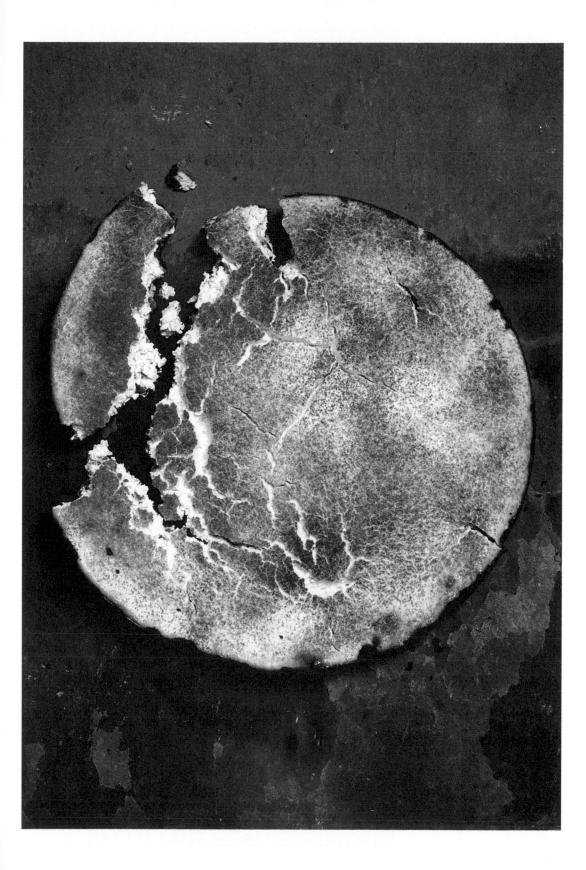

LAYERS

AFTER COUNTLESS ATTEMPTS to create the picture-perfect cake, it finally dawned on us that many 'scratch'-made cakes are usually two layers, not three like the ones pictured on the boxes of cake mix found at every US supermarket. If you've ever tasted a cake made from a mix, you'd appreciate why we set out from the other direction. Not that our two-layer experiments were bad, mind you – we ate every last crumb – but we were also drowning our sorrows over all that effort almost gone to waste and still not arriving at a photo-worthy cake. How could something that tasted so good look so puny? Could it be that the camera adds another layer? NAH. So we set out to develop recipes that never disappoint when consumed visually or via one's mouth. Having said that, the recipes included in this chapter can be down-sized to accommodate those with a different definition of cake perfection. Heathens though they are.

Don't despair if you're not seeing recipes you had hoped for, like a simple vanilla or chocolate layer. Those building blocks form the base for many of our Free Spirits, outright indulgent, once-a-year (the semblance of restraint can't be underestimated) celebration cakes, and will appear in that chapter. Here we have focused on slightly unusual recipes suitable for any occasion or lack thereof. And DON'T PANIC if you're not seeing frosting recipes to accompany the layer recipes included here. Nick Malgieri's *Perfect Cakes* remains one of our favorite cake books precisely because it separates layers from frostings, thus allowing your mind to wander and dream up your own favorite combinations. Sure, we'll make suggestions along the way, but by all means toss them aside if you feel inspiration tugging you in another direction. Just as one butters a brick to build a wall (look it up, it's true), so does one butter a layer to build a cake: take one layer, schmear it with frosting, place the next layer atop it, squish it a little, JIGGLE it a little; repeat. If you choose to spackle the sides with frosting, go for it (yes, it's also true that cake books use 'spackle' as a verb). If not, get some plates and forks.

MOM'S BANANA LAYERS

One of the things we both learned from watching our mothers bake is just how versatile and resourceful they were. If they didn't have any or enough of a particular ingredient they made do in any number of ways: they simply did without; they made up any difference with another ingredient; or they made a flat-out substitution. We see the exact opposite with the folks who work with us who are all schooled and trained in baking. Apparently baking curricula don't include anything about pragmatism. Who knew?

This recipe was made by Momma Lesniak all the time. She would always finish this with an Orange Buttercream (page 191) for a weekday dessert, but it lends itself to any number of other options as well. Speaking of options, the sour cream can easily be replaced with yoghurt, clotted cream, mascarpone, crème fraîche, coconut milk, buttermilk and even good old full-fat milk. The texture and taste will vary slightly, given your choice, but you will still end up with a perfectly delicious cake. Sour cream lends a tang to sweet bananas but if you prefer a smoother taste, ditch it and try something else. Serves 12–16

INGREDIENTS

all-purpose or plain flour
21oz / 600g / 4 cups
baking powder
4 teaspoons
bicarbonate of soda
1 teaspoon
kosher salt
1 teaspoon
unsalted butter, softened
8oz / 225g / 1 cup
granulated sugar
20oz / 550g / 2½ cups
large eggs, at room temperature
4
vanilla extract
2 teaspoons
sour cream
4oz / 115g / ½ cup
mashed banana (about 4)
16oz / 450g / about 2 cups

Preheat the oven to 180°C/350°F/gas mark 4. Butter three 9in/23cm round cake pans, line the bottoms with baking parchment, dust with flour and tap out any excess.

Sift together the flour, baking powder, bicarbonate of soda and salt. Set aside.

In a electric mixer, cream together the butter and sugar on medium–high speed until light and fluffy, about 5 to 6 minutes. Add the eggs, one at a time, beating thoroughly after each addition. Scrape the bowl as you go. On low speed, add the vanilla followed by the sour cream, mixing until just combined. Alternately add the flour mixture and bananas in 3 to 4 portions, mixing only until just combined. Divide the batter evenly among the prepared pans and smooth with a small offset spatula.

Bake for 25 to 30 minutes or until a knife inserted in the center comes out clean. It's best to rotate the pans front to back, top to bottom about ⅔ of the way through to ensure even baking. Let the layers cool in the pans for about 15 minutes before releasing them. Let them cool completely on wire racks.

ALMOND LAYERS

This is our preferred recipe when we want something nutty. Any nut will do; we opted for almonds because of their versatility: they pair well with almost any flavor frosting, be it light and lemony or rich and chocolatey. Macadamias do a pretty good job of it too. When grinding nuts in a processor, the only trick is to pulse them – do not let the motor run continuously otherwise you will end up with a paste, and that won't work here. (There's another recipe for that coming up.) If you're lucky enough to have a hand-held nut grinder, no additional flour is needed. Just patience. Hand-held grinders make great texture at the expense of your wrists. We've only found small ones available: fill, grind, repeat. And repeat, repeat, repeat. As nuts go, almonds have the least amount of fat so we typically process them solo. When it comes to fattier nuts like macadamias (the fattiest), walnuts or pecans, we toss a tablespoon or two of flour in with the nuts before turning the motor on. This prevents them turning into a paste prematurely and keeps the ground nuts loose so they are incorporated into the batter more evenly. Serves 12–16

INGREDIENTS

all-purpose or plain flour
  21oz / 600g / 4 cups
almonds, finely ground
  6oz / 175g / 1 cup
baking powder
  1½ teaspoons
bicarbonate of soda
  1½ teaspoons
kosher salt
  1½ teaspoons
sour cream
  12oz / 340g / 1½ cups
vanilla extract
  1½ teaspoons
almond extract
  ½ teaspoon
granulated sugar
  24oz / 675g / 3 cups
lemon zest,
  freshly grated (optional)
  1 tablespoon
unsalted butter, softened
  16oz / 450g / 2 cups
large eggs
  5

Preheat the oven to 180°C/350°F/gas mark 4. Butter three 9in/23cm round cake pans, line the bottoms with baking parchment, dust the sides with flour and tap out any excess.

Whisk together the flour, ground almonds, baking powder, bicarbonate of soda and salt. In a large, glass measuring jug, combine the sour cream, vanilla and almond extracts. Set both aside.

In the bowl of an electric mixer, combine the sugar and lemon zest, if using, on low speed until fragrant. Slowly add the butter and cream the mixture on medium–high speed until light and fluffy, about 6 to 8 minutes. On medium speed, add the eggs, one at a time, beating well after each addition. Reduce the speed to low again, and alternately add the flour and sour cream mixtures in 3 to 4 additions. Begin and end with the dry ingredients and mix only until just combined. Divide the batter evenly among the prepared pans.

Bake the layers for 30 to 35 minutes or until a small knife emerges clean from the center of each. Let the layers cool in the pans for about 10 minutes before releasing them to cool completely on wire racks.

COCONUT BUTTERMILK LAYERS

When you're raised by a mother who baked all the family birthday cakes from scratch, you quickly learn a thing or two about her favorite cake when her birthday rolls around. Every single year it's the same damned thing: lemon coconut. Which, of course, means making lemon curd as well. But, it keeps her happy and that's all that matters. At least we were varied in our requests, which no doubt kept things interesting for her. To satisfy her wish(es), we spread painstakingly prepared Lemon Curd (page 198) between the layers and Italian Meringue (essentially homemade marshmallow crème – only 7 minutes of constant slaving over a hot stove – page 184) on the entire outside, then carefully encrusted it with sweetened, flaked coconut. One strand at a time. Would it be in poor taste to mention Mom's use of store-bought pie crust at a time like this? Serves 12–16

INGREDIENTS

all-purpose or plain flour
24oz / 675g / 4½ cups
baking powder
1½ teaspoons
bicarbonate of soda
1 teaspoon
kosher salt
1 teaspoon
buttermilk, at room temperature
12fl oz / 350ml / 1½ cups
vanilla extract
2 teaspoons
granulated sugar
24oz / 675g / 3 cups
lemon zest, freshly grated
2 tablespoons
unsalted butter, softened
16oz / 450g / 2 cups
large eggs, at room temperature
8
shredded coconut, toasted or not
8oz / 225g / 2 cups

Preheat the oven to 160°C/325°F/gas mark 3. Butter three 9in/23cm round cake tins, line the bottoms with baking parchment, dust the sides with flour and tap out any excess.

Sift together the flour, baking powder, bicarbonate of soda and salt. In a large, glass measuring jug, combine the buttermilk and vanilla extract. Set both aside.

In the bowl of an electric mixer, combine the sugar and lemon zest on low speed until fragrant. Slowly add the butter and increase the speed to medium–high. Cream the butter and sugar until light, pale and fluffy, about 5 to 6 minutes. Turn the speed down a notch and add the eggs, one at a time, beating well after each addition. Scrape the bowl as necessary to dredge up anything stuck on the bottom. On low speed, alternately add the flour and buttermilk mixtures in 3 to 4 additions. Mix until just combined. With a rubber spatula, scrape the bowl to check for complete mixing then fold in the shredded coconut. Divide the batter evenly among the prepared pans and smooth with an offset spatula.

Bake for 45 to 50 minutes or until a knife inserted in the center of each comes out clean. The tops will be golden brown. It's best to rotate the pans front to back, top to bottom about ⅔ of the way through, for even baking. Cool the layers in their pans set on wire racks for 30 minutes before turning them out to cool completely.

ORANGE SPICE LAYERS

Every so often you'll find a recipe for Spice Cake that produces a lovely cube of a cake. Caramel Cake is another example, and one that typically uses square cake pans for baking four layers instead of the usual three round ones. While we don't know where the tradition comes from, we just know it to be so. Kind of like many traditions. Most people won't have this equipment in their baking arsenal, so we have adapted our preferred method to suit most home kitchens. Add dried cranberries and an Orange Buttercream (page 191) for a special holiday treat. *Serves 12–16*

INGREDIENTS

molasses, sorghum or cane syrup
 12fl oz / 350ml / 1½ cups
boiling water
 16fl oz / 460ml / 2 cups
orange juice
 4fl oz / 120ml / ½ cup
all-purpose or plain flour
 26oz / 750g / 5 cups
bicarbonate of soda
 4 teaspoons
kosher salt
 1 teaspoon
ground ginger
 2 tablespoons
cinnamon
 2 teaspoons
nutmeg, freshly grated
 1 teaspoon
allspice or cardamom
 1 teaspoon
ground cloves
 ½ teaspoon
light brown sugar
 8oz / 225g / 1 cup, packed
orange zest, freshly grated
 1 tablespoon
unsalted butter, softened
 8oz / 225g / 1 cup
large eggs
 4
dried cranberries (optional)
 6oz / 175g / 1 cup

Preheat the oven to 180°C/350°F/gas mark 4. Butter three 9in/23cm round cake pans, line the bottoms with baking parchment, dust the sides with flour and tap out any excess.

In a large measuring jug, combine the molasses, boiling water and orange juice. In a medium bowl, whisk together the flour, bicarbonate of soda, salt and spices. Set both aside.

In the bowl of an electric mixer, combine the sugar and orange zest until fragrant. Slowly add the butter and cream it on medium–high speed until light and fluffy, about 6 to 8 minutes. Reduce the speed to low and add the eggs, one at a time, beating well after each addition. Scrape the bowl from the bottom up as needed. Alternately add the flour and molasses mixtures in 3 or 4 additions, beginning and ending with the dry ingredients. Mix only until just combined. Now is the time to fold in the dried cranberries if you're using them. Divide the batter equally among the prepared pans.

Bake the layers for about 30 minutes or until a small knife emerges clean from the center. Let the layers cool in the pans for about 5 minutes before turning them out to cool completely on wire racks.

Note: This recipe can be made in four 9in/23cm square pans and baked for 20 to 25 minutes.

WALNUT ESPRESSO LAYERS

At the shop, we run upstairs and brew fresh espresso when making these layers. Presumably most people don't have an espresso machine at the ready, so we've engineered this recipe using normal pantry staples. Go the extra mile with the 'espresso', since it's the best way to inject enough coffee flavor so it doesn't bake out. Using filter coffee just doesn't cut it. Another trick is to stop by a coffee bar and order up three double espressos – each one is 2fl oz/60ml/¼ cup – by the time you get home it will be cool enough to use. That trick we learned in New York. At the time, neither of us drank coffee, and while staring out the kitchen window pondering what to do, we realized we were staring directly at a Starbucks. Problem solved. Serves 12–16

INGREDIENTS

walnuts
  9oz / 250g / 1½ cups
all-purpose or plain flour
  20oz / 550g / 3¾ cups
baking powder
  1½ teaspoons
bicarbonate of soda
  1½ teaspoons
kosher salt
  ¾ teaspoon
instant espresso powder
  3 tablespoons
buttermilk, at room temperature
  8fl oz / 240ml / 1 cup
brewed triple-strength espresso*
  6fl oz / 175ml / ¾ cup
vanilla extract
  1 tablespoon
unsalted butter, softened
  12oz / 340g / 1½ cups
granulated sugar
  12oz / 340g / 1½ cups
light brown sugar
  6oz / 175g / ¾ cup, packed
large eggs
  6

Preheat the oven to 180°C/350°F/gas mark 4. Butter three 9in/7.5cm round cake pans, line the bottoms with baking parchment, dust with flour and tap out any excess.

In a food processor, pulse the walnuts until finely ground. It's better to pulse versus running the motor to avoid making a paste. Whisk together the flour, baking powder, bicarbonate of soda, salt, espresso powder and the ground walnuts. In a large measuring jug, combine the buttermilk, brewed espresso and vanilla. Set both aside.

In a stand mixer, cream together the butter and both sugars on medium–high speed until light and fluffy, about 5 to 6 minutes. Add the eggs one at a time, beating thoroughly after each addition. Scrape the bowl as you go. On low speed, alternately add the flour/nut and buttermilk mixtures in 3 to 4 additions, until just combined. The batter may have a slightly curdled appearance, which is just fine. Divide the mixture evenly among the prepared pans.

Bake for 30 to 35 minutes, or until a knife inserted comes out clean. It's best to rotate the pans front to back, top to bottom, about ⅔ of the way through. Cool the layers in their pans for about 10 minutes before turning them out on to wire racks to cool completely.

* To brew triple-strength espresso, steep 3 heaped tablespoons ground Illy coffee in 6fl oz/175ml/1 cup boiling water. Once cooled, strain through a paper filter. Alternatively, dissolve 4 tablespoons/¼ cup instant espresso powder in 4½fl oz/130ml/¾ cup boiling water. Refrigerate in a covered jar until needed.

COKE LAYERS

Not everyone has the same preference when it comes to chocolate. Some enjoy milk, some dark and some the fake white stuff which isn't chocolate at all. When you need to please a crowd of real chocoholics, this would be our suggestion. It ticks all the boxes: a rich, deep, sweet chocolate flavour with just enough bitterness to please purists. Kids (also known as real men) love it too, if not for the taste then for what goes into it. For this we'd recommend a Chocolate Fudge Frosting (page 192). Serves 12–16

INGREDIENTS

unsalted butter
  12oz / 340g / 1½ cups
Coke (caffeine-free is fine, diet is not)
  12fl oz / 350ml / 1½ cups
mini marshmallows
  2¼oz / 65g / 1 cup
unsweetened chocolate, chopped
  3oz / 85g / ½ cup
all-purpose or plain flour
  19oz / 530g / 3½ cups
cocoa powder
  4oz / 115g / 1 cup
baking powder
  2¼ teaspoons
bicarbonate of soda
  1½ teaspoons
kosher salt
  ¾ teaspoon
granulated sugar
  24oz / 675g / 3 cups
canola or other flavorless oil
  6fl oz / 80ml / ¾ cup
vanilla extract
  1 tablespoon
large eggs, at room temperature
  5
buttermilk, at room temperature
  10fl oz / 300ml / 1¼ cups

Preheat the oven to 180°C/350°F/gas mark 4. Butter three 9in/7.5cm round cake pans, line the bottoms with baking parchment, dust with flour and tap out any excess.

In a medium saucepan, place the butter and Coke over medium heat until the butter melts. Add the marshmallows and chopped chocolate or chips and stir continuously until the chocolate and marshmallows are melted – the latter takes longer than you'd think but constant stirring will help expedite things. Let the mixture cool for about 10 minutes.

In a medium bowl, whisk together the flour, cocoa powder, baking powder, bicarbonate of soda and salt. Set aside.

In the bowl of an electric mixer fitted with a paddle, thoroughly combine the sugar, oil and vanilla on medium speed. Reduce the speed to low and add the eggs one at a time, beating well after each addition. Add the cooled chocolate mixture and stir until evenly incorporated. The mixture should have a consistent color. Alternately add the flour and buttermilk in 3 or 4 additions, beginning and ending with the dry ingredients and mixing only until just combined. Divide the batter evenly among the prepared pans.

Bake for 35 to 40 minutes or until a knife inserted into the center of each comes out clean. It's best to rotate pans front to back, top to bottom about ⅔ of the way through.

PEANUT BUTTER LAYERS

In our little corner of London there seems to be a love/hate relationship with peanut butter. Consistently we've found folks from other Commonwealth countries love it, so we're not entirely sure how it got such a bad reputation in Great Britain. In an effort to appease our host country, we've tried making this with Nutella, but it doesn't work, although there are other commercially available hazelnut pralines that are thicker and which get the job done beautifully. Many naysayers think the peanut butter stays intact somehow and gives you a mouthful of paste. Uh, no. Indeed that would be unpleasant. Like any ingredient that meets with an appliance, it gets incorporated. We use this recipe as a base for any number of cakes, including one finished with Chocolate Buttercream, one finished with Italian Meringue for a Fluffernutter Cake, and one finished with honey, banana and bacon (no typo that) for an Elvis Cake. His favourite combination … Serves 12–16

INGREDIENTS

large eggs, at room temperature
  6
whole milk
  12fl oz / 360ml / 1½ cups
peanut or canola oil
  4fl oz / 120ml / ½ cup
vanilla extract
  1 tablespoon
all-purpose or plain flour
  24oz / 675g / 4½ cups
baking powder
  4½ teaspoons
kosher salt
  1 teaspoon
granulated sugar
  12oz / 340g / 1½ cups
light brown sugar
  12oz / 340g / 1½ cups, packed
unsalted butter, softened
  6oz / 175g / ¾ cup
smooth peanut butter
  (crunchy makes mixing
  tricky)
  8oz / 225g / about 1 cup

Preheat the oven to 180°C/350°F/gas mark 4. Butter three 9in/23cm round cake pans, line the bottoms with baking parchment, dust the sides with flour and tap out any excess.

In a medium bowl, whisk together the eggs, milk, oil and vanilla until well combined.

In the bowl of an electric mixer, combine the flour, baking powder, salt and sugars on low speed until evenly mixed, about 1 minute. Add the butter and peanut butter to the bowl and beat on medium speed until the mixture is crumbly. Add ⅓ of the milk mixture and beat on medium speed for about 2 minutes. Scrape the bowl, add another ⅓ of the milk mixture and stir well. Again, scrape the bowl and finally add the last ⅓ of the milk mixture, blending well. The batter should be creamy and smooth when done. Divide the batter evenly among the prepared pans.

Bake for 35 to 40 minutes or until a small knife emerges clean from the center and the layers spring back when poked. Cool the layers in the pans for about 10 minutes before removing them to wire racks to cool completely.

RHUBARB LAYERS

During the formative years of Outsider Tart, we toured the London farmers' markets in search of inspiration. We couldn't help but notice the vast amounts of rhubarb happily being carted home. Off to a crumble, no doubt. Neither of us take to rhubarb all that well, but we couldn't deny that it appealed to many, so we endeavored to create a cake, since crumble isn't in our blood. We finish this with either Sweetened Whipped Cream (page 196), if we know it will be served relatively soon, or a Strawberry Buttercream (page 191), if it needs to travel or last a while longer. While it still hasn't won us over personally, rhubarb-lovers rave about this cake. Serves 12–16

INGREDIENTS

all-purpose or plain flour
  21oz / 600g / 4 cups
bicarbonate of soda
  2 teaspoons
kosher salt
  ½ teaspoon
cinnamon
  1 teaspoon
buttermilk
  16fl oz / 460ml / 2 cups
vanilla extract
  2 teaspoons
unsalted butter, softened
  12oz / 340g / 1½ cups
light brown sugar
  24oz / 675g / 3 cups, packed
large eggs
  2
rhubarb, coarsely chopped
  16oz / 450g / about 4 cups

Preheat the oven to 180°C/350°F/gas mark 4. Butter three 9in/23cm round cake pans, line the bottoms with baking parchment, dust the sides with flour and tap out any excess.

Whisk together the flour, bicarbonate of soda, salt and cinnamon in a medium bowl. In a large, glass measuring jug, combine the buttermilk and vanilla. Set both aside.

In the bowl of an electric mixer, cream the butter and sugar on medium–high speed until light and fluffy or, should we say, as light and fluffy as creamed brown sugar can be. Reduce the speed to medium and add the eggs, one at a time, beating well after each addition. On low speed, alternately add the flour and milk mixtures, beginning and ending with the dry ingredients. Blend only until just incorporated. Remove the bowl from the mixer and fold in the chopped rhubarb, making sure to scrape the bowl thoroughly to finish mixing the batter if the mixer hasn't done so already. Divide the batter evenly among the prepared pans.

Bake for about 30 minutes or until a small knife emerges clean from the center. Cool the layers in their pans for about 30 minutes before turning them out to cool completely on wire racks. The rhubarb will poke through here and there and cause these layers to look dimpled on top. They need extra cooling time in the pan for the layers to set enough so they don't fall apart when turning them out. You can thank the extra moisture from the rhubarb for that.

GRAHAM CRACKER LAYERS

S'mores are the quintessential American campfire treat. In the States they are a rite of passage on your first overnight camping experience. Of course, for some this meant the backyard, but still, a ritual is a ritual. The first known recipe dates back to 1927 from a Girl Scout guide entitled *Tramping and Trailing with the Girl Scouts*. One has to wonder what all would be included in a new guide by the same name these days. Anyhow, the basic ingredients for a s'more ('some more' contracted) are Graham Crackers, chocolate and marshmallow. We've devised many recipes using this combination and these layers are the basis for a S'mores Cake which we finish with a Marshmallow Meringue (page 184) then toast using a blow torch. When we're not in the mood for that, we add pecans to the batter and finish it with Caramel Frosting (page 189) for another delicious option. We stock Graham Crackers at the shop, but you can find them through a variety of online shops as well. Digestive biscuits are a close second, but for the real deal they fall a bit short. Serves 12–16

INGREDIENTS

Graham Cracker crumbs
  16oz / 450g / 3 cups
all-purpose or plain flour
  5½oz / 160g / 1 cup
baking powder
  1 tablespoon
kosher salt
  ½ teaspoon
whole milk
  12fl oz / 350ml / 1½ cups
vanilla extract
  2 teaspoons
unsalted butter, softened
  12oz / 340g / 1½ cups
granulated sugar
  6oz / 175g / ¾ cup
light brown sugar
  6oz / 175g / ¾ cup, packed
large eggs, separated
  5
cream of tartar
  scant ¼ teaspoon
semi-sweet chocolate chips
  (optional)
  9oz / 250g / 1½ cups

Preheat the oven to 180°C/350°F/gas mark 4. Butter three 9in/23cm round cake pans, line the bottoms with baking parchment, dust the sides with flour and tap out any excess.

Whisk together the cracker crumbs, flour, baking powder and salt in a medium bowl. In a large, glass measuring jug, combine the milk and vanilla. Set both aside.

Cream the butter and both sugars on medium–high speed until light and fluffy, about 6 to 8 minutes. Reduce the speed and add the egg yolks, one at a time, blending well after each addition. Scrape the bowl and mix for 1 minute more. Alternately add the flour and milk mixtures in 3 to 4 additions. Begin and end with the dry ingredients and mix only until just combined. Remove the bowl from the mixer.

In a separate bowl, whisk the egg whites with the cream of tartar until stiff (but not dry) peaks form. Stir ⅓ of the whites into the batter to loosen it up. Fold the remaining whites into the batter with a rubber spatula until evenly incorporated, followed by the chocolate chips, if using. Divide the batter evenly among the prepared pans.

Bake the layers for 25 to 30 minutes or until a small knife emerges clean from the center of each. Let the layers cool in the pans for 10 minutes before turning them out to cool completely on wire racks.

FROST

NGS & FINISHES

RUMOR (AND A FEW articles) have it that more and more bakeshops serve frosting as is. No pesky cupcake or other sponge to get in the way, just a cup of frosting. And, presumably, a spoon. The appeal is somewhat understandable, especially for those who have a tendency to start with dessert and work their way toward the entrée. If time allows … We toyed with putting this chapter first for that very reason, but tradition won out in the end. We did, however, separate frostings from their most likely recipients. At first glance it may seem odd, but the hope is it will set the wheels in motion to dream up unique combinations that suit individual palates. Ours might not necessarily be yours when it comes to taste or preference, so we've offered up the bits and pieces from which to build your own. In some instances, namely the Free Spirits chapter,

complete recipes appear intact because those DESSERTS are unique enough to warrant it. That said, we've also split them and used components wherever we wanted to. And that's the point. Part of the fun of baking is to experiment, and to try what you want versus achieving 'success' by making something that matches a pretty picture or is done to the letter. Relax. Enjoy. And use these suggestions however you see fit.

You'll note quantities vary a bit. Some recipes are enough to fill and frost the entire outside of a cake, top to bottom, where some are meant only to fill between the layers as they would in a Victoria Sponge – 'English style' as we call it. Others fill and top the cake. In a worst case scenario you'll have more to lick out of the bowl when you're done frosting.

BOSTON CREAM

This is a delicious alternative to the over-used pastry cream. In the States we have something called Boston Cream Pie. Not at all a pie, rather it is a rich vanilla sponge, split and filled with this – almost like a Victoria Sponge, only not as tall. The finished 'pie' is covered with a Dark Chocolate Glaze (page 193). Pastry cream is great, don't get us wrong, but once you've tried this extra-rich variation we think you'll see the wisdom of our ways. Plus, you don't have to stand at the stove and stir continuously. This is baked. How easy is that? Fills one 3-layer cake

INGREDIENTS

heavy or double cream
24fl oz / 700ml / 3 cups
cinnamon stick
1 (about 3in/7.5cm long)
vanilla bean/pod, split
1
granulated sugar
6 tablespoons
large egg yolks
6

In a small saucepan, add the cream and cinnamon stick. Split the vanilla bean lengthwise and scrape out the seeds using the back of a paring knife. Add the seeds and the bean to the saucepan. Slowly bring the mixture to a boil over a medium-low heat. Watch the pan closely because once the cream starts to boil it has a tendency to erupt out of it. Not good. Remove the pan from the heat, add the sugar and stir until it dissolves. Set aside to steep for about an hour.

Preheat the oven to 160°C/325°F/gas mark 3. Have at the ready a 9in/23cm glass pie plate or similar ovenproof dish which has been placed in a shallow baking pan. Boil a kettle of water.

Whisk the egg yolks in a medium bowl. Place the bowl on a damp dish towel to keep it from moving around later. If a skin has formed on the cream, stir it back in. Reheat the cream until almost boiling then slowly whisk it into the egg yolks – don't add all the hot cream at once or you'll cook the yolks. Strain the mixture into the pie plate. Add enough boiling water to the baking pan to come halfway up the sides of the pie plate.

Bake for about 20 minutes or just until set. The tip of a small knife should emerge clean from the center. The custard will still appear very jiggly but it will firm up considerably as it cools.

This can be made ahead and kept in the refrigerator for several days. Once it has been chilled, scrape it out of the pie plate when you need to spread it between layers. This is equally delicious served on its own with fresh berries on top, similar to a pannacotta.

NATILLA

Think of this as a slightly spiced, aromatic variation on vanilla custard.
It comes from the Cuban side of the family, courtesy of Abuela, OD's mother. Delicious
on its own with a dollop of Sweetened Whipped Cream (page 196), we have come to
use it for filling cupcakes and layers or adding into batters for a little something extra. Like
all good cooks, we think she left something out of the recipe since her's always tastes better,
but this is what she shared with us, so we share it with you.
Makes 48oz / 1350g / 6 cups – plenty to fill one 3-layer cake

INGREDIENTS

whole milk
  32fl oz / 960ml / 4 cups
kosher salt
  ¼ teaspoon
lime rind, freshly pared
  1–2 limes
cinnamon stick
  1 (about 3in/7.5cm long)
cornstarch
  8 tablespoons
water
  4fl oz / 120ml / ½ cup
large egg yolks
  8
light brown sugar
  12oz / 350g / 1½ cups, packed
cinnamon
  1 teaspoon
grated coconut (optional)
  6oz / 175g / about 1 cup
vanilla extract
  2 teaspoons
rum (for a touch of Havana)
  2 teaspoons

Combine the milk, salt, lime rind and cinnamon stick in a medium saucepan and bring to a boil. Reduce the heat and simmer/steep for about 10 minutes, stirring occasionally. Let cool to room temperature. Remove the cinnamon stick and lime rind.

Mix the cornstarch with the water in a large, glass measuring jug and set aside.

In an electric mixer, beat the egg yolks until fluffy. With the mixer running, slowly add the sugar and continue beating until creamy. In a steady stream, slowly pour in the cooled milk and whisk until smooth. Place the bowl over a pan of simmering water, heat and stir the mixture until it begins to splurt up from the bottom. Slowly pour in the cornstarch, stirring constantly, and continue cooking until the mixture thickens into a pudding-like consistency. (You may not need all the cornstarch.) Now would be a good time to add the cinnamon and coconut, if using it. Remove the natilla from the heat and stir in the vanilla and rum, if using. Cover with clingfilm and let cool to room temperature before refrigerating to cool completely.

Refrigerated this will easily keep for a week or more. Traditionally this would be served as a dessert on its own but we also use it to fill cakes and cupcakes for a little taste of home.

MARSHMALLOW MERINGUE

There are a variety of names for this deliciously sweet and creamy pillow of pleasure: Boiled Frosting, 7-minute Frosting, White Cloud Frosting or Italian Meringue. To us the most fitting is Marshmallow Meringue. We've used this countless times on Coconut Buttermilk Layers (page 171), Graham Cracker Layers (page 178), with or without things mixed in, as is, or toasted with a blow torch for a 'baked' meringue finish and added dramatic effect. It works perfectly with any curd dessert to offset the rich, tangy filling with just the right amount of sugar. One of our favourite combinations is Lemon Coconut Cake with sweetened, flaked coconut clinging to the meringue for a truly spectacular dessert. We make a cupcake version as well; dubbed Coconut Milk Cupcakes (page 100), that are trotted out any time in winter. Our Mom's Banana Layers (page 168) has this piled on and is then decorated with chocolate syrup, wet walnuts, cherries and sprinkles. The only thing missing is ice cream, but don't let that stop you.

Enough to fill and frost one 3-layer cake or frost 36 cupcakes

INGREDIENTS

granulated or caster sugar
16oz / 450g / 2 cups
large egg whites
6
kosher salt
a pinch

In the stainless-steel bowl of an electric mixer, combine the sugar, egg whites and salt. Place the bowl over a pot of simmering water, making sure the bottom of the bowl doesn't touch the water and the water doesn't boil. Using the whisk attachment, continuously stir the mixture over the heat until it gets frothy and becomes hot to the touch. This will take about 5 to 7 minutes. Remove the bowl and place it on the mixer. Whisk the mixture on high speed for upwards of 10 minutes until it is thick, bright white and glossy. It should be smooth and shiny as well. There are 2 other clues as to when it's done: the mixing bowl should feel cool to the touch and the sound of the mixer will change when the mixture thickens. When you remove the whisk from the bowl you should also see long, curly swoops of meringue flailing about. Okay, 3. We lied.

Spread and swoop 'til your heart's content.

RHUBARB STRAWBERRY PUDDING

For anyone who stops themselves from trying something they don't enjoy, we offer this recipe. Neither of us likes rhubarb but we recognize it's a popular option in the UK. This is the first step for our Rhubarb Strawberry Coffee Cake (page 136), but it's earned its own page given the fact neither of us can stop eating it whenever it's made. Plenty to fill one 3-layer cake

INGREDIENTS

rhubarb, cut in medium dice
16oz / 450g / about 4 cups
fresh strawberries, chopped
16oz / 450g / about 4 cups
water or orange juice
4fl oz / 120ml / ½ cup
granulated sugar
8oz / 225g / 1 cup
cornstarch
4 tablespoons

Combine the rhubarb, strawberries and liquid in a heavy-bottomed saucepan. Heat for about 5 minutes until the fruit begins to soften. Combine the sugar and cornstarch and then add it to the pot. Stir and heat everything for 5 to 10 minutes until bubbly and thick. Watch carefully, as this sticks to the bottom of the pan. A wooden or heatproof rubber spatula works best for stirring the bottom of the pan. Set aside to cool.

SPICED PECANS

INGREDIENTS

granulated sugar
12oz / 340g / 1½ cups
cinnamon
2 tablespoons
nutmeg, freshly grated
2 teaspoons
kosher salt
1 teaspoon
large egg whites
4
unsalted butter,
  melted and cooled slightly
8oz / 225g / 1 cup
pecan halves
32oz / 900g / about 8 cups

Preheat the oven to 160°C/325°F/gas mark 3. Butter the bottom of two 12 x 18 x 2in/30 x 45 x 5cm pans.

In a small bowl, combine the sugar, spices and salt.

In the bowl of an electric mixer, whisk the egg whites on medium–high speed until stiff. Slowly add the sugar mixture, 1 tablespoon at a time, and whisk – make sure the whites remain stiff. Adding sugar too quickly causes the whites to collapse, at which point they are history. That said, we have beaten the hell out of the mixture when that happens and proceed apace, getting better than average results. Remove from the mixer and fold in the butter and pecans. Spread the mixture evenly among the pans.

Bake for 15 minutes. Remove from the oven and, using a wide metal spatula, flip the mixture a little section at a time. Return to the oven and bake for 15 minutes more. Watch the pecans carefully toward the end as it is easy to overdo it. Cool in the pan then break chunks into nut-sized pieces.

BARRY'S GINGER PECAN CREAM CHEESE

We'll never forget the day our friend Lucy walked (more like paraded)
into the shop for the first time. To say she and mom, Jill, and dad, Barry, made a beeline
for the door would be an understatement. There's no mucking about with this lot (just
how British have we become?). One year, Lucy asked us to create something unique for
her father's birthday. We asked what all he liked and came up with this, in the spirit of all
good southern American frostings with their multiple inclusions. The original cake used
our Blackout Cake (page 202) with this frosting schmeared between the three layers and on
the outside, top to bottom. Either crystallized or stem ginger will work, but we opted for
crystallized since it's drier and won't change the texture, while stem is more tender but will
introduce added moisture. Depending on how you like your cream cheese frosting,
it may be necessary to add some heavy/double cream or milk to loosen things up to the
desired spreading consistency. Omit the ginger and pecans and you have our basic
Cream Cheese Mascarpone Frosting, which is used for all sorts of things from Carrot Cake
to Red Velvet Whoopies, or when you want something creamy, slightly sweet and fresh –
omit the cream/milk and use the zest and juice from one orange instead.

Enough to fill and frost one 3-layer cake or frost 36 cupcakes

INGREDIENTS

pecans
  9oz / 250g / 1½ cups
cream cheese, softened
  24oz / 675g / about 3 cups
mascarpone
  12oz / 340g / about 1½ cups
caster sugar
  10–12oz / 275–340g / 1¼–1½ cups
vanilla extract
  2 teaspoons
ground ginger
  1 teaspoon
milk or double cream,
  as needed
  up to 4 tablespoons
crystallized ginger,
  finely chopped
  4oz / 115g / ½ cup

Start by toasting the pecans. Preheat the oven to
180°C/350°F/gas mark 4. Spread the nuts on a baking
sheet and toast them in the oven for about 10 minutes or
until fragrant. Remove from the oven and let cool before
chopping. This will bring out the flavor and lend added
depth. Set aside.

Combine the cream cheese, mascarpone, sugar, vanilla
and ground ginger in the bowl of an electric mixer
and beat on medium speed until smooth. Increase the
speed to high and beat until you achieve the desired
consistency for spreading on the cake. You may need to
add a drop of milk or double cream to loosen it up if it
seems too thick. If you're using stem ginger, you could
add some of the syrup at this point instead, if you like.
Now you have 2 choices: either fold the pecans and
crystallized ginger into the frosting before spreading it,
or combine them in a small bowl and press the mixture
into the finished cream-cheese frosting once it has been
spread on the cake.

WHITE CHOCOLATE FROSTING

We've mentioned a time or two throughout this book, white chocolate is ostensibly the most luxurious vanilla you'll ever taste. Here is an elegant flourish that will dress up any cake for a special occasion. The beauty of this frosting is its simple understated color, so we leave it as is and let the taste do the talking. Think of this as grown-ups' vanilla frosting. While neither of us are fans of the stuff, this paired with Blackout Cake (page 202) has converted us; it is, bar none, the perfect balance. This frosting should be prepared once you are ready to frost your cake. It will firm up the longer it is left standing and become unworkable. Perfectly delicious, just not spreadable. Enough to fill and frost one 3-layer cake or frost 36 cupcakes

INGREDIENTS

white chocolate,
    chips or finely chopped
    9oz / 255g / 1½ cups
kosher salt
    ½ teaspoon
unsalted butter, softened
    12oz / 340g / 1½ cups
whole milk,
    at room temperature
    2 tablespoons
vanilla extract
    1 teaspoon
confectioner's or icing sugar
    12oz / 340g / about 2 cups

Melt the white chocolate and salt in the top of a double boiler or in a heatproof bowl set over simmering water. White chocolate can be very pernickety; it likes to be handled with care. If you still have bits of unmelted chocolate floating about, remove the bowl from the heat, let the mixture sit for a minute or so then stir it. More often than not there is enough heat already in the bowl to finish the job. Set aside and cool to room temperature.

In the bowl of an electric mixer, beat the butter until light and fluffy, about 5 to 7 minutes. While still beating the butter, slowly pour in the milk. Once combined, scrape up from the bottom of the bowl and continue beating until the mixture is once again light and fluffy. Mix in the cooled white chocolate until combined. Then add the vanilla. Slowly add the sugar, beating continually; the frosting will come together and is ready to spread.

SOUTHERN PEANUT BUTTER FROSTING

Peanuts and pecans reign supreme in the American South;
there is always an abundance of recipes using either. This is fantastic on Peanut Butter
Crunch Cake (page 129) or on any type of chocolate cake, whoopie or cupcake. Vanilla cakes
would work as well. Resist the temptation to use crunchy peanut butter and add chopped
peanuts at the end. We've tried it both ways and this works better, resulting
in a more consistent looking (and tasting) frosting. Crunchy peanut butter doesn't
cooperate in the mixing bowl, so things don't get as blended as they should.

Enough to fill and frost one 3-layer cake or frost 36 cupcakes

INGREDIENTS

smooth peanut butter
 12oz / 340g / about 1½ cups
cream cheese
 24oz / 675g / about 3 cups
vanilla extract
 1 tablespoon
kosher salt (if peanuts are unsalted)
 1 teaspoon
confectioner's or icing sugar
 30–36oz / 815–1050g / 5–6 cups
whole milk, only if or as needed
 2–4 tablespoons
roasted peanuts, chopped
 10–12oz / 275–340g / 2½ cups

In the bowl of an electric mixer, combine the peanut butter, cream cheese, vanilla, salt and half of the sugar on medium speed. Be careful not to overmix, which can sometimes cause the cream cheese to become too thin and almost liquidy. This is better stirred as opposed to beaten. Add the remaining sugar about 7oz/200g/1 cup at a time along with enough milk to create a smooth and spreadable consistency. If you've gone too far with the liquid, simply add additional sugar until you get the desired result. You can either add the nuts directly into the frosting or press them into the sides of the frosted cake.

CARAMEL FROSTING

Here is another southern classic. This one doesn't show up much north of the
Mason–Dixon line, but down south it's everywhere. OD has fiddled with this numerous times
and offers up two methods, depending on your preference. The first is more authentic, slightly
involved yet easier to work with, while the second is easier to make but you must apply it more
quickly. Overall both are about halfway toward making a southern Praline. Like its confectionery
cousin, a little goes a long way. In the end you will have a thin, flat layer of sweet perfection.
Use this with square Doberge Layers (page 210) for a Classic Caramel Cake. Unlike other
frostings and buttercreams, this one is quite thick and 'spreading' – it can be tricky.
When finishing a cake it spreads only so much before it sets, at which point you can
compress it with your fingers to smush it around and flatten it.
Enough to fill and frost one 3-layer cake or frost 36 cupcakes

INGREDIENTS

unsalted butter
  6oz / 175g / ¾ cup
dark brown sugar
  4oz / 115g / ½ cup, packed
buttermilk
  4fl oz / 120ml / ½ cup
molasses, treacle or golden syrup
  2fl oz / 60ml / ¼ cup
confectioner's or icing sugar
  36–42oz / 1050–1225g / 6–7 cups
vanilla extract
  2 teaspoons

Variation:

light brown sugar
  16oz / 450g / 2 cups, packed
unsalted butter
  4oz / 115g / ½ cup
evaporated milk
  4fl oz / 120ml / ½ cup
vanilla extract
  1 teaspoon

Slowly heat the butter, brown sugar and buttermilk with
the molasses, treacle or syrup in a medium saucepan until
it begins to boil. Stirring often to help the sugar dissolve,
continue heating until the mixture reaches 120°C/250°F
on a candy thermometer.

Measure the confectioner's sugar and vanilla into the bowl
of an electric mixer and slowly beat in the hot liquid.
Beat until smooth. This will set up rather quickly, so it's
best to spread the frosting while it is still warm. If the
frosting becomes stiff in the bowl, gently re-heat it until
it loosens up: either place the bowl over simmering water
or in a warm oven only until the mixture becomes pliable.
Alternatively, you can also blend in a bit of milk until you
have a workable consistency.

For the variation, combine all the ingredients in a medium
saucepan and bring to a gentle boil. Stir constantly and let
the mixture simmer for 7 minutes. Remove from the heat
and cool for 5 minutes. On low speed, beat the frosting
until it thickens, about 2 to 3 minutes. It's best and easiest
to use this frosting while it is still warm.

COCOA BUTTERCREAM

This is our go-to frosting when we're looking for something chocolatey but not in the mood to melt chocolate or wait around to cool it. As you beat this, the color will lighten to be like milk chocolate. It can be darkened some by adding more cocoa powder, but it's best to do that from the get go. Doing it later is near impossible because it will streak; by the time you beat it enough to even out the color you'll be back where you started. Use this on any cupcake or layer of your choosing. It takes well to additional decorations like sprinkles, just be sure to frost a little and decorate a little. All buttercreams develop a telltale skin, of sorts, when left standing – it's part of their irresistible charm – but it's not charming at all when you're trying to decorate. If it's a dark, rich chocolate look you want, then it would be best to turn to page 192 for our Chocolate Sour Cream Fudge frosting.

Enough to fill and frost one 3-layer cake or frost 36 cupcakes

INGREDIENTS

confectioner's or icing sugar
 36oz / 1050g / 6 cups
whole milk
 6fl oz / 175ml / ¾ cup
vanilla extract
 1 tablespoon
kosher salt
 a pinch
unsalted butter, softened
 12oz / 340g / 1½ cups
unsweetened cocoa powder
 2oz / 60g / ½ cup

In a mixing bowl, stir together the sugar, milk, vanilla and salt and mix on low speed until almost combined. (This will help reduce the mess of sugar exploding from the bowl.) Bit by bit, add the softened butter and increase the speed to medium–high. Beat for about 5 to 6 minutes or until light and fluffy. Continue mixing and add the cocoa. The reason we wait until this point to add the cocoa is color; the more you mix, the lighter the chocolate color of your frosting. Be sure to scrape the bowl up from the bottom to reduce/eliminate streaks of color in the frosting. Often we finish mixing by hand using a rubber spatula, which finishes incorporating the cocoa and helps to maintain a darker color. Once you achieve the desired consistency, spread the frosting with a metal spatula or palette knife.

This can be made ahead of time, but it may be necessary to beat it for 1 to 2 minutes to loosen it up again to a spreadable consistency.

VANILLA BUTTERCREAM

Talk about a staple of our repertoire! We practically make this one in our sleep.
Used for all sorts of things, this can easily be swayed anywhere in the spectrum by adding food
color, so it lends itself to a wide variety of uses, be it for cupcakes, layers or even whoopie pies.
Kids love this not only for the taste but because it's the one real chance we have to provide them
with bolder colors. Adding jam or fruit purée will also lend color, just not as intense.
If that's your preference, reduce the milk to 4fl oz/120ml/½ cup to compensate for the added
moisture. Nine times out of ten we fiddle with consistency toward the end by adding a bit more
powdered sugar. The water content of butter varies enough per brand and it's this
sort of recipe that reveals that kitchen factoid. For a Lemon or Orange Buttercream, substitute
freshly squeezed juice for the milk and add 1 tablespoon freshly grated zest to the butter and
sugar before creaming. The acid from the juice may require you to add a touch more icing sugar
to get the same consistency as the Vanilla Buttercream. Switch the milk to puréed strawberries
and, hey presto, you have another flavor entirely! How amazing is that?!
Enough to fill and frost one 3-layer cake or frost 36 cupcakes

INGREDIENTS

confectioner's or icing sugar
  36–48oz / 1050–1400g / 6–8 cups
whole milk
  6fl oz / 180 ml / ¾ cup
vanilla extract
  1 tablespoon
kosher salt
  just a pinch
food color for pastels
  (optional)
  1 teaspoon
food color, for bolder colors
  (optional)
  1–2 tablespoons
unsalted butter, softened
  12oz / 350g / 1½ cups

In a mixing bowl, stir together the sugar, milk, vanilla, salt and food color, if using, and mix on a low speed until almost combined. This will help reduce the mess of powdered sugar exploding from the bowl, as well as incorporate the color more evenly. Bit by bit, add the softened butter and increase the speed to medium–high. Beat for about 5 to 6 minutes or until light and fluffy. If you're tinting this frosting, be sure to scrape the bowl up from the bottom to reduce/eliminate streaks of color. Often we finish mixing by hand using a rubber spatula.

Once you achieve the desired consistency, spread the frosting with a metal spatula or palette knife. This can be made ahead of time, but if you do, it may be necessary to beat it for 1 to 2 minutes to loosen it up again to a spreadable consistency.

CHOCOLATE SOUR CREAM FUDGE FROSTING

Ostensibly this is a variation on chocolate ganache which is made by melting chocolate in hot cream. Sometimes it has butter, sometimes it doesn't. This is a looser version that doesn't harden once cool like ganache, but it does set into a thick, chewy layer. It's much easier to make than other fudgy frostings, mostly because it doesn't take as long. We've tried this with crème fraîche for a slightly sweeter version without the tang. Either variation is incredibly versatile. Enough to fill and frost one 3-layer cake or frost 36 cupcakes

INGREDIENTS

milk chocolate,
  chips or chopped
  12oz / 340g / 2 cups
semi-sweet chocolate,
  chips or chopped
  6oz / 175g / 1 cup
sour cream
  12oz / 340g / 1½ cups
vanilla extract
  1 teaspoon

Melt the chocolates in a heatproof bowl over a pan of simmering water. Stir occasionally to hasten the melting. Remove the bowl from the heat and whisk in the sour cream and vanilla. We sometimes do this in the bowl of a food processor, pulsing as needed to achieve a smooth, even color and consistency. Let the frosting cool to room temperature, stirring every once in a while when you pass the bowl. Avoid the urge to beat it to cool it faster as that will change the texture. Not that it will be awful, but the point of this frosting is its luxuriously smooth satin finish. Timing will vary depending on how warm the chocolate was before adding the sour cream, but for the most part you'll be ready to go in about 30 minutes.

Once it's thick enough to spread, frost the cake rather quickly. As you work, the frosting will set and thicken. If it has gone beyond the point of no return, gently re-heat the frosting over simmering water and start again.

DARK CHOCOLATE GLAZE

There are times when a little dab'll do ya. This is an elegant, simple finish that's perfect for the Boston Cream Pie mentioned on page 182. Thick, gooey and shiny, this glaze can be either spread or drizzled depending on the look you're after. We use this on Chocolate Chip Cupcakes (page 105). Once done, they don't always make their way to customers. Oddly, there seems to be an awful lot of quality control occurring rather suddenly ... Finishes 12 cupcakes

INGREDIENTS

granulated sugar
  2oz / 60g / ¼ cup
water
  6fl oz / 175ml / ¾ cup
dark chocolate,
  chips or finely chopped
  12oz / 340g / 2 cups
large egg, gently whisked
  1

Prepare all your ingredients first so you can add them to the mixture once everything reaches the right temperature. In a saucepan, combine the sugar and water over medium heat to dissolve the sugar and bring to a light simmer. (A light simmer is just before a full rolling boil; there will be many small bubbles in the bottom and around the perimeter of the pan.) It is not the end of the world if the mixture comes to a boil, you'll just have to wait 2 to 3 minutes before adding the chocolate. Remove from the heat and stir in the chocolate. Allow it to sit in the hot water for 4 minutes before stirring to combine.

Once all the chocolate is melted and combined, slowly add the egg, stirring constantly. The heat from the liquid will cook the egg and you must constantly stir to ensure you get a thick, smooth and glossy glaze. This thickens as it cools so use immediately if for a smooth finish. We either dip into it or pour it on. Otherwise it can be spread on once cooled.

PEACH JAM

When making a batch of peach jam, suddenly everyone comes out of the woodwork. It's a bit unusual since, at first glance, there's nothing really special about it. But when you reach the end of this recipe something inexplicable happens and the aroma becomes intoxicating – of course, it could just be the Bourbon fumes. When added into Peach Jam Scones (page 63) or Apple Stack Cake (page 212), the scent starts to waft through the kitchen all over again. And, again, creatures great and small come scurrying to see when they can partake.

Makes 32oz / 900g / 4 cups

INGREDIENTS

dried peaches
  16oz / 450g / about 4 cups
light brown sugar
  8oz / 225g / 1 cup, packed
Bourbon
  6fl oz / 175ml / ¾ cup
poaching liquid
  4fl oz / 120ml / ½ cup or more
cinnamon
  2 teaspoons
ground cloves
  ½ teaspoon

Place the dried peaches in a large, shallow saucepan. Cover with water (about 32fl oz/960ml/4 cups) and bring to the boil. Reduce the heat, cover the pan and simmer until the peaches have reconstituted and are very soft. Typically this takes 20 to 30 minutes. Strain the peaches, reserving 4fl oz/120ml/½ cup of the poaching liquid. Return the peaches to the pan and mash with a potato masher. Add the remaining ingredients along with half of the reserved liquid. Simmer on low heat for 15 minutes or until the mixture has thickened to resemble set jam. Stir frequently to prevent the peaches from sticking. Add more of the reserved liquid as necessary or if you prefer your jam to be looser in consistency.

Let cool to room temperature before placing in a jam jar to refrigerate. We won't even tell you how long we've kept this in the fridge, but let's just say it does fine for quite some time.

ALMOND PASTE

We're not big fans of almond paste, let's just get it out in the open.
There, we said it. However, we came across this idea courtesy of Nick Malgieri whose lovely
books help take the stigma out of baking. Plus, he complimented us on our cinnamon buns
when we took a class at the Institute of Culinary Education in Manhattan, so we owe him one.
For an earthier flavor, we use sorghum instead of golden syrup. For earthier still,
try roasting (then cooling) the nuts first. If you prefer, you can make this paste using hazelnuts –
just substitute the almonds for the same weight of either whole or ground hazelnuts.

Makes 32oz / 900g / 4 cups

INGREDIENTS

almonds, blanched or whole
  16oz / 450g / about 4 cups
granulated sugar
  16oz / 450g / 2 cups
golden or light corn syrup
  2fl oz / 60ml / ¼ cup
vanilla extract
  2 teaspoons
almond extract or more to taste
  (not our personal favourite)
  ½ teaspoon
large egg whites,
  at room temperature
  4

Pulse almonds and sugar in a food processor until somewhat pasty. Sometimes it gets pasty, sometimes it doesn't. Not to worry. Add syrup or sorghum and the extract(s) and process for another minute. With the motor running, pour in the egg whites and process until smooth and well combined. Scrape the inside of the bowl if the mixture sticks so all is evenly distributed. If not using immediately, store in an airtight container in the fridge for about a month.

We've always wondered if it would be possible to make this with other ground nuts and/or inverted sugars such as maple syrup. Have a go, let us know …

SWEETENED WHIPPED CREAM

One of the few bits of formal training we've done is to take a 3-day intensive chocolate course at the Valrhona kitchens in the south of France. Most of what we learned was geared toward formal plated desserts for banquets, using all sorts of tricks and ingredients we'd rather not. However, one of the most useful tidbits was how to properly whip cream. There is but one trick to it: patience. It only takes time. Nothing else. By doing it slowly you are creating zillions of smaller bubbles which build up to increase the volume of the cream. Smaller bubbles produce a silky smooth texture. In France it took nearly 30 minutes to get the job done. And that was with an electric mixer! We've expedited things without sacrificing the end result. Once you try this, we guarantee you will never whip fast again. It is worth every single second of anticipation.

Enough to fill and top one 3-layer cake or frost 24 cupcakes

INGREDIENTS

heavy or double cream
16fl oz / 460ml / 2 cups
confectioner's or icing sugar
4 tablespoons
vanilla extract
1–2 teaspoons or to taste

Before you whip the cream, chill the bowl and the beaters in the fridge or freezer for about an hour. For example, if you know you need to whip cream for a dinner-party dessert, chill everything when you sit down to eat. This will help the cream aerate as it gets whisked.

When you're ready, whisk together the cream, sugar and vanilla on low speed. As the volume of the cream begins to increase, slowly turn up the speed to medium. Continue whisking until you have soft peaks. This may take up to 10 minutes. If you're serving the whipped cream as an accompaniment, you could stop at the soft peak stage, in which case you'll have what some refer to as Chantilly Cream.

To finish a cake, remove the bowl from the mixer and finish whisking by hand until the cream firms up slightly more. It never takes long and it's the best way to avoid over beating. It should be luxuriously thick and smooth but not grainy. The latter is a sign of overdoing it. Properly whipped cream will maintain its texture if kept in the fridge. Improperly whipped cream will turn to butter as it chills.

CHOCOLATE WHIPPED CREAM

When developing the Strawberry Meringue Torte recipe (page 205) it originally called for melting and spreading chocolate followed by whipping and spreading cream, but we thought why not just combine the two and get the job done in less time? We sometimes omit the vanilla and use 1 tablespoon of liqueur instead, such as Kahlùa, rum or brandy. Fresh, delectable and (possibly) naughty. Enough to fill and top one 3-layer cake or frost 24 cupcakes

INGREDIENTS

heavy or double cream
16fl oz / 480ml / 2 cups
confectioner's or icing sugar
4 tablespoons
vanilla extract
½ teaspoon
bittersweet chocolate,
chips or chopped
4oz / 115g /   cup

In the bowl of an electric mixer, slowly heat the cream and sugar over a pot of simmering water until it just begins to boil. Remove from the heat and stir in the vanilla and chocolate. Let sit for a few minutes until the chocolate melts, then whisk vigorously until even in color and smooth in texture. If there are still bits of unmelted chocolate, let the mixture sit a few minutes longer and whisk again. Alternatively (though unlikely), you may need to pop the bowl back over the hot water for a little extra heat to get the job done. Cool to room temperature, then cover and refrigerate for at least 4 hours but preferably overnight.

Remove the bowl from the fridge, place it on the mixer and whisk the chocolate cream on medium–low speed until almost thick. Because of the chocolate, this thickens more quickly than Sweetened Whipped Cream, so keep a close eye on it. We finish the job by hand so we can literally feel the cream thicken to the point where it is spreadable but not resistant. It should still be light and creamy. It's best to use once it's ready. At most we've finished a cake with this just before people arrive for a dinner party, popped it back in the fridge, and then once finished with the main meal, removed it to serve dessert – in all, about 4 to 6 hours 'storage'.

CITRUS CURDS

Curds must be the reason meringues were invented. More often than not they use a whole lot of egg yolks, so presumably something had to be done with the whites. We like to have flexibility so we keep curds on hand to add to batters, fill cupcakes or spread between layers. Variations are only limited by imagination. Lemons and limes are more acidic than oranges and grapefruits, which is why the methods differ from one to the next. Limes need more sugar than you would think because they pack more punch per fruit than a lemon. Believe us, we've tried and it's not a pleasant pucker. Another handy recipe to have nearby when making this is Marshmallow Meringue (page 184). It uses up the whites and is a perfect complement to anything curd. Makes 32oz / 900g / 4 cups

LEMON CURD

INGREDIENTS

granulated sugar
   12oz / 340g / 1½ cups
lemon zest, freshly grated
   5–6 tablespoons
lemon juice, freshly squeezed
   (6-ish lemons)
   10fl oz / 300ml / 1¼ cups
kosher salt
   ½ teaspoon
large eggs
   6
large egg yolks
   12
unsalted butter,
   softened and diced
   10oz / 275g / 1¼ cups

Combine all the ingredients except the butter in the top of a double boiler or heatproof glass bowl. Place over simmering water, being careful not to let the bowl touch the water or let the water boil. Whisk continuously for about 15 minutes until thick. Turn the heat off and add the butter piece by piece until melted and thoroughly incorporated. Pour the mixture into a food processor and blitz it for 1 to 2 minutes until smooth. This will smooth out the mixture and make a better emulsion. If you opt not to use a food processor or don't have one, not to worry. Once the butter has been added, strain the curd if required (to get out any cooked egg bits) or desired (to remove the zest).

Pour the finished curd into a plastic tub or glass bowl and place clingfilm directly on top. Let cool to room temperature before refrigerating. This will keep in the refrigerator for up to 3 weeks.

ORANGE CURD

Same as above, but use the zest of 1 to 2 lemons and 2 large oranges along with 6fl oz/175ml/¾ cup fresh orange juice and 3fl oz/85ml/½ cup of fresh lemon juice. Once off the heat, add up to 1 teaspoon orange oil or liqueur. With curd, the delicate orange flavor might need to be enhanced amidst all the butter and egg, hence we sometimes resort to this 'cheat'.

LIME CURD

INGREDIENTS

lime zest, freshly grated
  8 limes
granulated sugar
  24oz / 675g / 3 cups
lime juice
  8fl oz / 240ml / 1 cup
large eggs
  8
kosher salt
  ¼ teaspoon
unsalted butter
  8oz / 225g / 1 cup

In a large heatproof bowl, whisk together the zest and sugar until evenly incorporated and fragrant. Mix in the lime juice, eggs and salt, whisk thoroughly and then add the butter. Place the bowl over a pot of simmering water. With a whisk or rubber spatula, stir continuously while you heat the mixture and the butter melts. Continue stirring and heating until the curd thickens. You will feel the resistance increase while you are stirring; this happens all of a sudden, so be prepared. Once thick, remove from the heat and pour into a bowl. Immediately cover the surface with clingfilm to prevent a skin forming on the top of the curd. Set aside to cool completely before refrigerating.

GRAPEFRUIT CURD

INGREDIENTS

fresh grapefruit juice
  20fl oz / 600ml / 2½ cups
large egg yolks
  12
granulated sugar
  16oz / 450g / 2 cups
grapefruit zest,
  freshly grated
  2 grapefruits
unsalted butter,
  softened and diced
  8oz / 225g / 1 cup

In a large saucepan, simmer the grapefruit juice until reduced by half. Let cool to room temperature. Add to the cooled juice all the ingredients except the butter and stir to combine. Heat the mixture over a medium–low heat, stirring constantly with a rubber spatula, until the mixture thickens to a custard consistency, about 15 to 20 minutes. Be sure not to boil the mixture, to avoid curdling. Remove the pan from the heat and whisk in the butter, bit by bit, until it is melted and fully incorporated. Transfer to a heatproof bowl and cover with clingfilm. Cool to room temperature before refrigerating until needed.

EVERY NOW AND again you need to pull out all the stops. Sometimes you literally have to and at other times it just needs to look like you did. These recipes will satisfy even the most demanding of circumstances and earn you top honors with those who don't already have you atop the pedestal on which, no doubt, you rightfully belong. Unlike our layer recipes, which are meant to be mixed and matched with your frosting(s) of choice, these are more complete cakes which rarely have other variants. Not that you shouldn't be tempted to experiment if inspiration strikes – by all means, anything can be improved upon – but we've found ourselves coming back to these recipes time and time again when the need to IMPRESS is paramount. We've opted for elaborate layer cakes, a few tortes and the odd duck here and there that defies being labelled

as anything. As can be the case with preparing for important events, timing is of the essence, so we've included recipes and tips for doing things ahead whenever possible. Many, if not all, of the components of a recipe can be made a day or two in advance if stored properly.

Layers should be kept in airtight containers and fillings should be refrigerated until you're ready to use them. FROSTINGS are at their best when made at the time they are needed. More elaborate recipes, like the Lady Baltimore Layers (page 217), are often made less daunting if you chip away at them over a few days. In that particular case, we chop and soak dried fruit up to a week in advance. While these recipes may seem and/or be more complicated, none are difficult. All are well worth the added effort and all will make a lasting impression.

SPIRTs

BLACKOUT CAKE

If ever a dessert deserved the stupid moniker 'Death by Chocolate' this would be it. Another silly option would be 'Chocolate Decadence'. We prefer a simpler version of the original Chocolate Blackout Cake. It is a New York classic, originally conceived in a Brooklyn bakery called Ebingers, long since closed. It is uniquely elegant, very rich and aimed at true chocoholics. It's fun to make and lasts for about a week – not that that ever gets put to the test. This can easily be finished several days in advance of serving. If that's your choice, be sure and refrigerate it in a covered cake container or under a cake dome set on a baking sheet, otherwise the crumb finish will take on any stronger flavors lurking in the fridge. Start by making the filling and frosting, since it's best if chilled overnight. Which is not to say it can't be chilled for several nights – these extra-moist layers can also be made several days ahead if it should help with scheduling. The only caveat is to let the cake chill for a minimum of 4 hours before serving so everything has a chance to glue together. If not, you might end up with a slippery slice. Serves 12–16

INGREDIENTS

For the filling and frosting:

milk or equal parts milk/single cream
32fl oz / 960ml / 4 cups
granulated sugar
12oz / 340g / 1½ cups
unsweetened cocoa powder
6 tablespoons
cornstarch
6 tablespoons
unsweetened chocolate,
finely chopped
6oz / 175g / 1 cups
unsalted butter, room temperature
2oz / 60g / ¼ cup
vanilla extract
1 tablespoon

For the layers:

instant espresso powder
1½ teaspoons
unsalted butter, melted and cooled
6oz / 175g / ¾ cup
all-purpose or plain flour
15oz / 425g / 2¾ cups
unsweetened cocoa powder
9½oz / 260g / 1¾ cups

Combine all the filling ingredients but the vanilla in a large saucepan. Set the pan over a medium–low heat and whisk constantly until the chocolate and butter are melted and the mixture begins to bubble and thicken, about 5 to 10 minutes – more if you've doubled the recipe. Off the heat, stir in the vanilla. Transfer the mixture to a glass bowl and place clingfilm directly on the surface of the filling. Let cool before refrigerating until cold, at least 4 hours. There are times when, despite your best efforts, the filling may be lumpy. Not to worry. Pour it into a food processor and whiz until it smooths out. This will take 2 or 3 pulses, or about 30 seconds. A hand whisk may also get the job done.

Preheat the oven to 180°C/350°F/gas mark 4. Butter three 9in/23cm round cake pans and line the bottom with parchment. Dust the sides with flour, tapping out any excess.

Dissolve the espresso powder in 8fl oz/240ml/1 cup of boiling water. Set aside to cool. Add more water if some should evaporate while cooling. Melt the butter in a small saucepan, then turn off the heat.

Sift together the dry ingredients and set aside. Put the buttermilk into a large, glass measuring jug then add the brewed espresso, melted butter and vanilla. Stir or whisk to combine. The varying temperatures of the liquids will even out the mixture to room temperature.

baking powder

2 teaspoons

bicarbonate of soda

4 teaspoons

kosher salt

1 teaspoon

granulated sugar

27oz / 760g / 3 3/8 cups

buttermilk, cold

18fl oz / 540ml / 2¼ cups

vanilla extract

4½ teaspoons

large eggs, at room temperature

5

In the bowl of an electric mixer on medium speed, beat the eggs well. Add in the remaining liquids and mix until evenly combined. On low speed, add the flour mixture in thirds, mixing only until just combined. Scrape the bowl as needed. Depending on the temperature of the liquid, this batter can be a bit thin. Divide the batter evenly between the 3 prepared pans.

Bake for 35 to 40 minutes or until a knife inserted comes out clean. It's best to rotate the pans in the oven front to back, top to bottom about ⅔ of the way through. Don't be concerned by cracks in the cake top. Cool in the pans for 20 minutes, then turn out to cool completely on wire racks.

To finish the cake, slice off the domed tops and set aside. Using a long serrated knife, slice each layer in half horizontally. If your layers were flat, keep 5 of the layers for assembling the cake and set 1 aside. Take the domed tops and/or the reserved cake layer and crumble it with your fingers until you have a bowl of even crumbs. They should be slightly larger than breadcrumbs, but they will vary.

Cut thin strips of baking parchment and place 4 on a serving plate or cake stand about 7in/18cm apart. This will keep things neat and tidy for presentation later. Place one of the cut layers on the parchment strips. Using a small offset spatula, spread a thin layer of filling on top of the layer. Repeat with all the layers. Once you're done stacking, cover the top and sides with the filling. Take a handful of cake crumbs and press them into the filling to cover the cake completely. Word to the wise, this is a messy proposition – it helps to place a baking sheet or aluminium foil underneath the cake stand to catch the crumbs that fall. If need be, you can recycle fallen crumbs to help cover the cake. When all the crumbs are in place, remove the parchment strips from under the cake. Refrigerate the finished cake for at least 4 hours before serving so it can set. A thin slice of this goes a long way as it is very rich.

STRAWBERRY MERINGUE TORTE

Many things came to mind when this recipe was evolving. Ostensibly, for you British folk, this is Eton Mess in cake form. To others it is a variation on a Pavlova. For the cook who wants to impress for a dinner party but not loose his/her mind doing so, this is a gift: This needs to be made a day in advance. Ideally this should be stored in the fridge under a cake dome or lightly wrapped in cling film to keep it from absorbing other aromas wafting through the fridge plus it keeps the strawberries looking bright. Serves 12–16

INGREDIENTS

For the meringues:
large egg whites
  6
kosher salt
  a pinch
cream of tartar
  ¼ teaspoon
cider vinegar
  1½ teaspoons
vanilla extract
  1½ teaspoons
granulated sugar
  12oz / 340g / 1½ cups

For the filling:
1 batch Chocolate Whipped Cream
  (see page 197)
strawberries,
  washed and hulled
  3–4 punnets

Preheat the oven to 130°C/275°F/gas mark 1. Line 2 or 3 baking sheets with baking parchment. Trace three 9in/23cm circles on the paper to use as guides.

In the bowl of an electric mixer, whisk the egg whites, salt, cream of tartar, vinegar and vanilla until soft peaks form. With the mixer running, slowly add in the sugar, about 1 tablespoon at a time, and continue whisking until stiff and glossy. Spread the meringue on top of each circle outline.

Bake the meringues for about 60 minutes or until firm. Turn off the oven and let the meringues sit in the oven for another 15 to 20 minutes. Transfer to wire racks to cool. If they don't want to budge, let them sit another 5 minutes or gently run a long, flat, metal palette knife under them to release them from the paper.

To assemble the torte, place one meringue on a serving plate or cake stand. Spread a layer of the chocolate cream over the meringue followed by half the strawberries. Repeat with another meringue. Place the third meringue on to the second layer of strawberries then cover it and the stacked sides with cream. Refrigerate for at least 4 hours (if you're pressed for time) but preferably overnight. The top can be left as is, dusted with cocoa powder or sprinkled with grated chocolate.

ABUELA'S ITALIAN CREAM CAKE

For our first Christmas spent with the Latino side of the family, we got to
New Orleans after 24 hours of driving with two dogs and an overnight stay in a truly revolting
hotel. Upon arrival, we were confronted with this glorious cake. Famished, we wanted to dig in
immediately. However, we were told it had just been removed from the freezer.
Intact. Not at all our preference, but both our mothers are prone to saying 'it freezes beautifully'
when talking about almost anything. Truth be told, this does indeed freeze beautifully.
Once we were allowed to slice it, we polished this off in two days. Both of us were the only ones
doing the polishing. If freezing is your choice, the best method for thawing is to remove it from
the freezer to the refrigerator for one day, and then one day on the counter, preferably
under a cake dome. Absolutely no one will know. As for the name, if there is one thing to be
learned spending time in Southern Louisiana, sometimes it's best not to ask.
It is what it is and that's that. Serves 12–16.

INGREDIENTS

For the cake layers:

all-purpose or plain flour
24oz / 675g / 4½ cups

baking powder
1½ teaspoons

bicarbonate of soda
1 teaspoon

kosher salt
1 teaspoon

cinnamon
1 teaspoon

nutmeg, freshly grated
1 teaspoon

buttermilk, at room temperature
12fl oz / 260ml / 1½ cups

vanilla and almond extract
2 teaspoons of each

unsalted butter, softened
18oz / 500g / 2 cups plus 2 tablespoons

granulated sugar
24oz / 675g / 3 cups

large eggs, at room temperature
8

shredded coconut (optional)
8oz / 225g / about 2 cups

Spiced Pecans, chopped (page 185)
8oz / 225g / 2 cups

Preheat the oven to 160°C/325°F/gas mark 3. Butter three
9in/23cm round cake pans, line the bottoms with baking
parchment, dust with flour and tap out any excess.

Whisk together the flour, baking powder, bicarbonate
of soda, salt and spices in a medium bowl. Set aside.

Combine the buttermilk and vanilla and almond extracts
in a large measuring jug. Set aside.

In the bowl of an electric mixer on medium–high speed,
cream together the butter and sugar until light, pale
and fluffy, about 6 to 8 minutes. Turn the mixer down a
notch and add eggs, one at a time, beating well after each
addition. Scrape the bowl as necessary. On low speed,
alternately add the flour and buttermilk mixtures in 3 to 4
additions. Begin and end with the dry ingredients and mix
only until just combined. With a rubber spatula, scrape any
leftover gunk from the bottom of the bowl then fold in the
shredded coconut and pecans until everything is evenly
incorporated. Divide the batter evenly among the pans
and smooth with an offset spatula.

Bake for 45 to 50 minutes or until a knife inserted comes
out clean. It's best to rotate pans front to back, top to
bottom about ⅔ of the way through. Cool on racks for
30 minutes before turning out layers to cool completely.

For the Spiced Pecan frosting:

cream cheese
  12oz / 340g / about 3 cups
unsalted butter, softened
  4oz / 115g / ½ cup
confectioner's or icing sugar
  16oz / 450g / about 4 cups
vanilla extract
  1 teaspoon
kosher salt
  ½ teaspoon
Spiced Pecans, chopped
  8oz / 225g / 2 cups

Meanwhile, make the frosting. In the bowl of an electric mixer, combine the cream cheese, butter, half of the sugar, the vanilla and salt on medium speed. Be careful not to over-mix, which can sometimes cause the cream cheese to become too thin and almost liquidy. Slowly add the remaining sugar, about 4oz/115g/1 cup at a time, to create a smooth and spreadable consistency. You can either fold the nuts directly into the frosting or use them to press into the sides of the frosted cake. If the frosting seems soft, add about 1 teaspoon of lemon juice in order to regain the thick cream cheese consistency.

To finish the cake, cut thin strips of parchment paper and place 4 of them on a serving plate or cake stand about 7in/18cm apart. This will keep things neat and tidy for presentation later. Place one layer flat-side down on the parchment strips. Slice off the domed top and enjoy snacking on it while moving along. Using an offset spatula, spread the frosting on top of the de-domed layer and repeat with the second layer. For the third and final layer, slice off the domed top. Place the cut side down on top of the frosted second layer. (Inverting the final layer helps reduce cake crumbs from working their way into the frosting. This particular frosting is lumpy and bumpy so it doesn't matter as much, but it makes for good practice.) Frost the top and sides of the entire cake. Remove the parchment strips from underneath the cake. Let the cake stand for about 4 hours before serving.

Wrap twice in clingfilm and then aluminium foil if you want to pop it in the freezer. This can also be refrigerated before serving, but remove it about 1 hour before serving so it can soften up for ideal enjoyment.

UGLY CAKE

This is what happens when you try to bake a cheesecake and cake layer simultaneously.
It ain't pretty, but boy is it good. Serves 12–16

INGREDIENTS

For the streusel crumbs:

all-purpose or plain flour
10oz / 300g / 2 cups

light brown sugar
12oz / 340g / 1½ cups, packed

unsalted butter, melted
4oz / 115g / ½ cup

For the cake base:

all-purpose or plain flour
18oz / 500g / 3½ cups

baking powder
1 tablespoon

kosher salt
¾ teaspoon

whole milk
14fl oz / 420ml / 1¾ cups

vanilla extract
1 tablespoon

unsalted butter, softened
8oz / 225g / 1 cup

granulated sugar
16oz / 450g / 2 cups

large eggs, at room temperature
4

For the filling:

cream cheese, at room temperature
24oz / 675g / about 3 cups

granulated or caster sugar
8oz / 225g / 1 cup

large eggs
3

lemon zest, freshly grated
1 tablespoon

lemon juice, freshly squeezed
3 tablespoons

vanilla extract
1½ teaspoons

Preheat the oven to 160°C/325°F/gas mark 3. Butter a 12in/30cm springform pan or round pan with removable bottom. If the latter, line the bottom with baking parchment.

Start by making the streusel: combine all the ingredients in a large bowl and mix until you have a crumby mess. You should have lumps and bumps of all sizes but no streaks of flour. Set aside or refrigerate until needed.

To make the cake base, whisk together the flour, baking powder and salt. In a large measuring jug, combine the milk and vanilla. Set both aside.

In the bowl of an electric mixer, cream together the butter and sugar on medium–high speed until light and fluffy, about 5 to 6 minutes. Add the eggs, one at a time, beating thoroughly after each addition. Scrape the bowl as you go. On low speed, alternately add the flour and milk mixtures in 3 to 4 additions until just combined. Spread the batter evenly into the pan.

To make the filling, beat the cream cheese and sugar on low speed until well blended. Add the eggs and incorporate them fully before adding in the lemon zest, juice and vanilla. You're good to go. Pour the filling over the batter already in the pan. Take a fistful of crumbs, clench them and then distribute evenly over the filling.

Bake for 60 to 70 minutes or until golden. The center should appear set but it will still wiggle. A small knife should emerge with no traces of cake batter but it will have a smear on it from the filling. The crumbs will be golden brown. Let the cake cool completely in the pan before removing it to serve at room temperature. We also serve this slightly chilled.

DOBERGE

One of Crescent City's finest! Doberge (say it with us, doe-bazsh) is what
New Orleans is known for when it comes to cake. Up north we would call this 7-layer cake,
but when any New Orleanian explains the difference, all you get is an earful of unrecognizable
syllables. At least, to ears untrained, in Cajun patois. Most often, Doberge is made by stacking
vanilla layers with chocolate custard and enveloping it in a thick, chocolate icing/frosting hybrid,
but some use chocolate layers instead. Here we've opted for the classic, since the only syllable
we'd like to hear (and can recognize) is 'yum'. Like our Blackout Cake (page 202),
you can chip away at preparation by making the layers and filling a day or two in advance. The
finished cake can be assembled the day before serving so everything can bond together. Genuine
Doberge is square, as we've done here. If you only have two square pans you can bake half the
batter first, refrigerate the remaining batter until the first two layers are cooled (as are the pans),
and repeat. Chilled batter needs about another 5 minutes baking time. Alternatively,
you can do this as three 9in/23cm round layers. Again, since the pans will have more batter,
add another 5 or so minutes to the baking time. Serves 16–18

INGREDIENTS

For the filling:

all-purpose or plain flour
  3½oz / 90g / ⅔ cup
granulated sugar
  20oz / 550g / 2½ cups
large egg yolks
  8
whole milk
  20fl oz / 600ml / 2½ cups
light or single cream
  20fl oz / 600ml / 2½ cups
semi-sweet chocolate chips
  6oz / 175g / 1 cup
unsalted butter, softened
  6oz / 175g / ¾ cup
vanilla extract
  2 teaspoons
almond extract (optional)
  ½ teaspoon

Start with the filling. In a medium bowl, whisk together
the flour and sugar. In another bowl, beat the egg yolks
slightly. Set aside.

In a medium saucepan over a medium heat, heat the milk,
cream and chocolate until the chocolate melts and the
mixture is combined. Gradually add 8fl oz/240ml/1 cup
of the chocolate to the flour mixture and stir to make a
thick paste. Return the paste to the saucepan and continue
cooking until everything comes together and the mixture
thickens, about 3 to 4 minutes. Take 8fl oz/240ml/1 cup of
the new chocolate mixture and add it to the egg yolks to
warm them. Pour the egg mixture back into the saucepan
and incorporate quickly. Continue cooking for 3 to 4
minutes more until the filling is thick, shiny and smooth.
Remove from the heat, add the butter and vanilla (almond,
too, if you're using it) and mix well. Cool to room
temperature. If you chill this overnight, let it come back to
room temperature before assembling the finished cake.

Preheat the oven to 180°C/350°F/gas mark 4. Butter four
9in/23cm square cake pans, line the bottoms and 2 sides
with parchment, dust with flour and tap out any excess.
Square layers tend to stick, so we line 2 sides to lift out
cooled layers as opposed to flipping them out.

For the layers:

all-purpose or plain flour
27oz / 780g / 5¼ cups

baking powder
1½ tablespoons

kosher salt
1 teaspoon

whole milk
20fl oz / 600ml / 2½ cups

vanilla extract
1½ tablespoons

unsalted butter, softened
12oz / 340g / 1½ cups

granulated sugar
24oz / 675g / 3 cups

large eggs, at room temperature
6

For the frosting:

confectioner's or icing sugar
48oz / 1400g / about 8 cups

unsalted butter
8oz / 225g / 1 cup

cocoa powder
2oz / 60g / ½ cup

buttermilk
8fl oz / 240ml / 1 cup

vanilla extract
2 teaspoons

Whisk together the flour, baking powder and salt in a medium bowl. In a large, glass measuring jug, combine the milk and vanilla. Set both aside.

In the bowl of an electric mixer, cream the butter and sugar on medium–high speed until light and fluffy, about 6 to 8 minutes. Add the eggs, one at a time, beating thoroughly after each addition. Scrape the bowl as you go. On low speed, alternately add the flour and buttermilk mixtures in 3 to 4 additions, beginning and ending with the dry ingredients and mixing only until just combined. Divide the batter evenly among the prepared pans.

Bake for 20 to 25 minutes (25 to 30 minutes for chilled batter or round layers) or until a knife inserted into the center emerges clean. It's best to rotate pans front to back, top to bottom about ⅔ of the way through for even baking. Cool the layers in their pans for about 10 minutes before releasing them from the pans to cool completely on wire racks.

To assemble the cake, slice off the domed tops. Using a long serrated knife, slice each layer in half horizontally. Cut thin strips of baking parchment and place 4 on a serving plate or cake stand about 8in/21cm apart. This will keep things neat and tidy for presentation later. Place one of the cut layers on the parchment strips. Using a small offset spatula, spread a thin layer of filling on top of the layer. Repeat with all the layers.

Once the cake is assembled, make the frosting. The consistency will be somewhere between a thin icing and a thick buttercream. Place the sugar in the bowl of an electric mixer. Heat the butter, cocoa and buttermilk slowly until it begins to boil. Remove from the heat and gently pour it into the bowl with the mixer on low speed. Beat until smooth. Stir in the vanilla. Let the frosting stand for no more than 5 minutes before spreading it over the top of the cake first. If the mixture is still too warm and soft it won't adhere to the sides of the cake – by starting on top you've bought yourself some time. Then cover the sides of the cake. Let the finished cake stand at room temperature for several hours before serving. If you've opted to refrigerate it, remove it 1 hour before serving so it has a chance to soften up.

APPLE STACK CAKE

Known as Tennessee or Kentucky Apple Stack Cake, versions of this recipe frequently appear in southern American cookbooks. Given a Yankee sensibility, it appealed as a curiosity that had to be tried. When all is said and done, it will appear to be little more than a pile of pancakes with applesauce. Far from it. This makes a show-stopping finish to any autumnal celebration. For a touch of late summer, try it with our Peach Jam instead (page 194). Prolonged simmering reduces the 'applesauce' to something we call apple butter. A thicker, more intensely flavored compote used for adding to recipes, filling cakes or slathering onto anything. Serves 16–18

INGREDIENTS

For the filling:

dried apples
16oz / 450g / about 4 cups

water or apple juice or cider
32–48fl oz / 960–1440ml / 4–6 cups

light or dark brown sugar
12oz / 340g / 1½ cups, packed

cinnamon
1½ teaspoons

nutmeg, freshly grated
1 teaspoon

ground ginger
1 teaspoon

allspice
½ teaspoon

ground cloves
¼ teaspoon

kosher salt
½ teaspoon

dark rum or brandy (optional)
2oz / 60ml / ¼ cup

Start by making the filling, which can be done several days ahead. Place the dried apples in a large saucepan and cover with the liquid. Bring to a gentle boil over medium heat, stirring when you happen to walk past the pot. Reduce to a simmer and cook for another 30 minutes or so until the apples are soft and the liquid has almost completely evaporated. Sometimes the reverse happens and we need to toss in some more liquid. In all, this first step can take anywhere from 30 to 60 minutes. There is no magic to this, nor any place to fail. Remove from the heat and stir in the sugar, spices and salt. Smush the mixture with a potato masher until you get a fairly smooth sauce. You can also do this in batches in a food processor. If the mixture still appears too liquidy, return it to the pan and simmer until the liquid evaporates. Stir frequently to prevent the mixture sticking to the bottom of the pan. It's best to use a flat heatproof rubber spatula for this so you can scrape and stir all at once. If you're opting to use the alcohol, stir it in and cook for another 10 minutes or so to let the alcohol burn off. Remove from the heat and cool to room temperature before refrigerating until needed.

Preheat the oven to 180°C/350°F/gas mark 4. Butter six 9in/23cm round cake pans, line the bottoms with baking parchment, dust the sides with flour and tap out any excess. Alternately, you can do this in 2 or 3 passes, depending on how many pans you have. Just remember to let the pans cool before re-filling them with batter. Whisk together the dry ingredients in a medium bowl. In a large measuring jug, combine the buttermilk and eggs. Set both aside.

For the layers:

all-purpose or plain flour
32oz / 900g / 6 cups

baking powder
1 tablespoon

bicarbonate of soda
1 teaspoon

kosher salt
1 teaspoon

buttermilk
12fl oz / 350ml / 1½ cups

large eggs
5

unsalted butter, softened
12oz / 340g / 1½ cups

light or dark brown sugar
12oz / 340g / 1½ cups, packed

molasses, sorghum or cane syrup
12fl oz / 350ml / 1½ cups

In the bowl of an electric mixer, cream the butter, sugar and molasses on medium–high speed until well combined. Reduce the speed to low and alternately add the flour and buttermilk mixtures, beginning and ending with the dry ingredients, and mix only until just combined. Divide the batter equally among the prepared pans. You will use about 8fl oz/240ml/1 cup of batter per pan so don't be alarmed by quantities or looks. Smooth the batter with a small offset spatula or the back of a spoon. If it looks like you're baking pancakes, to a degree you *are*.

Bake for 10 to 12 minutes until they spring back when poked in the center and begin to pull away from the sides of the pan. For the most part, these layers will not dome in the middle. To be honest, they don't look like much when they come out of the oven. Cool in the pans for about 10 minutes before turning them out to cool completely. These remain quite moist and almost sticky on top.

To complete the cake, place one layer on a serving plate or cake stand. Smother the layer with apple filling then repeat until all the layers have been used. The top layer is the finish. Refrigerate for at least 4 hours but preferably overnight so it can ripen – meaning all the flavours can come together. Remove the cake from the fridge about 1 hour before serving and dust the top with confectioner's or icing sugar. Appearances aside, a thin slice of this will stay intact for serving. Of course, a dollop of whipped cream would cover any sins should there be any, plus it is the perfect accompaniment. Because of the fruit filling, it will keep for about a week if refrigerated. This may well be the tallest cake we make.

CANNOLI CAKE

A favourite New York treat is devouring a cannoli while walking and people watching and attempting not to have luscious filling ooze down your chin. For the uninitiated, cannoli can be found at almost any Italian bakery: a crunchy outer shell is deep-fried batter somehow (miraculously?) rolled into a hollow tube which is then filled with a slightly sweet ricotta cheese filling studded with chocolate and orange. There is nary a drop of Italian blood between us so we've never ventured into making traditional cannoli shells, but in the spirit of many southern American frostings bursting with all sorts of things, one day we thought of doing an inside-out cannoli cake by using the filling as the frosting. A true sponge seemed the logical choice for its texture and ability to absorb moisture from the cheese filling. Like our Blackout Cake (page 202), this will set into a squidgy slice of pure indulgence. Serves 16–18

INGREDIENTS

For the sponge:

all-purpose or plain flour
  16oz / 450g / 3 cups
baking powder
  1 teaspoon
kosher salt
  ½ teaspoon
large eggs, separated
  10
cold water
  8fl oz / 240ml / 1 cup
granulated sugar
  20oz / 550g / 2½ cups
vanilla extract
  1 tablespoon
cream of tartar
  1 teaspoon

To make the sponge, preheat the oven to 160°C/325°F/gas mark 3. Butter three 9in/23cm round cake pans, line the bottoms with baking parchment, dust with flour and tap out any excess.

In a medium bowl, whisk together the flour, baking powder and salt. Set aside.

In the bowl of an electric mixer fitted with a paddle, beat the egg yolks at medium–high speed until thick, creamy and pale yellow, about 4 to 5 minutes. Slowly pour in the cold water – this will make the mixture foamy, so don't panic. Gradually add in the sugar and continue to beat for about 3 minutes until it dissolves. Stir in the vanilla. On low speed, add in the flour a little at a time. Remove the bowl from the mixer and finish mixing by folding with a rubber spatula. In another mixing bowl, beat the egg whites and cream of tartar with a whisk until stiff, shiny peaks form. Fold the whites into the batter thoroughly and divide evenly among the prepared pans.

Bake for 25 to 30 minutes or until a knife inserted comes out clean. It's best to rotate pans front to back, top to bottom about ⅔ of the way through. Cool the layers in the pans for about 10 minutes before turning them out to cool completely on wire racks. Peel off the liners only after the layers have cooled completely, otherwise they might tear apart.

For the filling/frosting:

ricotta cheese
32oz / 900g / about 4 cups

confectioner's or icing sugar
14oz / 400g / 2¼ cups

cinnamon
½ teaspoon

vanilla extract
1 teaspoon

bittersweet chocolate,
chips or finely chopped
6oz / 175g / 1 cup

candied orange peel,
finely chopped
4oz / 115g / ½ cup

While the layers are in the oven, make the filling. In the bowl of an electric mixer, beat the ricotta on low speed until it loosens up and smoothes out. Add the sugar, cinnamon and vanilla and continue beating until evenly combined. Fold in the chocolate chips and candied peel. Cover and refrigerate until firm. This can easily be made in advance as well.

To assemble the cake, using a long serrated knife, slice each layer in half horizontally. Once cooled, these layers are pretty sturdy, so don't panic as you slice them – it may seem like they'll tear apart. On the off-chance they do, still, don't worry.

Cut thin strips of baking parchment and place 4 of them on a serving plate or cake stand about 7in/18cm apart – this will keep things neat and tidy for presentation later. Place one of the cut layers on the parchment strips. Using a small offset spatula, spread a thin layer of the filling on top of the layer. Repeat with all the layers. Once you're done stacking, cover the top and sides with the remaining filling. Take a handful of cake crumbs and press them into the filling to cover the cake completely. Refrigerate the finished cake for at least 4 hours before serving so it can set. A thin slice of this goes a long way as it is very rich.

LADY BALTIMORE LAYERS

Truth be told, Lady Baltimore is the Queen of Southern American cakes. Most likely the name comes from an early 20th-century novel of the same name in which a young man flirts with a young woman who made this as a wedding cake for her customers. Apparently it was his way of broaching the topic of his affection. He got a little ahead of himself as he ordered it as a wedding cake for his nuptials. To her. Another far less interesting theory is it was created in Charleston, South Carolina (those Huguenots sure could bake) in the eponymous tearoom. One way or another, this became and remains a favorite wedding cake in the South. Lord Baltimore is another delicious confection using yolks for the batter instead of whites called for here. But the layers aren't really the point. It's all about the frosting. Traditionally Lady Baltimore is finished with Marshmallow Meringue into which marinated fruits and nuts are folded. We've opted for a buttercream version only because it's better when preparing in advance – this entire cake can sit assembled for several days before serving. For Purists, use the same amount of marinated fruit and nuts folded into a batch of Marshmallow Meringue (page 184). Serves 12 to 16

INGREDIENTS

For the frosting:

dried apricots, chopped
  6oz / 175g / 1 cup
golden raisins, chopped
  6oz / 175g / 1 cup
dark raisins, chopped
  6oz / 175g / 1 cup
lemon or orange juice
  2fl oz / 60ml / ¼ cup
orange or lemon zest, freshly grated
  1 tablespoon
dark rum, to cover the fruit
  12–16fl oz / 350–460ml / 1½ cups

For the layers:

all-purpose or plain flour
  24oz / 675g / 4½ cups
baking powder
  4½ teaspoons
kosher salt
  1½ teaspoons
walnuts, finely chopped
  6oz / 175g / 1½ cups
whole milk
  12oz / 350ml / 1½ cups
vanilla extract
  1½ teaspoons

Place all the chopped dried fruit in a medium bowl and add the juice and rum. Cover with clingfilm and let stand at room temperature for at least 4 hours but preferably overnight. Stir occasionally and add additional liquids if required. Strain and reserve the liquid for brushing the layers before frosting.

Preheat oven to 180°C/350°F/gas mark 4. Butter three 9in/23cm round cake pans, line the bottoms with baking parchment, dust the sides with flour and tap out any excess.

Sift together the flour, baking powder and salt. Add finely chopped nuts and stir until evenly distributed.

Combine the milk, vanilla and 2 tablespoons of the reserved juice and rum mixture.

In the bowl of an electric mixer on medium–high speed, cream the butter and 20oz/550g/2½ cups of the granulated sugar until light, pale and fluffy, about 5 to 6 minutes. Turn the mixer down a notch and add the egg yolks, one at a time, beating well after each addition and scraping the bowl as necessary. On low speed, alternately add in flour–nut and milk mixtures in 3 to 4 additions. Mix until just combined. With a rubber spatula, scrape the bowl up from the bottom to ensure everything is mixed evenly.

For the layers (cont.):

unsalted butter, softened

12oz / 340g / 1½ cups

granulated sugar

24oz / 675g / 3 cups

large egg yolks

3

large egg whites

9

For the frosting:

unsalted butter, softened

16oz / 450g / 2 cups

kosher salt

½ teaspoon

vanilla extract

1 teaspoon

reserved juice and rum

1–2 tablespoons

confectioner's or icing sugar, sifted

36–42oz / 1050–1225g / 6–7 cups

walnuts, chopped

6oz / 175g / 1½ cups

In a separate bowl, whisk the egg whites on slow speed. As the eggs develop foam, increase the speed to medium and then medium–high until soft peaks form, which will take about 3 minutes. Slowly add the remaining 4oz/115g/½ cup granulated sugar and beat until the peaks are stiff but not dry. Fold the egg whites into the batter in thirds. We mix in the first ⅓ with the electric mixer on low speed to loosen things up a bit, then take the bowl off and fold in the remaining ⅔ of the whites by hand with a rubber spatula. Divide the batter evenly among the pans. Smooth the batter with the back of a spoon or a small offset spatula if necessary.

Bake for 35 to 40 minutes or until a small knife emerges clean. Remove from the oven and let the layers cool in their pans for 10 minutes before removing layers to cool completely.

Meanwhile, make the frosting. Put the butter, salt, vanilla, 1–2 tablespoons of reserved juice–rum mixture and half the sugar into the bowl of an electric mixer. With a paddle attachment, start out on low speed to combine ingredients and gradually increase the speed until the sugar is incorporated. Add the remaining sugar, 6oz/175g/1 cup at a time. With each addition, start out at low speed and increase gradually to medium–high. Using a rubber spatula, fold in the rum-soaked dried fruits and the coarsely chopped walnuts until evenly incorporated.

To finish the cake, cut the dome off 2 of the 3 cake layers, or all 3 if you wish. Brush the cut side of each layer with the reserved juice-rum liquid. Slather the fruit- and nut-buttercream on to the bottom layer and spread evenly with an offset spatula. Set the second layer atop the bottom and repeat. If the third layer is still domed, place the flat side on top of the 2 stacked layers and repeat frosting the top and sides of the cake. If you have domed all 3 layers, brush the cut side with the reserved liquid then invert it so the cut side faces down. This will reduce the amount of crumbs that might get worked into the finished frosting. Let the completed cake sit overnight as the flavors are best when allowed to ripen.

KING CHARLES PUDDING RECEIPT

A dessert by many names, we've taken the liberty to coin a new one. In a sense, we've come full circle. Many know this as Huguenot Torte, others as Ozark Pudding. A little bit of sleuthing tells us King Charles II sent 45 Huguenots to the new province of Carolina in 1680. His aim was to establish a British territory built on the know-how of his French Protestant subjects; their mission was to stake a claim and name it 'Charles Town'. In turn Charleston, South Carolina was born. One of its most famous cookbooks, Charleston Receipts, included a recipe for Huguenot Torte, so-called because it was first served at the Huguenot Tavern smack in the center of town. A bit more sleuthing gets us further back in time to suggest the torte was based on an earlier confection, Ozark Pudding, which may or may not be anything more than a regional variation, since the Ozark Mountains are due west of Charleston. Both are a combination of apples and walnuts with other bits and bobs varying in slight degrees. English walnuts would complete the circle just that much more. As we began with Potayto/ Potahto, it somehow seems fitting to end with Dessert is Pudding, Recipe is Receipt, and the Huguenot influence is the handiwork of a bloke named Charles who happened to be king.

A quick word about our receipt: for a crowd we would double this, bake out two and slather sweetened whipped cream between the layers. Ozark Puddings are one layer while Huguenot Tortes are typically two. Serves 12–16

INGREDIENTS

all-purpose or plain flour
2½ oz / 70g / ½ cup

baking powder
1 tablespoon

kosher salt
½ teaspoon

large eggs
4

vanilla extract
2 teaspoons

granulated sugar
16oz / 450g / 2 cups

pecans, ground
4oz / 115g / 1 cup

walnuts, ground
4oz / 115g / 1 cup

apples, finely chopped
(2 medium)
12oz / 340g / 2 cups

Preheat the oven to 180°C/350°F/gas mark 4. Generously butter a 12in/30cm round springform or cheesecake pan with removable bottom.

Whisk together the flour, baking powder and salt in a medium bowl. In the bowl of an electric mixer, beat the eggs at high speed until pale yellow and thick. (Some refer to this as the ribbon stage because when you lift the beater, the thickened eggs will drip back down to create a ribbon in the bowl.) Be patient, as this can take about 10 minutes. The good news is you can't over-beat at this point. Add in the vanilla. Slowly add the sugar in 3 to 4 portions, beating well after each addition. It will take about 5 minutes to incorporate all the sugar. The mixture should be shiny, thick and almost triple in volume. Scrape the bottom of the bowl to incorporate anything lurking down below. Remove the bowl from the mixer and gently fold in the flour mixture only until it disappears. Sprinkle the nuts and apples into the bowl and, again, fold everything together gently. Pour the batter into the prepared pan and smooth it with a spatula.

Bake the pudding for 30 to 35 minutes or until it is golden brown, puffed and just beginning to pull away from the pan. Do not test with a knife or poke the middle with your finger since this is quite delicate and could collapse. Cool the torte completely in the pan set on a wire rack.

To serve, release the sides of the pan and transfer the torte to a serving plate. Either spread the top of the torte with Sweetened Whipped Cream (page 196) or serve each slice with a dollop on the plate. If you've doubled the recipe, place 1 torte on the serving plate, spread it with whipped cream, stack the second torte on top and finish by spreading more whipped cream on top. Leave the sides bare. The soonest we'd finish anything with whipped cream would be 4 hours before it is served. The assembled pudding can keep in the refrigerator for up to 2 days, but it's at its prime soon after it's made.

INDEX

ACKNOWLEDGEMENTS

Firstly we must acknowledge how ludicrous it is that we find ourselves in need of writing this section at all. We love to bake, we do it to our utmost ability and, apparently, it led us here. Who'd a thunk? This entire journey would not have been possible without the generosity and support from these kind folk: Abuela and Mom and Dad Lesniak who bid us farewell and offer their love alas from afar; our siblings for helping our parents tolerate the circumstances; Nina Diamond-Brown who finally realized there's more to life than savories and let us start at the Richmond Farmer's Market; Tiffany Young who pulled back the velvet ropes and let us in to the Suppliers' Club; our vendors who manage to accommodate our, how shall we say, quirks; our customers whose steadfast and vocal support garnered media attention; Rachel Allen who showered us with kindness on our first TV outing and has continued to support and encourage us; Susann Jerry who works her magic with the aforementioned media; Imogen Fortes who took note of Susann's handiwork and popped in one day asking us to write a book (a million thank yous and apologies for our insanity); Gordon Wise whose patient stewardship manages to keep us on the right side of the cliff; Lucy Dickens for her voracious appetite (boy, that girl can eat), her gift of gab (boy, that girl can talk) and her gift for taking care of us; Denise Van Outen who indulged Lucy's pleas and came to dinner one night and so kindly offered her two cents (or pence as the case may be); Adele and Louie for taking the time to come into the shop and enjoying what we do; Nick Knowles and Jessica Moore for their unbridled enthusiasm and support; Simon Silverwood for his penchants: pots and pedagogy; Jan Baldwin and her Johnny for their scrumptious photography; everyone at Ebury/Random House for, no doubt, listening to Imogen gripe about these two idiots; David Eldridge for hitting the perfect spot with his cover design; Charlotte Heal for designing these gorgeous pages; Helena Caldon for gently (more or less) guiding us through copy edits; Helena's friend JC just because; our staff for putting up with us both (OD's worse), (OD: I just like things perfect); and our friends who've suffered one too many a declined invitation. Though prone to being verbose, we are suddenly at a loss to aptly convey our gratitude.

10 9 8 7 6 5 4 3 2 1

Published in 2011 by Ebury Press,
an imprint of Ebury Publishing

A Random House Group Company

Text copyright © David Lesniak and David Muniz 2011
Photography copyright © Jan Baldwin 2011

David Lesniak and David Muniz have asserted their right to be
identified as the authors of this Work in accordance with the
Copyright, Designs and Patents Act 1988

The Random House Group Limited Reg. No. 954009

Addresses for companies within the Random House Group
can be found at: www.randomhouse.co.uk

A CIP catalogue record for this book is available
from the British Library

The Random House Group Limited supports The Forest Stewardship
Council (FSC), the leading international forest certification
organisation. All our titles that are printed on Greenpeace approved
FSC certified paper carry the FSC logo. Our paper procurement policy
can be found at www.randomhouse.co.uk/environment
To buy books by your favourite authors and register
for offers visit: www.randomhouse.co.uk

Printed and bound in China by C&C Offset Printing Co., Ltd

ISBN 9780091940966

Design: Charlotte Heal
Photography: Jan Baldwin
Production: Lucy Harrison